Show Me Microsoft Office Access 2003

Steve Johnson

Perspection, Inc.

Que Publishing
800 East 96th Street
Indianapolis, IN 46240 USA

Show Me Microsoft® Office Access 2003

International Standard Book Number: 0-7897-3004-9

Library of Congress Catalog Card Number: 2003108705

Printed in the United States of America

First Printing: September 2003

09 08 07   8 7 6 5 4 3

Que Publishing offers excellent discounts on this book when ordered in quantity for bulk purchases or special sales. For information, please contact:

U.S. Corporate and Government Sales

1-800-382-3419

corpsales@pearsontechgroup.com

For sales outside the U.S., please contact:

International Sales

1-317-428-3341

International@pearsontechgroup.com

Trademarks

All terms mentioned in this book that are known to be trademarks or service marks have been appropriately capitalized. Que cannot attest to the accuracy of this information. Use of a term in this book should not be regarded as affecting the validity of any trademark or service mark.

Microsoft and the Microsoft Office logo are a registered trademarks of Microsoft Corporation in the United States and/or other countries.

Warning and Disclaimer

Every effort has been made to make this book as complete and as accurate as possible, but no warranty or fitness is implied. The authors and the publishers shall have neither liability nor responsibility to any person or entity with respect to any loss or damage arising from the information contained in this book.

Publisher
Paul Boger

Associate Publisher
Greg Wiegand

Managing Editor
Steve Johnson

Author
Steve Johnson

Project Editor
Holly Johnson

Technical Editors
Nicholas Chu
Melinda Lankford

Production Editor
Beth Teyler

Page Layout
Kate Lyerla
Joe Kalsbeek
Ryan Suzuki
Matt West

Interior Designers
Steve Johnson
Marian Hartsough

Indexer
Katherine Stimson

Proofreaders
Beth Teyler
Melinda Lankford

Team Coordinator
Sharry Lee Gregory

Acknowledgements

Perspection, Inc.

Show Me Microsoft Office Access 2003 has been created by the professional trainers and writers at Perspection, Inc. to the standards you've come to expect from Que publishing. Together, we are pleased to present this training book.

Perspection, Inc. is a software training company committed to providing information and training to help people use software more effectively in order to communicate, make decisions, and solve problems. Perspection writes and produces software training books, and develops multimedia and Web-based training. Since 1991, we have written more than 60 computer books, with several bestsellers to our credit, and sold over 4.5 million books.

This book incorporates Perspection's training expertise to ensure that you'll receive the maximum return on your time. You'll focus on the tasks and skills that increase productivity while working at your own pace and convenience.

We invite you to visit the Perspection Web site at:

www.perspection.com

Acknowledgements

The task of creating any book requires the talents of many hard-working people pulling together to meet impossible deadlines and untold stresses. We'd like to thank the outstanding team responsible for making this book possible: the writer, Steve Johnson; the editor, Holly Johnson; the technical editors, Melinda Lankford and Nicholas Chu; the production team, Kate Lyerla, Joe Kalsbeek, Ryan Suzuki, and Matt West; the proofreaders, Beth Teyler and Melinda Lankford; and the indexer, Katherine Stimson.

At Que publishing, we'd like to thank Greg Wiegand for the opportunity to undertake this project, Sharry Gregory for administrative support, and Sandra Schroeder for your production expertise and support.

Perspection

Dedication

Most importantly, I would like to thank my wife Holly, and my three children, JP, Brett, and Hannah, for their support and encouragement during the project. I would also like to thank Sarah Bartholomaei for her tender loving care and dedication towards our children during the deadline times.

About The Author

Steve Johnson has written more than twenty books on a variety of computer software, including Microsoft Office XP, Microsoft Windows XP, Macromedia Director MX and Macromedia Fireworks, and Web publishing. In 1991, after working for Apple Computer and Microsoft, Steve founded Perspection, Inc., which writes and produces software training. When he is not staying up late writing, he enjoys playing golf, gardening, and spending time with his wife, Holly, and three children, JP, Brett, and Hannah. When time permits, he likes to travel to such places as New Hampshire in October, and Hawaii. Steve and his family live in Pleasanton, California, but can also be found visiting family all over the western United States.

We Want To Hear From You!

As the reader of this book, *you* are our most important critic and commentator. We value your opinion and want to know what we're doing right, what we could do better, what areas you'd like to see us publish in, and any other words of wisdom you're willing to pass our way.

As an associate publisher for Que, I welcome your comments. You can email or write me directly to let me know what you did or didn't like about this book—as well as what we can do to make our books better.

Please note that I cannot help you with technical problems related to the topic of this book. We do have a User Services group, however, where I will forward specific technical questions related to the book.

When you write, please be sure to include this book's title and author as well as your name, email address, and phone number. I will carefully review your comments and share them with the author and editors who worked on the book.

Email: feedback@quepublishing.com

Mail: Greg Wiegand
         Que Publishing
         800 East 96th Street
         Indianapolis, IN 46240 USA

For more information about this book or another Que title, visit our Web site at *www.quepublishing.com*. Type the ISBN (excluding hyphens) or the title of a book in the Search field to find the page you're looking for.

Contents

Introduction   *xv*

1 Getting Started with Access   1

Understanding How Databases Store Data   2
Starting Access   4
Using Tasks Panes   5
Opening a Database   6
Finding a File or Contents in a File   7
Viewing the Access Window   8
Arranging Windows   9
Choosing Menu Commands   10
Choosing Dialog Box Options   11
Working with Toolbars   12
Viewing Database Objects   14
Getting Help While You Work   16
Getting Help from the Office Assistant   18
Getting Access Updates on the Web   20
Saving Your Work   22
Recovering an Office Program   23
Detecting and Repairing Problems   24
Closing a Database and Quitting Access   26

2 Touring Access Databases   27

Opening a Sample Database   28
Using a Switchboard   29
Working with Database Objects   30
Grouping Database Objects   32
Hiding Windows   33
Touring a Table   34
Touring a Form   36
Entering Data   37

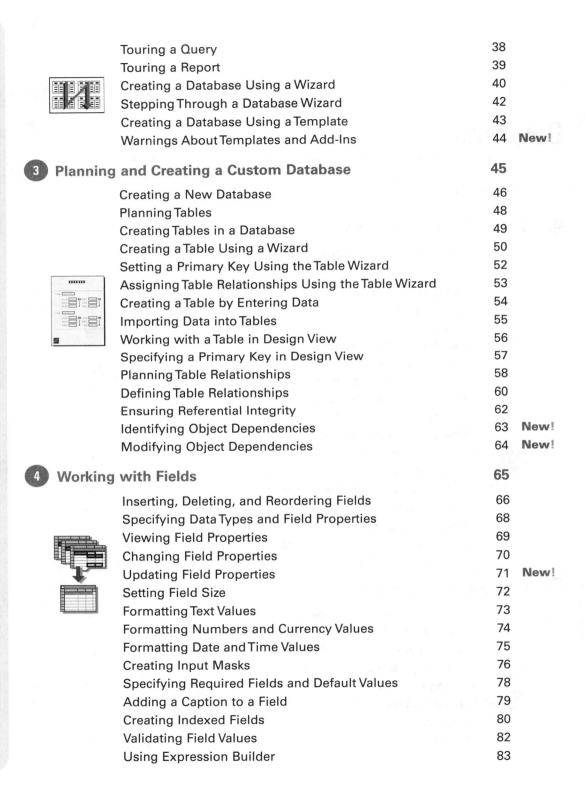

Touring a Query	38	
Touring a Report	39	
Creating a Database Using a Wizard	40	
Stepping Through a Database Wizard	42	
Creating a Database Using a Template	43	
Warnings About Templates and Add-Ins	44	**New!**

3 Planning and Creating a Custom Database — 45

Creating a New Database	46
Planning Tables	48
Creating Tables in a Database	49
Creating a Table Using a Wizard	50
Setting a Primary Key Using the Table Wizard	52
Assigning Table Relationships Using the Table Wizard	53
Creating a Table by Entering Data	54
Importing Data into Tables	55
Working with a Table in Design View	56
Specifying a Primary Key in Design View	57
Planning Table Relationships	58
Defining Table Relationships	60
Ensuring Referential Integrity	62

Identifying Object Dependencies	63	**New!**
Modifying Object Dependencies	64	**New!**

4 Working with Fields — 65

Inserting, Deleting, and Reordering Fields	66	
Specifying Data Types and Field Properties	68	
Viewing Field Properties	69	
Changing Field Properties	70	
Updating Field Properties	71	**New!**
Setting Field Size	72	
Formatting Text Values	73	
Formatting Numbers and Currency Values	74	
Formatting Date and Time Values	75	
Creating Input Masks	76	
Specifying Required Fields and Default Values	78	
Adding a Caption to a Field	79	
Creating Indexed Fields	80	
Validating Field Values	82	
Using Expression Builder	83	

Creating a Lookup Field 84

Setting Lookup Properties 86

5 Working with Tables 87

Working with a Table 88

Moving to a Specific Record in a Table 89

Searching for and Replacing Text 90

Entering Data Accurately with AutoCorrect 92 **New!**

Using Smart Tags 94 **New!**

Editing Text 96

Working with the Clipboard 98

Checking Spelling 100

Arranging Columns 102

Changing the Size of Rows and Columns 104

Managing Columns in Datasheet View 105

Formatting a Datasheet 106

Repairing Renaming Errors 107

Sorting Records 108

Copying and Pasting Records 110

Viewing a Subdatasheet 111

Filtering Out Records 112

Creating Complex Filters Using Forms 114

6 Locating Specific Information Using a Query 115

Understanding Types of Queries 116

Creating a Query in Design View 117

Getting Information with a Query 118

Modifying a Query in Design View 119

Creating a Query Using a Wizard 120

Changing the Query Fields 122

Specifying Criteria for a Single Field 124

Specifying Criteria for Multiple Fields 125

Creating Queries with Comparison and Logical Operators 126

Performing Calculations in Queries 128

Creating a Parameter Query 129

Finding Duplicate Fields 130

Finding Unmatched Records 131

Creating New Tables with a Query 132

Contents **ix**

Adding Records with a Query   133
Deleting Records with a Query   134
Updating Records with a Query   135
Summarizing Values with Crosstab Query   136
Creating SQL-Specific Queries   138

7 Simplifying Data Entry with Forms   139

Creating Forms   140
Working with Form Controls   141
Creating a Form Using AutoForm   142
Creating a Form Using a Wizard   144
Creating a Form in Design View   146
Editing an Existing Form   147
Adding and Modifying Controls   148
Using the Control Wizards   150   New!
Creating a Subform   152
Editing in Form View   154
Entering and Editing Data in a Form   155
Using Windows XP Themes in Forms   156   New!

8 Creating Reports to Convey Information   157

Exploring Different Ways to Create a Report   158
Creating a Report Using a Wizard   160
Using Sections in Design View   162
Working with Controls   163
Creating a Report in Design View   164
Using Toolbox Buttons and Controls   166
Arranging Information   168
Creating Mailing Labels   170
Setting Properties   171
Performing Calculations in Reports   172
Grouping Records   174
Inserting a Header or Footer   176
Assigning a Shortcut Key to a Control   177
Checking for Errors in Reports and Forms   178   New!
Changing the Page Setup   180
Previewing Information   181
Printing Information   182

9 **Improving the Appearance of Forms and Reports**   **183**

      Formatting a Form or Report   184
      Adding Lines and Rectangles   186
      Changing Line or Border Thickness   187
      Changing Colors   188
      Applying Special Effects to Controls   190
      Applying Conditional Formatting   191
      Aligning and Grouping Controls   192
      Sharing Information Between Documents   194
      Copying and Pasting Objects   195
      Inserting a New Object   196
      Inserting an Object from a File   197
      Inserting a Picture   198
      Inserting Excel Charts and Worksheets   200
      Inserting a Graph Chart   202
      Formatting Chart Objects   204
      Moving and Resizing an Object   206

10 **Working on the Web**   **207**

      Integrating Access and the Internet   208
      Creating a Hyperlink Field   210
      Inserting a Hyperlink to a File or Web Page   211
      Linking to an Object in a Database   212
      Linking to a New Document   214
      Navigating Hyperlinks   215
      Working with the Web Toolbar   216
      Exporting Database Objects to HTML   217
      Exporting Database Objects to ASP Files   218
      Holding an Online Meeting   220
      Creating a Data Access Page Using a Wizard   222
      Working with a Data Access Page in Design View   224
      Adding a Theme to a Page   225
      Grouping a Data Access Page   226
      Viewing a Data Access Page   228
      Analyzing Pivot Data from the Web   230

11 Importing and Exporting Information　　　231

　　　Importing and Linking Data　　　232
　　　Importing or Linking Data from an Access Database　　　234　New!
　　　Importing or Linking Data from an Excel Spreadsheet　　　236
　　　Importing or Linking Data from a Mail Program　　　237
　　　Getting Data from Other Programs　　　238
　　　Importing and Exporting XML Data　　　240　New!
　　　Exporting Data to Other Programs　　　242
　　　Merging Data with Word　　　244
　　　Analyzing Data in Excel　　　246

12 Managing a Database　　　247

　　　Securing a Database　　　248
　　　Creating a Workgroup Information File　　　250
　　　Joining a Workgroup　　　251
　　　Creating User and Group Accounts　　　252
　　　Activating User Logons　　　253
　　　Setting User and Group Permissions　　　254
　　　Setting Object Ownership　　　256
　　　Setting a Database Password　　　257
　　　Encoding a Database　　　258
　　　Locking Database Records　　　259
　　　Replicating a Database　　　260
　　　Backing Up a Database　　　262　New!
　　　Compacting and Repairing a Database　　　263
　　　Splitting a Database　　　264
　　　Documenting a Database　　　265
　　　Analyzing a Database　　　266
　　　Converting Access Databases　　　268
　　　Using Add-Ins　　　270
　　　Creating a Database Switchboard　　　271
　　　Managing a Switchboard　　　272
　　　Creating a Splash Screen　　　273
　　　Setting Access Startup Options　　　274

13 **Customizing Access** 275

Adding and Removing Toolbar Buttons 276
Customizing a Toolbar 278
Customizing the Menu Bar 280
Editing Toolbar Buttons and Menu Entries 282
Learning About Macros 283
Creating a Macro 284
Running and Testing a Macro 286
Creating Macro Groups 288
Creating Conditional Macros 289
Assigning a Macro to a Button 290
Assigning a Macro to an Event 292
Creating a Message Box 294
Controlling Access with Your Voice 295
Executing Voice Commands 296
Dictating Text 297
Recognizing Handwriting 298 New!
Using Multiple Languages 300

14 **Enhancing a Database with Programming** 301

Enhancing a Database with VBA 302
Creating a Standard Module 304
Understanding Parts of the Visual Basic Editor 305
Creating a Sub Procedure 306
Writing VBA Commands 307
Running a Sub Procedure 308
Copying Commands from the Object Browser 309
Creating a Custom Function 310
Running a Custom Function 311
Creating a Class Module for a Form or Report 312
Setting Project Properties 313
Debugging a Procedure 314
Identifying VBA Debugging Tools 315
Optimizing Performance with an MDE File 316

15 **Working Together on Office Documents** **317**

Viewing SharePoint Team Services	318	New!
Administering SharePoint Team Services	320	New!
Storing Documents in the Library	322	New!
Viewing Team Members	323	New!
Setting Up Alerts	324	New!
Assigning Project Tasks	325	New!
Creating an Event	326	New!
Creating Contacts	328	New!
Holding Web Discussions	330	New!
Importing and Exporting Access Data with SharePoint	331	New!
Installing Windows 2003 and SharePoint Server 2003	332	

Microsoft Office Specialist	*333*
New Features	*337*
Troubleshooting	*341*
Index	*347*

Introduction

Welcome to *Show Me Microsoft Office Access 2003*, a visual quick reference book that shows you how to work efficiently with Microsoft Office Access 2003. This book provides complete coverage of basic and intermediate Access 2003 skills.

Find the Best Place to Start

You don't have to read this book in any particular order. We've designed the book so that you can jump in, get the information you need, and jump out. However, the book does follow a logical progression from simple tasks to more complex ones. Each task is no more than two pages long. To find the information that you need, just look up the task in the table of contents, index, or troubleshooting guide, and turn to the page listed. Read the task introduction, follow the step-by-step instructions along with the illustration, and you're done.

What's New

If you're searching for what's new in Access 2003, just look for the icon: New! The new icon appears in the table of contents so you can quickly and easily identify a new or improved feature in Access 2003. A complete description of each new feature appears in the New Features guide in the back of this book.

How This Book Works

Each task is presented on no more than two facing pages, with step-by-step instructions in the left column and screen illustrations in the right column. This arrangement lets you focus on a single task without having to turn the page.

How You'll Learn

Find the Best Place to Start

What's New

How This Book Works

Step-by-Step Instructions

Real World Examples

Troubleshooting Guide

Show Me Live Software

Microsoft Office Specialist

Step-by-Step Instructions

This book provides concise step-by-step instructions that show you "how" to accomplish a task. Each set of instructions include illustrations that directly correspond to the easy-to-read steps. Also included in the text are timesavers, tables, and sidebars to help you work more efficiently or to teach you more in-depth information. A "Did You Know?" provides tips and techniques to help you work smarter, while a "See Also" leads you to other parts of the book containing related information about the task.

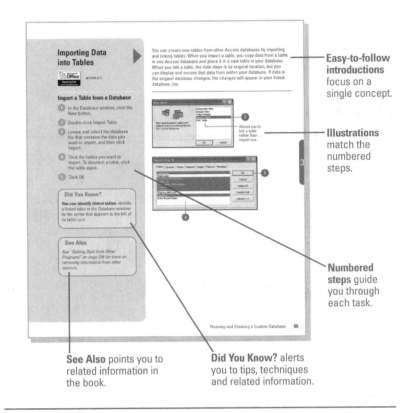

Easy-to-follow introductions focus on a single concept.

Illustrations match the numbered steps.

Numbered steps guide you through each task.

See Also points you to related information in the book.

Did You Know? alerts you to tips, techniques and related information.

Real World Examples

This book uses real world examples to help convey "why" you would want to perform a task. The examples give you a context in which to use the task. You'll observe how *Home Sense, Inc.*, a fictional home improvement business, uses Access 2003 to get the job done.

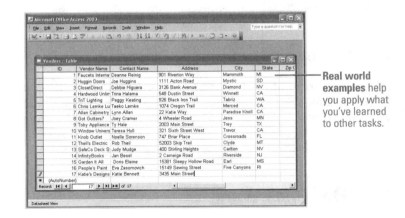

Real world examples help you apply what you've learned to other tasks.

Troubleshooting Guide

This book offers quick and easy ways to diagnose and solve common Access 2003 problems that you might encounter. The troubleshooting guide helps you determine and fix a problem using the task information you find. The problems are posed in question form and are grouped into categories that are presented alphabetically.

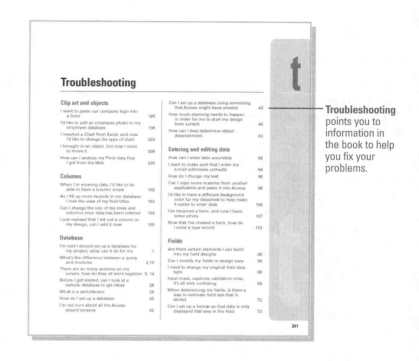

Troubleshooting points you to information in the book to help you fix your problems.

Show Me Live Software

In addition, this book offers companion software that shows you how to perform most tasks using the live program. The easy-to-use VCR-type controls allow you to start, pause, and stop the action. As you observe how to accomplish each task, Show Me Live highlights each step and talks you through the process. The Show Me Live software is available free at *www.perspection.com or www.quepublishing.com/showme.*

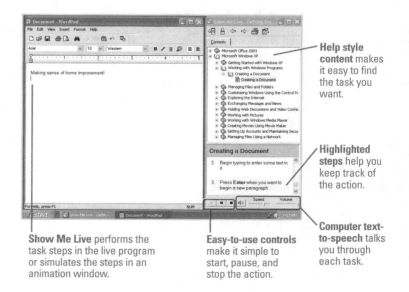

Help style content makes it easy to find the task you want.

Highlighted steps help you keep track of the action.

Computer text-to-speech talks you through each task.

Show Me Live performs the task steps in the live program or simulates the steps in an animation window.

Easy-to-use controls make it simple to start, pause, and stop the action.

Microsoft Office Specialist

This book prepares you fully for the Microsoft Office Specialist exam at the specialist level for Microsoft Office Access 2003. Each Microsoft Office Specialist certification level has a set of objectives, which are organized into broader skill sets. To prepare for the certification exam, you should review and perform each task identified with a Microsoft Office Specialist objective to confirm that you can meet the requirements for the exam. Throughout this book, content that pertains to an objective is identified with the Microsoft Office Specialist logo and objective number next to it.

Microsoft Office Specialist

About the Microsoft Office Specialist Program

The Microsoft Office Specialist certification is the globally recognized standard for validating expertise with the Microsoft Office suite of business productivity programs. Earning an Microsoft Office Specialist certificate acknowledges you have the expertise to work with Microsoft Office programs. To earn the Microsoft Office Specialist certification, you must pass one or more certification exams for the Microsoft Office desktop applications of Microsoft Office Word, Microsoft Office Excel, Microsoft Office PowerPoint, Microsoft Office Outlook, or Microsoft Office Access. The Microsoft Office Specialist program typically offers certification exams at the "specialist" and "expert" skill levels. (The availability of Microsoft Office Specialist certification exams varies by program, program version, and language. Visit *www.microsoft.com-officespecialist* for exam availability and more information about the program.) The Microsoft Office Specialist program is the only Microsoft-approved program in the world for certifying proficiency with Microsoft Office programs.

What Does This Logo Mean?

It means this book has been approved by the Microsoft Office Specialist program to be certified courseware for learning Microsoft Office Access 2003 and preparing for the certification exam. This book will prepare you fully for the Microsoft Office Specialist exam at the specialist level for Microsoft Office Access 2003. Each certification level has a set of objectives, which are organized into broader skill sets. Throughout this book, content that pertains to a Microsoft Office Specialist objective is identified with the Microsoft Office Specialist logo and objective number below the title of the topic:

 AC03S-1-1
AC03S-2-2

Logo indicates a task fulfills one or more Microsoft Office Specialist objectives.

333

Getting Started with Access

Introduction

Microsoft Office Access 2003 is a database program that allows you to:

- ◆ Store an almost limitless amount of information.
- ◆ Organize information in a way that makes sense for how you work.
- ◆ Retrieve information based on selection criteria you specify.
- ◆ Create forms that make it easier to enter information.
- ◆ Generate meaningful and insightful reports that can combine data, text, graphics, and other objects.
- ◆ Share information easily over the Web.

What Is a Database?

Database is a rather technical word for a collection of information that is organized as a list. This definition might be oversimplified, but whenever you use or make a list of information—names, addresses, products, customers, or invoices—you are using a database. A database that you store on your computer, however, is much more flexible and powerful than a simple list you keep on paper, in your card file, or in your address book.

What You'll Do

Understand How Databases Store Data

Start Access

Use Task Panes

Open a Database

Find a File or Contents in a File

View the Access Window

Arrange Windows

Choose Menu Commands

Choose Dialog Box Options

Work with Toolbars

View Database Objects

Get Help While You Work

Get Help from the Office Assistant

Get Access Updates on the Web

Save Your Work

Recover an Office Program

Detect and Repair Problems

Close a Database and Quit Access

Understanding How Databases Store Data

Storing Data on a Computer

Some lists can serve a much more useful purpose when stored on a computer. For example, the names, addresses, and phone numbers you jot down on cards or in a paper address book are only be used when you have the paper list in your hand. Suppose you currently store names and addresses on cards. All the information about a particular person is stored in one place.

If you store that list on a computer, however, you can do much more with it than just refer to it. For example, you can generate lists of your most important phone numbers to put next to every phone in the house, you can print mailing labels for greeting cards, you can create lists of this month's birthdays, and so on.

There are a number of ways to store lists on a computer. For example, you can store a list in a Microsoft Word table or on a Microsoft Excel spreadsheet.

If you place this information in a Word table or on an Excel spreadsheet, you are faced with a problem: you end up repeating some of the information. Consider what happens if a family moves or a last name is changed. You have to ensure that information is updated everywhere it's stored. For a small list that might not matter, but for a large list with information that requires constant updating (such as an address list), it is a huge task to keep data up-to-date in this way.

Storing Data in a Database

If, on the other hand, you save address information in an Access database, you can ensure that each piece of information is entered only once.

An Access database consists of objects, such as tables, forms, queries, reports, pages, macros, and modules.

- A **table** is a collection of related information about a topic, such as names and addresses. A table consists of fields and records. A field stores each piece of information in a table, such as first name, last name, or address. A record is a collection of all the fields for one person.

- A **form** provides an easy way to view and enter information into a database. Typically, forms display one record at a time.

- A **query** is a method to find information in a database. The information you find with a query is based on conditions you specify.

- **Reports** are documents that summarize information from the database.

- **Pages** enable you to access a database on the Internet using a Web browser.

- A **macro** saves you time by automating a series of actions into one action.

- **Modules** are programs you create in a programming language called Visual Basic for Applications (VBA), which extend the functionality of a database.

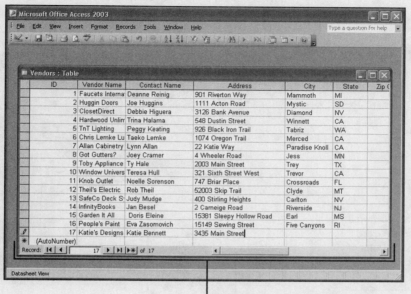

A database table with fields and records

Frequently Asked Questions

What is a Microsoft Access Project?

A Microsoft Office Access project is an Access data file that provides access to a Microsoft SQL Server database through the OLE DB component architecture, which provides network and Internet access to many types of data sources. An Access project is called a project because it contains only code-based or HTML-based database objects: forms, reports, the name and location of data access pages, macros, and modules. Unlike an Access database, an Access project doesn't contain any data or data objects, such as tables, views, database diagrams, stored procedures, or user-defined functions. Working with an Access project is virtually the same as working with an Access database, except you need to connect to an SQL Server database, which stores the data.

Starting Access

You can start Access from the Start menu or the desktop. When you're choosing how to start Access, you need to decide if you want to create a new database or open an existing one. When you open Access from the Start menu, you make this choice from within Access.

Start Access from the Start Menu

1. Click the Start button on the taskbar.

2. Point to All Programs.

3. Click Microsoft Office.

4. Click Microsoft Office Access 2003.

   The first time you start an Office program, an Activation Wizard opens; follow the instructions to activate the product.

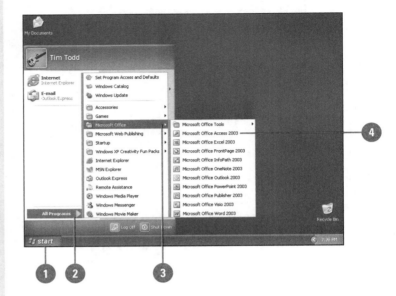

Did You Know?

You can create a program shortcut from the Start menu to the desktop. Click the Start menu, point to All Programs, point to Microsoft Office, right-click Microsoft Office Access 2003, point to Send To, and then click Desktop (Create Shortcut).

You can start Access and open a database from Windows Explorer. Double-clicking any Access database icon in Windows Explorer opens that file and Access.

Using Task Panes

When you start Access, a task pane appears by default on the right side of the program window. The task pane displays various options that relate to the current task. There are several types of options available on the task pane. You can search for information, select options, and click links, like the ones on a Web page, to perform commands. You can also display different task panes, move back and forth between task panes, and close a task pane to provide a larger work area.

Use the Task Pane

1. When you start Access, the task pane appears on the right side of your screen.

2. Click an option on the task pane.

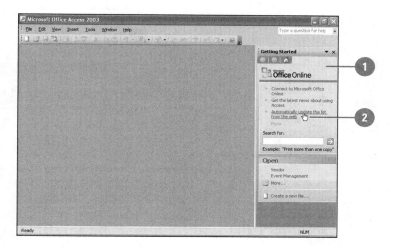

Open and Close Task Panes

1. Click the View menu, and then click Task Pane.

2. To open another task pane, click the list arrow on the task pane title bar, and then click the task pane you want.

3. To switch between task panes, click the Back and Forward task pane buttons.

4. Click the Close button on the task pane.

Opening a Database

You can open an existing database from the Getting Started task pane you see when you first start Access or by navigating to this task pane at any point. You can also open an existing database by clicking Open on the File menu, or by using the Open button on your toolbar. If you were recently working with the database you want to open, you can start Access and the database by using My Recent Documents on the All Programs menu, or open the database by clicking the database name listed at the bottom of the File menu from within Access.

Open a Database

1. Click the Open button on the Database toolbar.

2. Click the Look In list arrow, and then click the appropriate folder containing the database you want to open.

3. Click the database you want to open.

4. Click Open.

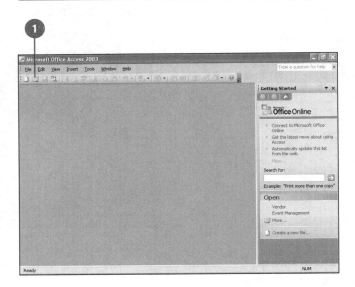

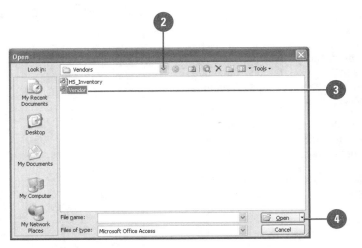

Did You Know?

You can open a sample database. Click the Open button on the Database toolbar, click the Look In list arrow, open the Samples folder located in *C:/Program Files/Microsoft Office/Office*, click the database you want to open, and then click Open.

See Also

See "Warnings About Templates and Add-Ins" on page 44 for information on security alerts that appear when you open a database.

Finding a File or Contents in a File

The search feature available in the Open dialog box is also available using the Search task pane. You can use the Search task pane to find a files name or location as well as search for specific text or property in a database. This becomes handy when you recall the content of a database, but not the name. When you perform a search, try to use specific or unique words to achieve the best results.

Find a File or Contents in a File

1. Click the File menu, and then click File Search.

2. Type the name of the file you are looking for or any distinctive words or phrases in the database.

3. Click the Search In list arrow, and then select or clear the check boxes to indicate where you want the program to search.

    Click the plus sign (+) to expand a list.

4. Click the Results Should Be list arrow, and then select or clear the check boxes to indicate the type of files you want to find.

5. Click Go.

6. To revise the find, click Modify.

7. When the search results appear, point to a file, click the list arrow, and then click the command you want.

8. When you're done, click the Close button on the task pane.

Did You Know?

You can use wildcards to search for file names. When you recall only part of the file name you want to open, type a question mark (?) for any one unknown character or an asterisk (*) for two or more unknown characters.

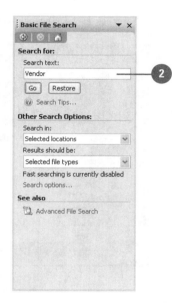

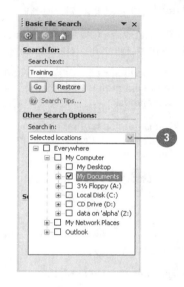

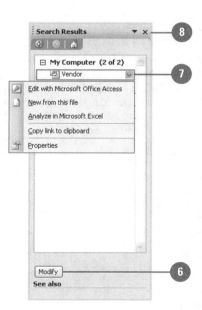

Viewing the Access Window

When you open a database, the Access program window opens and displays a title bar, menus, toolbars and either the Database window or a switchboard. The **Database window** is where you can create and edit your databases using the Database toolbar and database objects. A **switchboard** is a window that gives easy access to the most common actions a database user might need to take.

Parts of the Access Window

◆ The **Database title bar** displays the name of the open database.

◆ The **menu bar** contains menus that represent groups of related commands.

◆ The **Database toolbar** contains buttons that you can click to carry out commands.

◆ The **status bar** displays information about the items you click or the actions you take.

Did You Know?

You can customize Access startup.
Click the Tools menu, click Startup, set the startup options you want, and then click OK. Close and open the database to see the new startup.

You can view the Database window.
All the databases that come with Access 2003 open with a switchboard. You can open the Database window by clicking the Window menu and then clicking the name of the database.

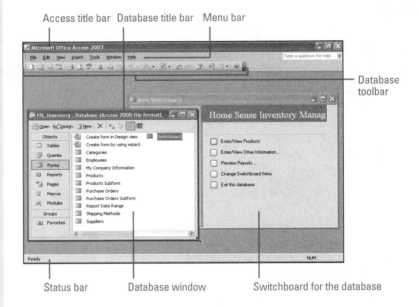

Access title bar   Database title bar   Menu bar

Database toolbar

Status bar   Database window   Switchboard for the database

Arranging Windows

When you want to work with information in a database, or move or copy information between databases or programs, it's easier to move windows out of the way or display several windows at once. You can use the sizing button on the title bar or the pointer to resize and move windows around for easier viewing. You can also arrange two or more windows, from within Access or from different programs, on the screen at the same time.

Resize a Window

All windows contain the same sizing buttons and mouse functionality:

◆ **Maximize button.** Click to make a window fill the entire screen.

◆ **Restore Down button.** Click to reduce a maximized window to a reduced size.

◆ **Minimize button.** Click to shrink a window to a taskbar button. To restore the window to its previous size, click the taskbar button.

◆ **Close button.** Click to shut a window.

◆ **Mouse pointer.** Position the pointer over the edge of a window (changes to a two-headed arrow), and drag to resize a window.

Maximize/Restore Down button

Close button

Minimize button

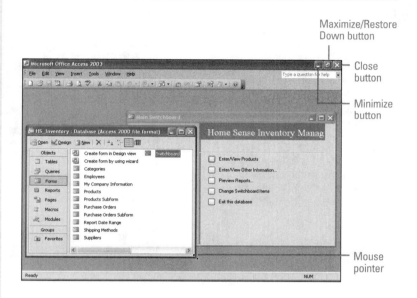

Mouse pointer

Move a Window

1 Position the pointer over the title bar of the window you want to move.

2 Drag the window to a new location.

Choosing Menu Commands

A **menu** is a list of related commands or options, located at the top of the window. The menus are personalized as you work—when you click a menu name, you first see the commands you use most frequently. After a few moments, you see the entire list of commands. You can right-click a word or object to open a **shortcut menu,** which contains menu commands related to the specific item.

Choose a Command from a Menu

1. Click a menu name on the menu bar.

2. If necessary, click the double-headed arrow to expand the menu, or wait until the expanded list of commands appears.

3. Click the command you want. If the command is followed by an arrow, point to the command to see a list of related options, and then click the option you want.

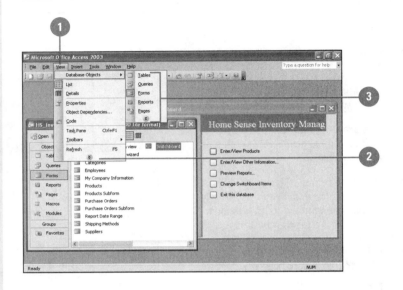

Choose a Command from a Shortcut Menu

1. Right-click an object (a text or graphic element).

2. Click a command on the shortcut menu. If the command is followed by an arrow, point to the command to see a list of related options, and then click the option you want.

    TIMESAVER *You can use a shortcut key to choose a command. Press and hold down the first key, and then press the second key. For example, press and hold the Ctrl key, and then press S to select the Save command.*

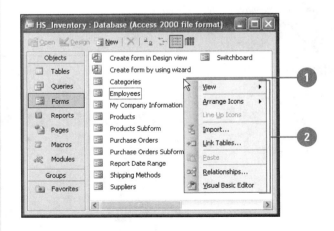

Choosing Dialog Box Options

A **dialog box** is a window that opens when you choose a menu command followed by an ellipsis (. . .). The ellipsis indicates that you must supply more information before the program can carry out the command you selected. After you enter information or make selections in a dialog box, click the OK button to complete the command. Click the Cancel button to close the dialog box without issuing the command. In many dialog boxes, you can also click an Apply button to apply your changes without closing the dialog box.

Choose Dialog Box Options

All dialog boxes contain the same types of options, including the following:

◆ **Tabs.** Click a tab to display its options. Each tab groups a related set of options.

◆ **Option buttons.** Click an option button to select it. You can usually select only one.

◆ **Up and down arrows.** Click the up or down arrow to increase or decrease the number, or type a number in the box.

◆ **Check box.** Click the box to turn on or off the option. A checked box means the option is selected; a cleared box means it's not.

◆ **List box.** Click the list arrow to display a list of options, and then click the option you want.

◆ **Text box.** Click in the box and type the requested information.

◆ **Button.** Click a button to perform a specific action or command. A button name followed by an ellipsis (...) opens another dialog box.

◆ **Preview box.** Many dialog boxes show an image that reflects the options you select.

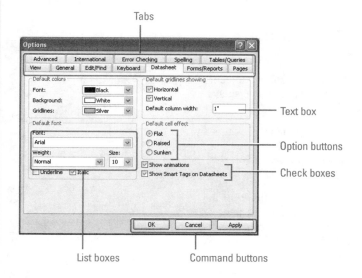

Tabs

Text box

Option buttons

Check boxes

List boxes

Command buttons

For Your Information

Navigating a Dialog Box

Rather than clicking to move around a dialog box, you can press the Tab key to move from one box or button to the next. You can also use Shift+Tab to move backward, or Ctrl+Tab and Ctrl+Shift+Tab to move between dialog box tabs.

Working with Toolbars

A **toolbar** contains a collection of buttons you click to select frequently used menu commands. Most programs open with a Standard toolbar (with commands such as Save and Print) and a Formatting toolbar (with commands for selecting fonts and sizes) side by side. You can also display toolbars designed for specific tasks, such as drawing pictures, importing data, or creating charts. If you're not using a toolbar or want to reposition it, you can dock it to the edge of a window or allow it to float in a separate window. The toolbars are personalized as you work, showing only the buttons you use most often. Additional toolbar buttons are available by clicking the Toolbar Options list arrow at the end of the toolbar.

Choose a Command Using a Toolbar Button

1. If you are not sure what a toolbar button does, point to it to display a ScreenTip.

2. To choose a command, click the button or click the Toolbar Options list arrow, and then click the button.

   When you select a button from the Toolbar Options list arrow, the button appears on the toolbar, which shows only the buttons you use most often.

Did You Know?

Toolbar buttons and keyboard short-cuts are faster than menu commands. You can learn the toolbar button equivalents of menu commands by looking at the toolbar button icon to the left of a menu command. Keyboard shortcuts (such as Ctrl+V) appear to the right of their menu commands. To use a keyboard shortcut, press and hold the first key (such as Ctrl), press the second key (such as V), and then release both keys.

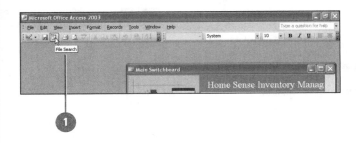

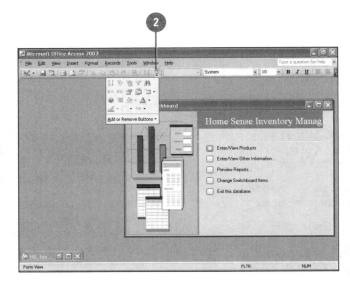

Display or Hide a Toolbar

1 Click the View menu, and then point to Toolbars.

2 Click the toolbar you want to display or hide.

A check mark next to the toolbar name indicates that it is currently displayed on the screen.

> ### Did You Know?
>
> **You can choose a toolbar quickly.** To quickly display the list of available toolbars, right-click a toolbar, and then click the toolbar you want to use.

Move and Reshape a Toolbar

◆ To move a toolbar that is docked (attached to one edge of the window), click the gray dotted edge bar on the left edge of the toolbar, and then drag it to a new location.

◆ To move a toolbar that is floating (unattached) over the window, drag the title bar to a new location.

◆ To return a floating toolbar to its previously docked location, double-click its title bar.

◆ To change the shape of a floating toolbar, drag any border until the toolbar is the shape you want.

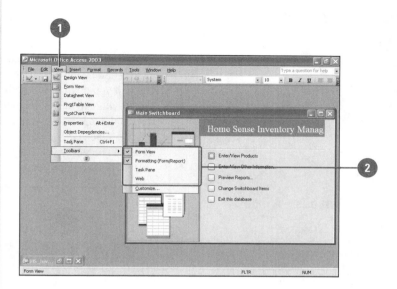

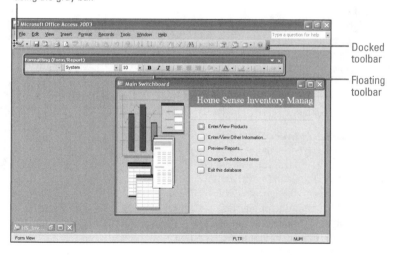

Drag any docked toolbar using the gray bar.

Docked toolbar

Floating toolbar

Viewing Database Objects

When you open an existing database, the first thing you usually see is the Database window. However, if the database was created with a switchboard, you need to close or minimize the switchboard before you can view the Database window. To view an open database or other database related windows, such as a switchboard, you can use the Window menu. If you need to switch between open databases or other open programs, you can click document buttons on the taskbar. Once you view the database window, you can view database objects, which are the building blocks of a database. Access databases can contain seven database object types. The table on the next page identifies the database objects that you use when creating and working with a database.

View the Database Window

① Open the database.

If no special startup options are specified, the Database window opens automatically.

② Click the Window menu.

③ Click the name of the database to view the Database window.

Databases with multiple users might have security measures in effect that prevent some users from accessing the Database window.

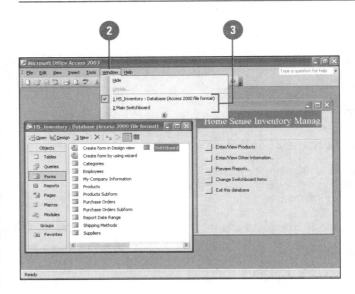

Did You Know?

You can switch between Datasheet and Design view. For many of the tasks you do in Access, you will switch back and forth between Design and Datasheet view. In Design view, you format and set controls for queries, reports, forms, or tables that you are creating from scratch or modifying from an original wizard design. In Datasheet view, you observe the result of the modifications you have made in Design view. To switch between the two, click the View button on the toolbar, and then select the view.

View a List of Database Objects

① Open the database whose objects you want to view.

② Click Tables, Queries, Forms, Reports, Pages, Macros, or Modules on the Objects bar.

◆ The **Database window toolbar** contains buttons for commands that allow you to create, open, and manage database objects.

◆ The **Objects bar** lists the types of objects in a database.

◆ The **Groups bar** allows you to group database objects the way you want them, creating shortcuts to objects of different types.

Objects bar

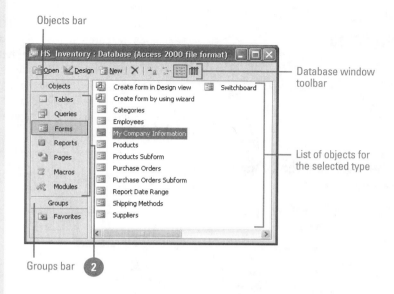

Database window toolbar

List of objects for the selected type

Groups bar ②

Database Objects	
Database Object	**Description**
Tables	Grids that store related information, such as a list of customer addresses
Queries	A question you ask a database to help locate specific information
Forms	A window that is designed to help you enter information easily and accurately
Reports	Summaries of information that are designed to be readable and accessible
Pages	Separate files outside the Access database in HTML format that can be placed on the Web to facilitate data sharing with the Web community
Macros	Stored series of commands that carry out an action
Modules	Programs you can write using Microsoft Visual Basic

Getting Help While You Work

At some time, everyone has a question or two about the program they are using. The Office Online Help system provides the answers you need. You can search an extensive catalog of Help topics using a table of contents to locate specific information, or you can get context sensitive help in a dialog box. You can also ask your question in the Type A Question For Help box located on the right side of the menu bar. When you use any of these help options, a list of possible answers is shown to you in the Search Results task pane, with the most likely answer to your question at the top of the list.

Get Help Without the Office Assistant

1. Click the Help button on the Standard toolbar.

2. Locate the Help topic you want.

   ◆ Type one or more keywords in the Search For box, and then click the Start Searching button.

   ◆ Click Table Of Contents, and then click a topic.

   The topic you want appears in the right pane.

3. Read the topic, and then click any hyperlinks to get information on related topics or definitions.

4. When you're done, click the Close button.

5. Click the Close button on the task pane.

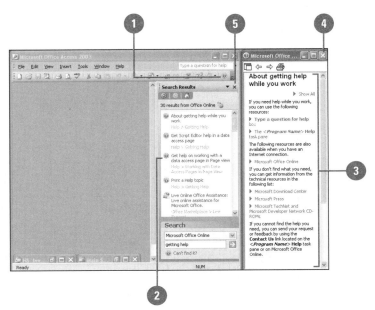

Get Help While You Work

1. Click the Type A Question For Help box.

2. Type your question, and then press Enter.

3. Click the topic that you want to read about.

4. When you're done, click the Close button on the task pane.

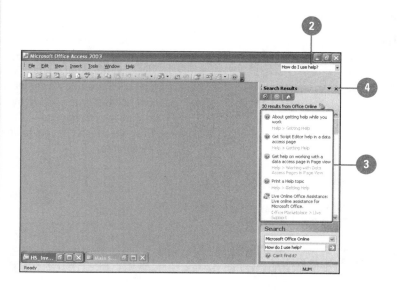

Get Help in a Dialog Box

1. Display the dialog box in which you want to get help.

2. Click the Help button.

3. Click the item in the dialog box in which you want information.

   A ScreenTip displays information about the dialog box item.

4. Click a blank area to remove the ScreenTip.

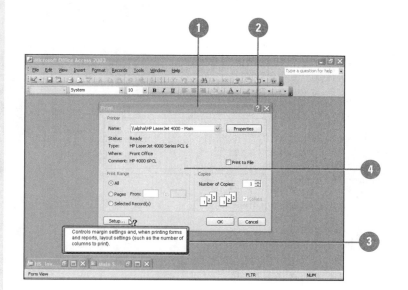

Getting Help from the Office Assistant

Often the easiest way to learn how to accomplish a task is to ask someone who knows. Now, with Office, that knowledgeable friend is always available in the form of the Office Assistant. The **Office Assistant** is an animated Help feature that you can use to access information that is directly related to the task you need help with. Using everyday language, just tell the Office Assistant what you want to do and it walks you through the process step by step. You can turn this feature on and off whenever you need to. If the personality of the default Office Assistant—Clippit—doesn't appeal to you, choose from a variety of other Office Assistants.

Ask the Office Assistant for Help

1. Click the Help menu, and then click Show Office Assistant.

2. Click the Office Assistant, if, necessary, to display the help balloon.

3. Type your question about a task you want help with.

4. Click Search.

5. Click the topic you want help with, and then read the information.

6. After you're done, click the Close button.

7. To refine the search, click the Search list arrow, select a search area, and then click the Start Searching button.

8. When you're done, click the Close button on the task pane.

9. Click the Help menu, and then click Hide The Office Assistant.

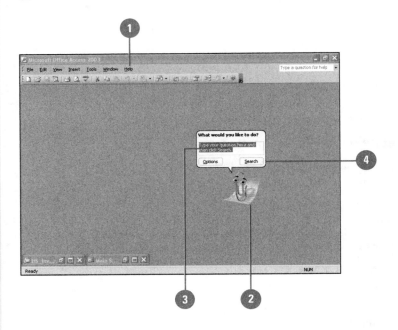

Hide the Office Assistant

1. Right-click the Office Assistant.

2. Click Hide.

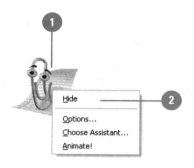

Turn Off the Office Assistant

1. Right-click the Office Assistant and then click Options, or click the Options button in the Assistant window.

2. Click the Options tab.

3. Clear the Use The Office Assistant check box.

4. Click OK.

Did You Know?

You can change the Assistant character. Right-click the Assistant, and then click Choose Assistant. Click the Next and Back buttons to view the available Assistants, and then click OK. You might be asked to insert the original installation CD.

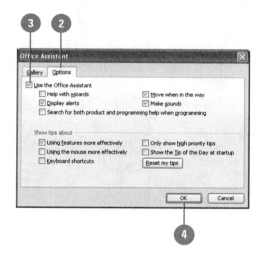

Getting Access Updates on the Web

Access offers a quick and easy way to update Access with any new software downloads that improve the stability and security of the program. From the Help menu, simply select the Check For Updates command to connect to the Microsoft Office Online Web site, where you can have your computer scanned for necessary updates, and then choose which Office updates you want to download and install. To help you stay as current and efficient as possible, Microsoft extends its Access help by giving you direct access to other areas on the Microsoft Office Online Web site. Using the Office online links on the Access Help task pane, you can check out Access-related news, obtain the most up-to-date help from Microsoft, and locate training and assistance with any aspect of Access.

Get Access Updates on the Web

1 Click the Help menu, and then click Check For Updates.

The Microsoft Office Online Web site opens, displaying the Downloads page.

2 Click Check For Updates to find out if you need Access updates, and then choose the updates you want to download and install.

3 When you're done, click the Close button.

Get the Latest Information on Access

1. Click the Help button on the toolbar.

2. Click one of the Office online links for information on an Access feature.

   ◆ Click Assistance to go to the Assistance Home Web page for information on ways to maximize the features you want to use in Access for greater efficiency.

   ◆ Click Training to go to the Training Home Web page to learn how to use the tools in Access more effectively.

   ◆ Click Communities to go to the Microsoft Office Newsgroup Web page to communicate with other Access users.

   ◆ Click Downloads to go to the Downloads Web page and get the very latest information on Access.

3. When you're done, click the Close button on the task pane.

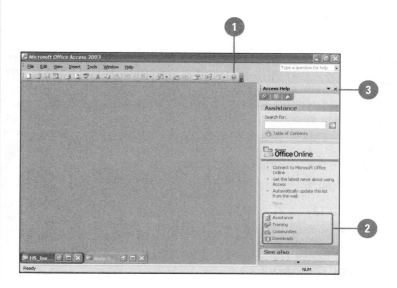

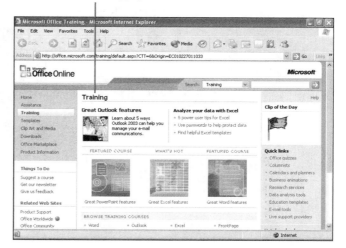

Training page on the Office Online Web site

Saving Your Work

Saving your work is generally a very important part of working with a program. If you don't save your work, you might lose important data. With Access, it's also important to save your work, but you don't have to do it. Access automatically saves your work as you do it. You don't have to worry about losing your changes, but you do have to remember that any changes you make are permanent and can be undone by using the Undo button on the Database toolbar or Undo command on the Edit menu, or changing your data again. The Undo command provides multiple undos, where you can step back through your changes.

The Save button on the Database toolbar and the Save As command on the File menu allow you to save the design aspects of new or existing database objects, such as a table, query, form, or report, but not the data the object contains.

When Access saves a new database created in Access 2003, the default file format is Access 2000, which provides maximum compatibility with existing databases. If you want a different default file format, you can change it using the Options command on the Tools menu.

Click to save the table design and structure.

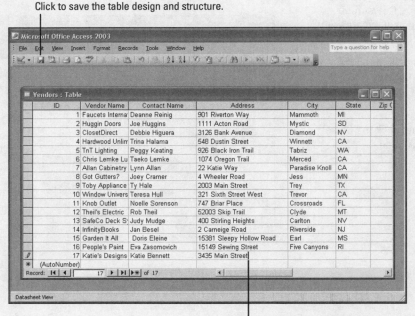

Access automatically saves the data in a database object as you type it.

Recovering an Office Program

Recover an Office Program

1. Click the Start button on the taskbar, point to All Programs, and then point to Microsoft Office.

2. Point to Microsoft Office Tools, and then click Microsoft Office Application Recovery.

3. Click the Office program you want to recover.

4. Click Restart Application or End Application.

If an Office program gets stuck exiting or stops responding during an operation, you can use the Microsoft Office Application Recovery program to exit the program, send an error report to Microsoft, and try to recover your unsaved work.

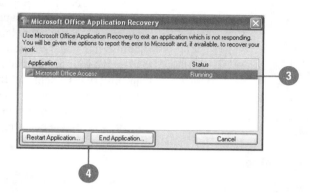

1

Detecting and Repairing Problems

To help you keep your Office 2003 suite of programs running at its best, Office comes with its own diagnostic and repair tools. If you find that Access is not behaving as you think it should, its core files might have been damaged or inadvertently deleted. If Access encounters a problem itself, it prompts you to run its self-diagnostic tool, **Detect and Repair**. Running the Detect and Repair tool restores Access' default settings and finds and fixes problems that might diminish the performance of Access. When you run Detect and Repair, you can choose to preserve any of the shortcuts that you have created. You can also choose whether you want to preserve your customized settings or return Access to its default settings. Before you begin the Detect and Repair procedure, make sure you close all programs that are running (if not, you will be prompted to do so during the procedure). If the Detect and Repair procedure doesn't fix the problem you are encountering, try reinstalling Access.

Detect and Repair Problems

1. Click the Help menu, and then click Detect And Repair.

2. To save your shortcuts, select the Restore My Shortcuts While Repairing check box.

3. To save the settings you have specified for your Outlook features, clear the Discard My Customized Settings And Restore Default Settings check box.

4. Click Start to begin the process.

5. If necessary, insert the Microsoft Office 2003 CD.

6. Click OK when the procedure is complete.

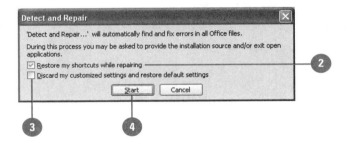

Perform Maintenance on Office Programs

1 In Windows Explorer, double-click the Setup icon on the Office CD.

2 Click one of the following maintenance buttons:

◆ Add Or Remove Features to determine which, and when, features are installed or removed

◆ Reinstall Or Repair to repair or reinstall Office

◆ Uninstall to uninstall Office

3 Click Next and then follow the wizard instructions to complete the maintenance.

Did You Know?

You can set Detect and Repair to run automatically. In the Control Panel (Classic view), double-click Add Or Remove Programs, click Microsoft Office 2003, and then click Change/Remove. Click Repair Office, click Repair Errors In My Office Installation, and then click Finish.

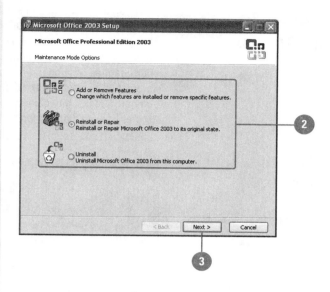

Closing a Database and Quitting Access

After you finish working in a database, you can close it. You can then choose to open another database or quit Access. If you made any changes to the structure of the database—for example, if you changed the size of any rows or columns in a table—Access prompts you to save your changes. Any changes you make to the data in a table are saved automatically as you make them. When you close a database or when you quit Access, any objects that are still open, such as tables or queries, will also be closed.

Close a Database

1. Click the Close button on the Database window.

2. If necessary, click Yes to save any changes you made or No to ignore any changes.

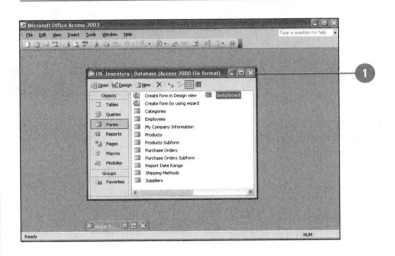

Quit Access

1. Click the Close button on the Access window title bar.

2. If necessary, click Yes to save any changes you made or No to ignore any changes.

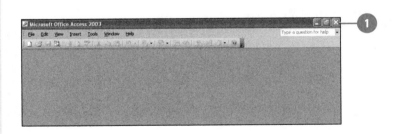

Touring Access Databases

Introduction

Microsoft Office Access 2003 helps you get started working with databases right away by providing sample database applications that you can use to store your own personal or business data. Access also offers a set of database wizards that aid you in creating common business databases. You can study these sample databases and wizards to get ideas for the databases you might want to design for other types of data that aren't covered by the existing samples and wizards.

When you are working with an existing database, however, you don't need to worry about the complexities of database design. You just need to know how to get around the database you are using. The tasks you are likely to perform with an existing database include entering and viewing data or subsets of data, creating and printing reports, and working efficiently with all the windows in front of you.

What You'll Do

Open a Sample Database

Use a Switchboard

Work with Database Objects

Group Database Objects

Hide Windows

Tour a Table

Tour a Form

Enter Data

Tour a Query

Tour a Report

Create a Database Using a Wizard

Step Through a Database Wizard

Create a Database Using a Template

Warnings About Templates and Add-ins

Opening a Sample Database

Access provides a sample database application called Northwind Traders—a database and project version—for you to explore. The Northwind Traders contains sample data and database objects for a specialty foods company. If you have specialized database needs, you can study the structure of the sample database, and then use them as models for your own.

Open a Sample Database

1. Click the Help menu.

2. Point to Sample Databases.

3. Click the sample database you want.

4. If necessary, read the introduction screen, and then click OK to continue.

   A switchboard opens for the sample database.

See Also

See "Warnings About Templates and Add-Ins" on page 44 for information on security alerts that appear when you open a database.

Did You Know?

You can switch to the Database window. You can press F11 to switch to the Database window from a switchboard or any other window.

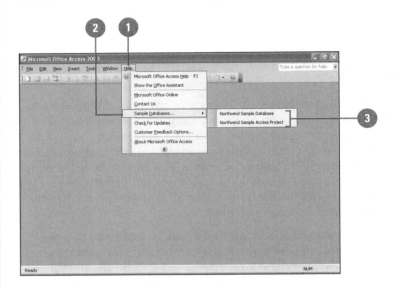

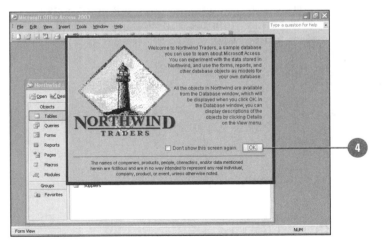

Using a Switchboard

The sample databases that come with Access all employ switchboards. A **switchboard** is a customized window that makes many features of a specific database available at the click of a button. The Address Book switchboard, for example, offers immediate access to printing mailing labels, merging addresses with a Word document, or locating an address quickly. Often, switchboard options open forms that allow you to view or enter data, reports that allow you to see summaries of data, or queries that allow you to view subsets of data.

Open a Switchboard

1. Open the database. If the database contains a switchboard, it usually appears automatically when the database is opened.

2. If necessary, click the Window menu, and then click Main Switchboard to view the switchboard.

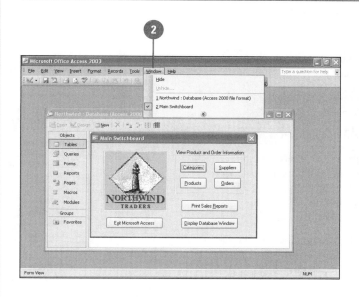

Select Switchboard Options

1. Read the descriptions on the switchboard to find the task you need to perform.

2. Click the button that corresponds to the task you want to perform.

   Access opens or starts whatever database object will help you perform that task.

3. When you're done, click the Close button on the window for the database object.

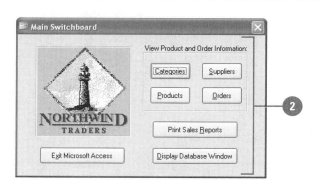

Working with Database Objects

The Database window is the container for all the objects in a database, including tables, forms, reports, queries, pages, macros, and modules. These database objects work together to help you store and manage your data. Objects are organized by object type on the Objects bar. You can open, group, rename, and delete database objects from the Database window. You can use the Open button in the Database window to view and enter object data, and the Design button to create the layout for the object data.

Open and View a Database Object

① If necessary, click the Objects bar in the Database window.

② Click the object type icon on the Objects bar.

③ Click the object you want to open.

④ Click the Open button on the Database window toolbar to view the object's data, or click the Design button to work with the object's design.

⑤ To close the object, click the Close button in the upper-right corner of the Object window.

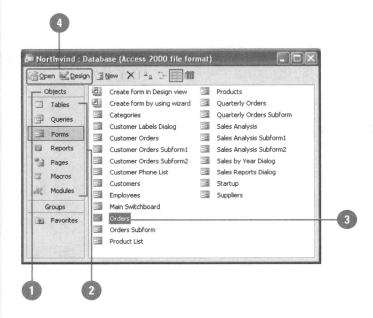

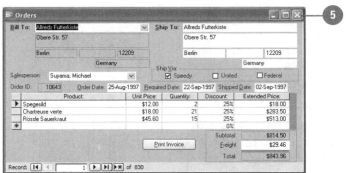

Manage Database Objects

◆ To create a new object, click the type of object you want to create on the Objects bar, and then click the New button on the Database window toolbar.

◆ To delete an object, right-click it in the Object list, and then click Delete.

◆ To rename a database object, right-click the object in the Object list, click Rename, and then type a new name.

◆ To change the Database view of the objects, click the Large Icons, Small Icons, List, or Details button on the Database window toolbar.

Did You Know?

You can use AutoCorrect to rename objects. When you rename a database object, you don't have to worry about other Access objects that use the object you just renamed. The Name AutoCorrect feature automatically fixes common side effects that occur when a user makes name changes. Click the Tools menu, click Options, click the General tab, and then work with the Name AutoCorrect settings to enable this feature.

Click to create a new database object.

The menu opens when you right-click an object.

Click to rename the selected object.

Click to delete the selected object.

View buttons

Grouping Database Objects

You can group shortcuts to related objects of different types together using the **Groups bar**. When you first create a group, it is empty until you populate it with shortcuts to the related objects. When you add an object to a group, you do not change the object's original location, nor are you creating a new object. Instead, you are simply creating a shortcut to an object that already exists.

Create a Group and Add a Group Shortcut

1. In the Database window, click the Groups bar.

2. Right-click anywhere under the Groups bar.

3. Click New Group, type a name for your group, and then click OK.

4. Drag an object from the Object list to the group.

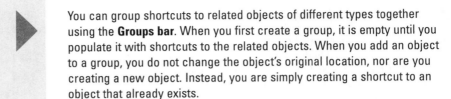

Remove a Group Shortcut

1. In the Database window, display the database group with the shortcut you want to remove.

2. Select the shortcut, press Delete, and then click Yes to confirm.

Did You Know?

You can delete or rename a group.
In the Database window, click the Groups bar, right-click anywhere under the Groups bar, and then click Delete Group or Rename Group. When you rename a group, type a new name, and then click OK.

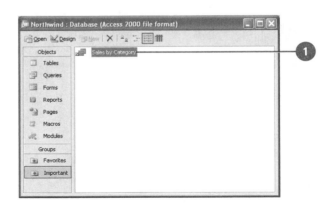

Hiding Windows

As you work with a database, you might find it difficult to work with so many windows on the screen. You can unclutter the Access program window by hiding a window. Hiding windows in Access does not affect the information in other parts of the database; all information in hidden windows is still referenced as necessary. When you need to view the window, you can unhide it.

Hide a Window

1 Display the window you want to hide.

2 Click the Window menu.

3 Click Hide.

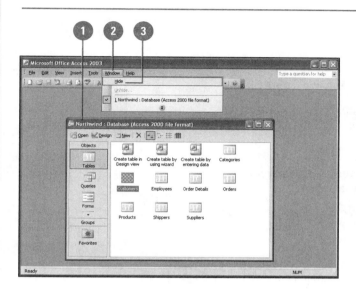

Unhide a Window

1 Click the Window menu, and then click Unhide.

2 Select the window you want to unhide.

3 Click OK.

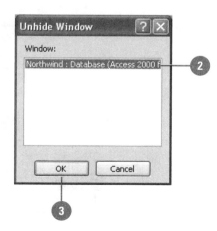

Touring a Table

A database is made up of groups of fields organized into tables. A **field** is a specific category of information, such as a name or a product. Related fields are grouped in tables. All the fields dealing with customers might be grouped in a Customer table, while fields dealing with products might be grouped in a Products table. You usually enter data into fields one entity at a time (one customer at a time, one product at a time, and so on). Access stores all the data for a single entity in a **record**. You can view a table in Datasheet or Design view. Design view allows you to work with your table's fields. Datasheet view shows a grid of fields and records. The fields appear as columns and the records as rows.

Open and View a Table

1. In the Database window, click Tables on the Objects bar.

2. Click the table.

3. Click Open. The table opens in Datasheet view.

   ◆ Drag the horizontal scroll box to scroll through the fields in a table.

   ◆ Drag the vertical scroll box to scroll through the records in a table.

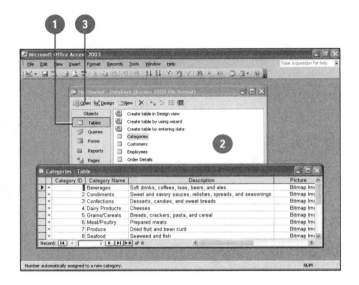

Select and Resize a Column or Row

◆ Click the column or row selector to select a column or row.

◆ Drag the border between the column or row selectors to resize a column or row.

Each record has a unique identification number, which appears in the Specific Record box when that record is selected.

Row selector   Column selector

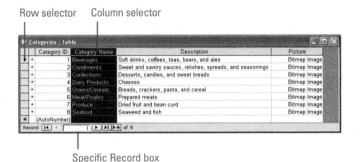

Specific Record box

Enter a New Record in a Table

1. Open the table in Datasheet view from a switchboard or from the Objects bar in the Database window.

2. Click the New Record button.

3. Press Tab to accept the AutoNumber entry.

4. Enter the data for the first field. If you make a typing mistake, press Backspace.

5. Press Tab to move to the next field or Shift+Tab to move to the previous field.

6. When you reach the end of the record, click the New Record button or press Tab to go to the next record. Access saves your changes when you move to the next record.

Delete a Record from a Table

1. Right-click the row selector.

2. Click Delete Record.

3. Click Yes to confirm the deletion.

Did You Know?

You can AutoNumber fields. The first field in a table is often an AutoNumber field, which Access uses to assign a unique number to each record. You can't select or change this value.

Touring a Form

Database designers often display data in forms that mimic the paper forms used to record data. Forms facilitate data entry and record viewing. They can also contain buttons that allow you to perform other actions, such as running macros, printing, or creating labels. The options that appear on a form depend on what features the database designer included. A form directs you to enter the correct information and can automatically check your entries for errors. Access places the data you've entered in the form into the proper table or tables. You can open a form in Form view or Design view. Form view allows you to view all the information associated with a record; Design view allows you to modify the form's design.

Enter a New Record in a Form

1. In the Database window, click Forms on the Objects bar, click the form you want to use, and then click the Open button.

2. Click the New Record button.

3. Enter the data for the first field.

4. Press Tab to move to the next field or Shift+Tab to move to the previous field.

5. When you have finished entering the data, you can close the form, click the New Record button to enter another record, or view a different record.

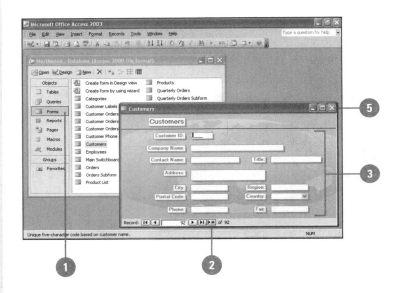

Delete a Record from a Form

1. Display the record you want to delete.

2. Click the Delete Record button on the Form View toolbar.

3. Click Yes to confirm the deletion.

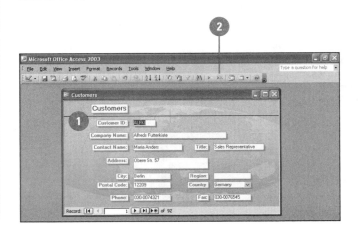

Entering Data

Normally you enter data into a form, because forms are specifically designed to facilitate data entry. You can, however, enter data into a table or a query. The methods are similar. How you enter data in a field depends on how the database designer created the field. Some fields accept only certain kinds of information, such as numbers or text. Some fields appear as check boxes or groups of option buttons; others appear as text boxes. Some text boxes only allow dates; others only allow certain predefined entries, such as a state or country. When you enter data, you don't have to click a Save button to save the data. Access automatically saves the data as you enter it.

Enter Data into a Field

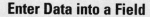

1. Open the query, table, page, or form into which you want to enter data.

2. Activate the field into which you want to enter data.

   ◆ Click a field to activate it.

   ◆ Press Tab to move to the next field or Shift+Tab to move to the previous field.

3. Enter data in the active field.

   ◆ Click a list arrow, and then click one of the available choices (such as a category).

   ◆ Click a check box or option button.

   ◆ Type text in a box. When you click a box, a blinking insertion point appears, indicating where the text will appear when you type.

   ◆ Enter dates in the required format (such as month/day/year).

Touring a Query

To locate and retrieve information in a table (or in multiple tables), you create a query. A **query** is simply a question that you ask a database to help you locate specific information. For example, if you want to know which customers placed orders in the last six months, you can create a query to examine the contents of the Order Date field and to find all the records in which the purchase date is less than six months ago. Access retrieves the data that meets the specifications in your query and displays that data in table format. You can sort that information or retrieve just a subset of its contents with still more specific criteria, so that you can focus on exactly the information you need—no more or less.

Open and Run a Query

1. In the Database window, click Queries on the Objects bar.

2. Click the query you want to run.

3. Click the Open button.

   The query opens in a table called a dynaset. The dynaset displays the records that meet the specifications set forth in the query.

View a Query in Design View

1. In the Database window, click Queries on the Objects bar.

2. Click the query you want to run.

3. Click the Design button.

   In Design view, you can see the criteria that specify what records to include in the dynaset.

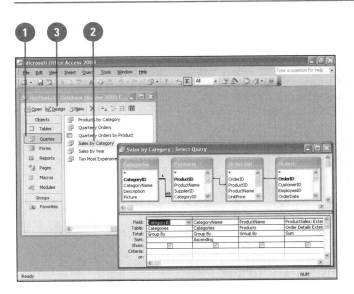

Touring a Report

After you have retrieved and organized only the specific information you want, you can display and print this information as a report. In Access you can create a simple report that displays each record's information, or you can customize a report to include calculations, charts, graphics, and other features to go beyond the numbers and really emphasize the information in the report. You can print a report, a table, a query, or any data in a single step using the Print button, in which case Access automatically prints a single copy of all pages in the report. If you want to print only selected pages or if you want to specify other printing options, use the Print command on the File menu.

Create a Report

1. In the Database window, click Reports on the Objects bar.

2. Click the report you want to view.

3. Click the Preview button.

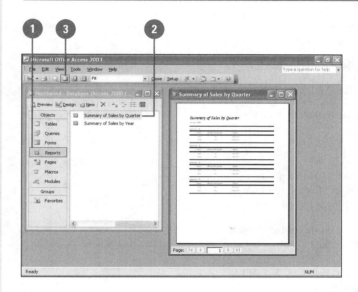

Print Data

1. Click the File menu, and then click Print.

2. If necessary, click the Name list arrow, and then select the printer you want to use.

3. To print selected pages in the report, click the Pages option, and then type the first page in the From box and the ending page in the To box.

4. Click OK.

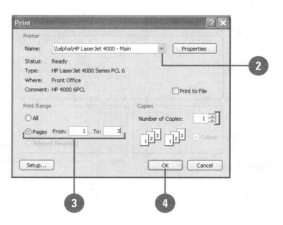

Creating a Database Using a Wizard

AC03S-1-1

You can use a wizard to create a database, or you can create a custom database from scratch. The Access database wizards help you create databases suited to your specific needs. Each wizard guides you through the process of selecting and creating fields, tables, queries, reports, and forms, which makes it easier to use the database. When you create a database, you need to assign a name and location to your database, and then you can create the tables, forms, and reports that make up the inner parts of the database.

Create a Database Using a Wizard

1 Click the New button on the Standard toolbar.

2 Click On My Computer.

3 Click the Databases tab.

4 Click the database wizard you want.

5 Click OK.

6 Click the Save In list arrow, and then select the location where you want to save the new database.

7 Type in a name for the database, and then click Create.

Did You Know?

The default file format is Access 2000. For maximum compatibility with existing databases, the default file format for new databases created with Access 2003 is Access 2000.

See Also

See "Converting Access Databases" on page 268 for information on changing the default file format and converting databases.

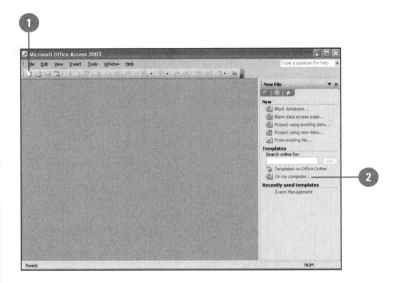

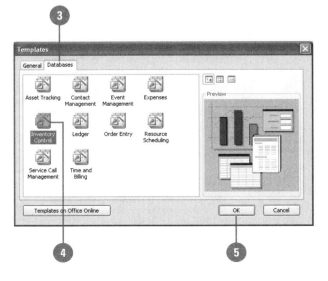

8 Read the introduction, and then click Next to continue.

9 Click a table to display the fields in the table, select the check boxes with the fields you want, and then click Next.

10 Select the style you want to use for screen displays, and then click Next.

11 Select the report style you want, and then click Next.

12 Type a name for the database, and then click Next.

13 Click Finish.

Access creates the database based on your responses to the wizard. Enter any additional information requested during the final process.

When Access finishes creating all the database objects, the Main Switchboard appears, where you can use the database.

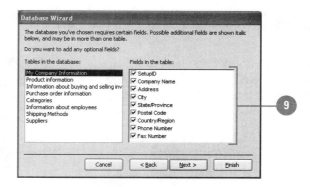

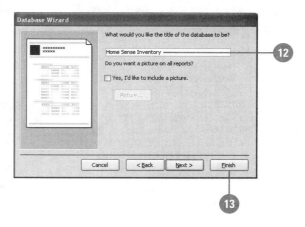

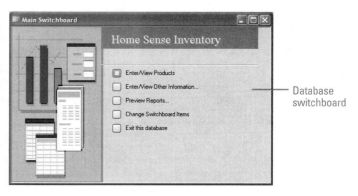

Database switchboard

Stepping Through a Database Wizard

The choices that appear as you progress through a database wizard depend on the kind of information the database is designed to manage. All the wizards, however, share certain features.

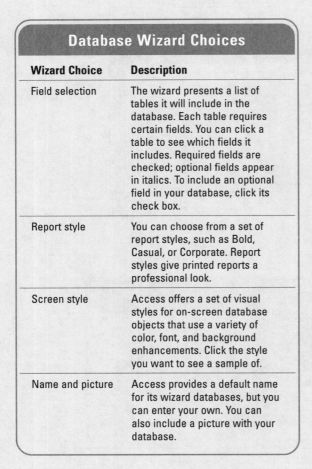

Database Wizard Choices

Wizard Choice	Description
Field selection	The wizard presents a list of tables it will include in the database. Each table requires certain fields. You can click a table to see which fields it includes. Required fields are checked; optional fields appear in italics. To include an optional field in your database, click its check box.
Report style	You can choose from a set of report styles, such as Bold, Casual, or Corporate. Report styles give printed reports a professional look.
Screen style	Access offers a set of visual styles for on-screen database objects that use a variety of color, font, and background enhancements. Click the style you want to see a sample of.
Name and picture	Access provides a default name for its wizard databases, but you can enter your own. You can also include a picture with your database.

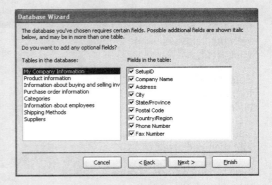

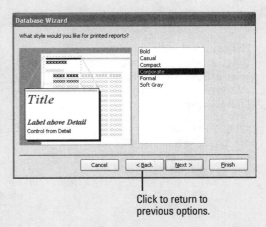

Click to return to previous options.

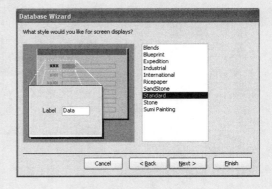

Creating a Database Using a Template

The quickest way to create a database is to use a template, which you can find on the Office Online Web site. Office Online provides database templates on a variety of subjects, including finance, inventory control, and order status. The New File task pane contains a link to access the templates area on the Office Online Web site. You can browse the site for templates, and then download the ones you want. Before you start the downloading process, be sure to carefully read the download and any installation instructions. Some of the templates on the site were created for earlier versions of Access, but you can use them with Office Access 2003.

Get Templates on the Web

1. Click the File menu, and then click New.

2. Click Templates On Office Online to open the Microsoft Web Office Online site in your browser.

3. Click the link to the template you want.

4. Click Download Now, and then follow the online instructions.

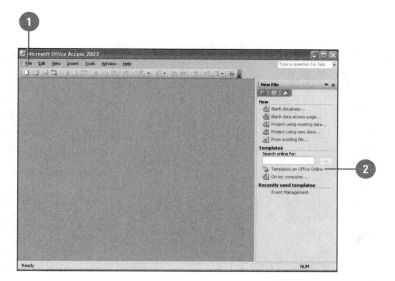

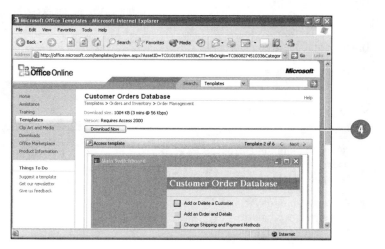

Warnings About Templates and Add-Ins

When you open a database or database template, you might be prompted with a security alert. Databases can include potentially unsafe functions using the Microsoft Jet Expression Service and additional programming code called macros, which can contain viruses. You can protect your computer from viruses by running up-to-date antivirus software and setting your macro security level to high for maximum protection or medium for lesser protection. When you set the macro security level to high, some database functionality, such as wizards, is disabled. If macro security is set to medium, database users will be prompted to enable macros. Prompts also might appear to block potentially unsafe functions.

Set Macro Security

1. Click the Tools menu, point to Macro, and then click Security.

2. Click Security Level tab, and then click the Medium option.

3. Click the Trusted Publishers tab.

4. Select or clear the Trust All Installed Add-ins And Templates check box.

5. Click OK, and then if necessary, click Yes to block unsafe expressions and click OK to restart Access.

Enable Macros When You Open a Database

1. Open a database with macros.

2. If a macro security alert appears, click one of the following:

   ◆ Open to enable macros and open the database.

   ◆ Cancel to keep the current macro security level and stop the open database task.

   ◆ More Info to open Access online Help with more information about macro security.

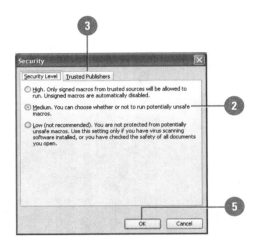

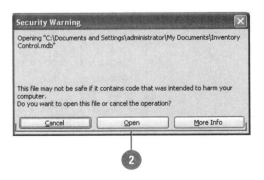

Planning and Creating a Custom Database

3

Introduction

The Microsoft Office Access 2003 database wizards make creating databases easy, but you may need to create a database that does not fit any of the wizard's predefined choices. In that situation, you may need to create the database "from scratch."

Creating a database from scratch involves careful planning. You must:

◆ Determine the purpose and scope of your database.

◆ Decide what tables your database will contain and what the content of those tables will be.

◆ Define how data in one table is related to data in another table.

When you create a database from scratch, you can take advantage of the tools that Access provides. If you don't plan to create a database from scratch but instead plan to use only existing Access databases, you might not need the information in this chapter. Understanding database design concepts, however, will help you better understand how to create effective queries later on.

What You'll Do

Create a New Database

Plan Tables

Create Tables in a Database

Create a Table Using a Wizard

Set a Primary Key Using the Table Wizard

Assign Table Relationships Using the Table Wizard

Create a Table by Entering Data

Import Data into Tables

Work with a Table in Design View

Specify a Primary Key in Design View

Plan Table Relationships

Define Table Relationships

Ensure Referential Integrity

Identify Object Dependencies

Modify Object Dependencies

Creating a New Database

AC03S-1-1

A database created without using one of the database wizards is empty; it doesn't contain any tables, forms, or reports. Unlike new documents created with other Microsoft Office 2003 programs, a blank Access database must be saved to a hard disk or floppy disk before you can work with it. Once you save the database, you can add the elements, such as fields, tables, queries, reports, and forms, and the features your database requires. If you already have a database that you want to use as the starting point for a new database, you can create a new database from an existing one.

Create a Blank Database

1. Click the New button on the Standard toolbar.

2. Click Blank Database.

3. Click the Save In list arrow, and then select the location where you want to save the new database.

4. Type in a name for the database.

5. Click Create.

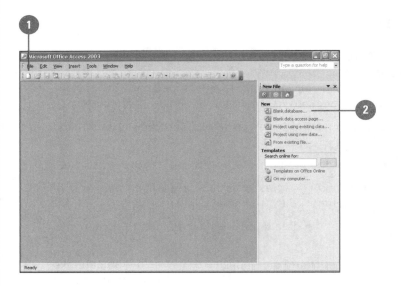

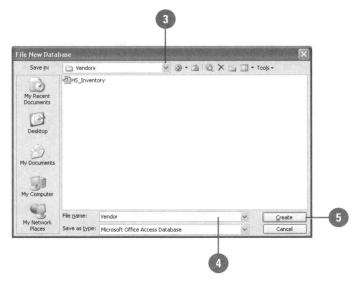

Create a New Database From an Existing Database

① Click the New button on the Standard toolbar.

② Click From Existing File.

③ Click the Look In list arrow, and then select the location where the database you want to use as the basis for a new database.

④ Click the the database file.

⑤ Click Create New.

Access creates a new database with the existing database name and a number at the end.

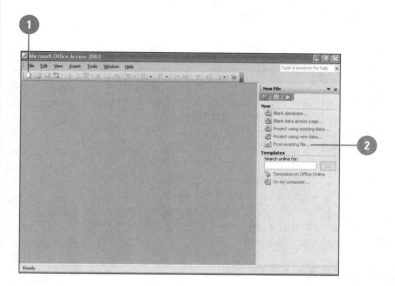

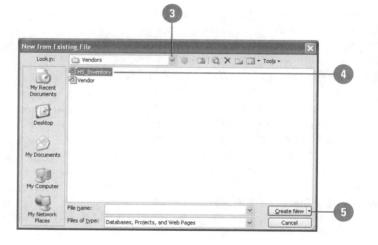

Planning Tables

Although you can always make changes to your database when necessary, a little planning before you begin can save time later on. When you plan a database, consider how you will use the data. What kind of data are you collecting? What kind of data are you entering? How are data values related to one another? Can your data be organized into separate, smaller groups? What kinds of safeguards can you create to ensure that errors do not creep into your data? As you consider these questions, you should apply the answers as you structure your database.

Plan Tables

Tables are one of the fundamental building blocks of a database. Database planning begins with deciding how many and what kinds of tables your database will contain. Consider organizing your database information into several tables—each one containing fields related to a specific topic—rather than one large table containing fields for a large variety of topics. For example, you could create a Customers table that contains only customer information and an Orders table that contains only order information. By focusing each table on a single task, you greatly simplify the structure of those tables and make them easier to modify later on.

Choose Data Types

When you create a table, you must decide what fields to include and the appropriate format for those fields. Access allows you to assign a data type to a field, a format that defines the kind of data the field can accept. Access provides a wide variety of data types, ranging from text and number formats to object-based formats for images, sounds, and video clips. Choosing the correct data type helps you manage your data and reduces the possibility of data-entry errors.

Specify a Primary Key

You should also identify which field or fields are the table's primary keys. **Primary keys** are those fields whose values uniquely identify each record in the table. A social security number field in a personnel table could be used as a primary key, since each employee has a unique social security number. A table with time-ordered data might have two primary keys—a date field and a time field (hours and minutes), which together uniquely identify an exact moment in time. Although primary keys are not required, using them is one way of removing the possibility of duplicate records existing within your tables.

Creating Tables in a Database

After creating a database file, you need to create the tables that will store the data. There are several ways to create a new table: in Design view, in Datasheet view, with a Table Wizard, or by importing a table from another Access database. Depending on the method you choose, creating a table can involve one or more of the following:

◆ Specifying the fields for the table

◆ Determining the data type for each field

◆ Determining the field size (for text and number fields only)

◆ Assigning the primary key

◆ Saving and naming the table

Methods for Creating a Table

Method	Description
Datasheet	When you create a table in Datasheet view, you can start viewing and entering data right away. Access automatically assigns a data type based on the kind of information you entered in the field, and it assigns a default field size for text and number fields. After you close and save the table, Access prompts you to identify a primary key or to allow Access to designate one for you.
Design	In Design view, you must specify the fields, specify the data type for each field, assign the size (for text and number fields), assign the primary key, and save the table yourself.
Table Wizard	Using a Table Wizard, you select fields from sample tables that are appropriate for the type of database you are creating. The data type and other field properties are already defined for each field.
Importing	If you want to use data from another Access database in the database you are creating, you can import it. When you import a table, all the field names and data types are retained with the imported data. However, you must name the new table and identify the primary key or have Access create a primary key for you. Also, you may need to change the field size and other properties after importing.
Linking	When you link a table, the data is retrieved from a table in another database. Linking a table saves disk space because there is only one table rather than multiple tables with the same data. Linking a table saves time because there is no need to update the same information in more than one table.

3

Creating a Table Using a Wizard

 AC03S-1-2

Create a Table Using the Table Wizard

1. In the Database window, click Tables on the Objects bar, and then double-click the Create Table By Using Wizard icon.

2. Click the Business or Personal option.

3. Scroll thru the list to find the table that best matches your needs.

4. Double-click each field you want to include in the table. Click Next to continue.

5. Type a new name for the table, or accept the suggested name.

6. Click the Yes option to have the Table Wizard assign the primary key, or click the No option to assign your own primary key. Click Next to continue.

> ### Did You Know?
>
> **You can select fields in the order you want them to appear in the table.** In the Sample Fields list, you can choose the fields you want to include in your table in any order. The fields you choose will appear in the table in the order you chose them.

One of the easiest ways to create a table is to use the Table Wizard. The **Table Wizard** walks you through a series of dialog boxes that help you choose the types of tables your database will contain and the fields present in each table. You can change table names, field names, and properties as you proceed through the wizard. The wizard also makes it easy to create a primary key for your table and to establish relationships between the new table and other tables in the database.

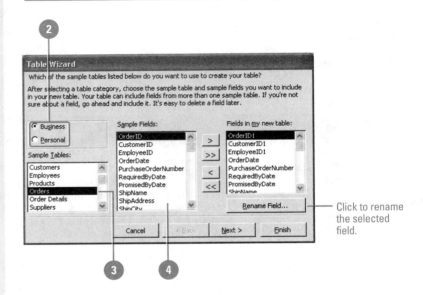

Click to rename the selected field.

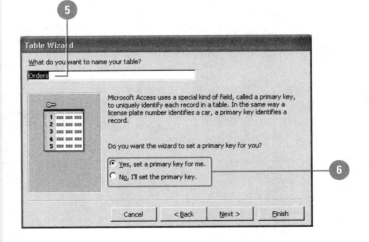

7. If you chose to set the primary key, select the field and data type. Click Next to continue.

8. If your database already contains at least one table and you want to make changes, select the relationship you want to change, click Relationships, specify the new table relationships, and then click OK. Click Next to continue.

9. In the final wizard dialog box, click one of the options, either to modify the table design (in Design view) before entering data, to enter data directly (in Datasheet view), or to enter data in a form that the wizard creates for you.

10. Click Finish.

See Also

See "Setting a Primary Key Using the Table Wizard" on page 52 to learn how to create a primary key with the Table Wizard.

See "Assigning Table Relationships Using the Table Wizard" on page 53 to learn how to relate tables to one another.

This dialog box appears only if your database already contains at least one table.

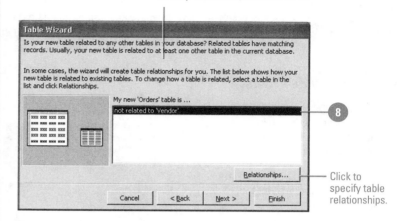

Click to specify table relationships.

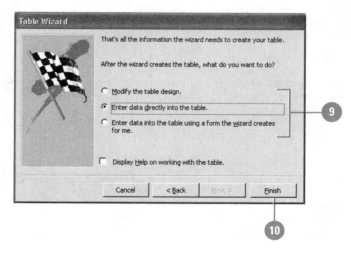

3

Setting a Primary Key Using the Table Wizard

When you create a table with the Table Wizard, you can choose either to set a primary key yourself or to have the wizard do it for you. If you set the primary key, a dialog box appears that allows you to select the primary key and define its data type. Access can generate primary key values automatically, or you can enter a unique value for each new record when you enter data.

Set the Primary Key Yourself

1. When the Table Wizard prompts you to set the primary key, click the No, I'll Set The Primary Key option. Click Next to continue.

2. Click the list arrow to select the field you want to use as the primary key.

3. Click the option corresponding to the data type you want to use for your primary key.

4. Click Next to continue.

5. Click the option corresponding to what you want to do after the wizard creates the table.

6. Click Finish.

See Also

See "Specifying a Primary Key in Design View" on page 57 for information on creating and altering primary keys.

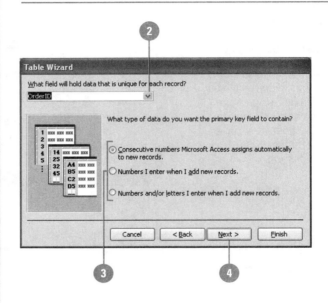

Primary Key Options

Option	Description
Consecutive Numbers	Access assigns the primary key value for a new record that is automatically one more than the primary key value in the previous record.
Numbers I Enter When I Add New Records	You enter a unique number for the primary key of each new record.
Numbers And/Or Letters I Enter When I Add New Records	You enter a unique string of text for the primary key of each new record.

Assigning Table Relationships Using the Table Wizard

When you create a table using the Table Wizard, you have the option to relate the new table to the other tables in the database. The Table Wizard displays a list of established tables. You can choose to create a relationship between the new table and any of the tables in the list. You can create relationships between the tables in which a record in one table matches with many in another. When you create a one-to-many relationship, the Table Wizard automatically adds new fields to the related table if necessary.

Create a Relationship Between Tables

1 When the Table Wizard displays the dialog box listing related and unrelated tables, select the table whose relationship you want to change, and then click the Relationships button.

2 Click one of the three options describing the relationship between the new table and the established table.

3 Click OK.

See Also

See "Defining Table Relationships" on page 60 for information about establishing table relationships.

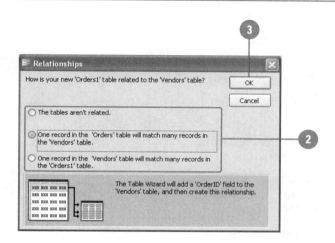

Relationship Options

Option	Description
The Tables Aren't Related	No relationship will exist between the new table and the established table.
One Record In The New Table Will Match Many Records In The Old Table	Create a one-to-many relationship. Access sets the new table as the primary table and the established table as the related table.
One Record In The Old Table Will Match Many Records In The New Table	Create a one-to-many relationship. Access sets the new table as the related table and the established table as the primary table.

Creating a Table by Entering Data

Access allows you to display many of its objects in multiple viewing modes. Datasheet view displays the data in your tables, queries, forms, and reports. Design view displays options for designing your Access objects. You can create a new table in both views. When you create a table in Datasheet view, you can enter data and Access creates the table as you type. Access determines the data type of each field based on the data you enter. When you finish entering data, Access will prompt you for the name of the table you've just created.

Enter Data to Create a Table

1. In the Database window, click Tables on the Objects bar.

2. Double-click the Create Table By Entering Data icon.

3. Enter the data.

   Press Tab to move from field to field or click in a cell.

4. To change a field name, double-click the field name, type the new name, and then press Enter.

5. Click the Save button on the toolbar.

6. Type a table name, and then click OK.

7. To have Access set the primary key, click Yes.

8. Close the Table window.

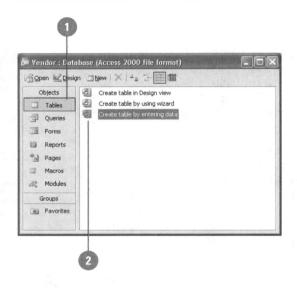

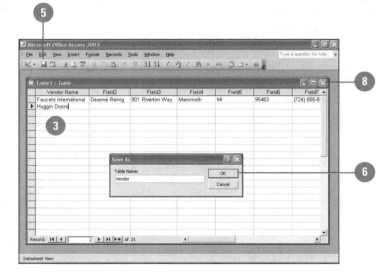

Did You Know?

You can select or resize a column or row like in Excel. To select a column or row in a table, click the Column or Row selector. To resize a column or row, drag the border between the Column or Row selectors.

Importing Data into Tables

You can create new tables from other Access databases by importing and linking tables. When you import a table, you copy data from a table in one Access database and place it in a new table in your database. When you link a table, the data stays in its original location, but you can display and access that data from within your database. If data in the original database changes, the changes will appear in your linked database, too.

Import a Table from a Database

1. In the Database window, click the New button.

2. Double-click Import Table.

3. Locate and select the database file that contains the data you want to import, and then click Import.

4. Click the tables you want to import. To deselect a table, click the table again.

5. Click OK.

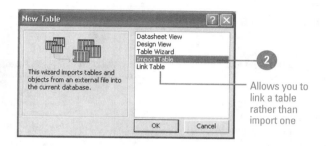

Allows you to link a table rather than import one

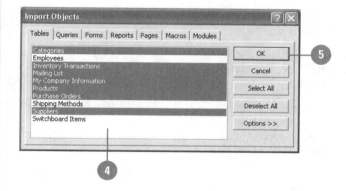

Did You Know?

You can identify linked tables. Identify a linked table in the Database window by the arrow that appears to the left of its table icon.

See Also

See "Getting Data from Other Programs" on page 238 for more on retrieving information from other sources.

Working with a Table in Design View

AC03S-1-2, AC03S-1-3

Create or Modify a Table in Design View

1. In the Database window, click Tables on the Objects bar.

2. Double-click the Create Table In Design View icon, or click the table you want to modify, and then click the Design button.

3. Click in a Field Name cell, and then type a modified field name.

4. Click in a Data Type cell, click the Data Type list arrow, and then click a data type.

5. Click in a Description cell, and then type a description. If the Property Update Options button appears, if necessary, select an option.

6. To insert a field, click the row selector below where you want the field, and then click the Insert Rows button on the Table Design toolbar.

7. To delete a field, click the row selector for the field you want to delete, and then click the Delete Rows button on the Table Design toolbar.

8. Click the Save button on the toolbar, and then if necessary, enter a table name and click OK.

9. When you're done, click the Close button in the Table window.

Most Access objects are displayed in Design view, which allows you to work with the underlying structure of your tables, queries, forms, and reports. To create a new table in Design view, you can define the fields that will comprise the table before you enter any data. In Design view for tables, each row corresponds to a field. You can edit, insert, and delete fields in your database tables in Design view. You can insert a field by adding a row, while you delete a field by removing a row. You can also change field order by dragging a row selector to a new position.

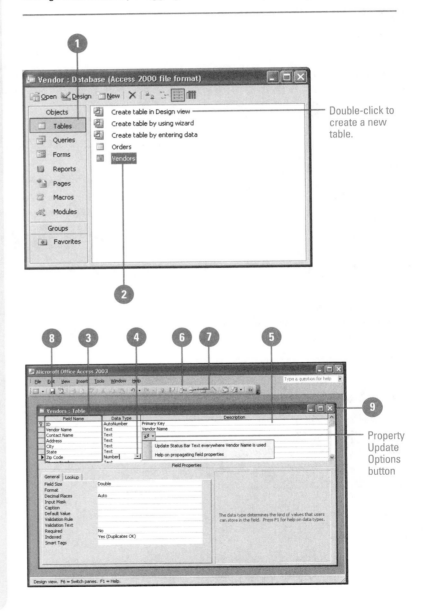

Double-click to create a new table.

Property Update Options button

Specifying a Primary Key in Design View

In Design view, you can use the Primary Key button to assign or remove the primary key designation for the selected field or fields. When you create a table in Design view, you can specify more than one field as a primary key. However, since you are not using the Table Wizard, you are responsible for determining the data type of the primary key. Whatever data type you choose, values for the primary key must be unique for each table record.

Specify a Primary Key

1. In Design view, create a field that will be that table's primary key, and then select an appropriate data type.

    ◆ If you choose the AutoNumber data type, Access assigns a value to the primary key for a new record that is one more than the primary key in the previous record.

    ◆ If you choose any other data type, such as Text, Number, or Date/Time, during data entry, you must enter a unique value in the appropriate format for the primary key of each new record.

2. Click the row selector of that field.

3. Click the Primary Key button on the Table Design toolbar.

3 Click to assign or remove a primary key.

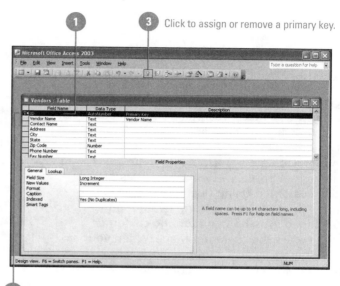

2 This symbol indicates the primary key field. Click to select the rowfill

Did You Know?

You can select more than one primary key. To create more than one primary key, press and hold Ctrl, click the row selector for each field you want to designate as a primary key, and then click the Primary Key button.

Planning Table Relationships

When you place data into separate tables, you need some way of merging this data together for forms and reports. You can do this by establishing table relationships that indicate how data in one table relates to data in another.

Specifying Common Fields

Data from several different tables is related through the use of common fields. A common field is a field existing in two or more tables, allowing you to match records from one table with records in the other tables. For example, the Customers table and the Orders table might both contain a Customer ID field, which functions as a primary key that identifies a specific customer. Using Customer ID as a common field allows you to generate reports containing information on both the customer and the orders the customer made. When you use a primary key as a common field, it is called a **foreign** key in the second table.

Building Table Relationships

Once you have a way of relating two tables with a common field, your next task is to express the nature of that relationship. There are three types of relationships: one-to-one, one-to-many, and many-to-many.

A table containing customer names and a second table containing customer addresses exist in a one-to-one relationship if each customer is limited to only one address. Similarly, a one-to-many relationship exists between the Customers table and the Orders table because a single customer could place several orders. In a one-to-many relationship like this, the "one" table is called the **primary table**, and the "many" table is called the **related table**.

Table Relationships	
Wizard Choice	**Description**
One-to-one	Each record in one table is matched to only one record in a second table, and visa versa.
One-to-many	Each record in one table is matched to one or more records in a second table, but each record in the second table is matched to only one record in the first table.
Many-to-many	Each record in one table is matched to multiple records in a second table, and visa versa.

Finally, if you allow several customers to be recorded on a single order (as in the case of group purchases), a many-to-many relationship exists between the Customers and Orders tables.

Maintaining Referential Integrity

Table relationships must obey standards of **referential integrity**, a set of rules that control how you can delete or modify data between related tables. Referential integrity protects you from erroneously changing data in a primary table required by a related table. You can apply referential integrity when:

- The common field is the primary table's primary key.

- The related fields have the same format.

- Both tables belong to the same database.

Referential integrity places some limitations on you.

- Before adding a record to a related table, a matching record must already exist in the primary table.

- The value of the primary key in the primary table cannot be changed if matching records exist in a related table.

- A record in the primary table cannot be deleted if matching records exist in a related table.

Access can enforce these rules by cascading any changes across the related tables. For example, Access can automatically copy any changes to the common field across the related tables. Similarly, if a record is deleted in the primary table, Access can automatically delete related records in all other tables.

As you work through these issues of tables, fields, and table relationships, you will create a structure for your database that will be easier to manage and less prone to data-entry error.

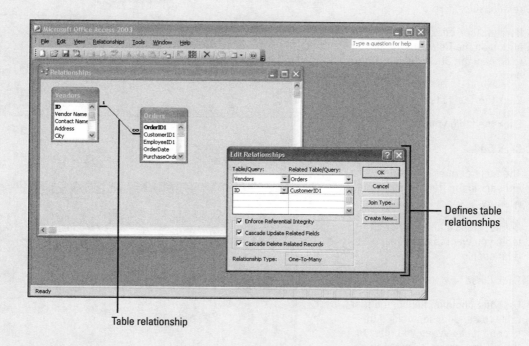

Table relationship

Defines table relationships

Defining Table Relationships

AC03S-1-5

You can define table relationships in several ways. When you first create tables in your database using the Table Wizard, the wizard gives you an opportunity to define table relationships. You can also define relationships in the Database window or in Design view. This method gives you more control over your table relationships and also gives you a quick snapshot of all the relationships in your database. After you define a relationship, you can double-click the connection line to modify or add to the relationship.

Define Table Relationships

① In the Database window, click the Relationships button on the Database toolbar.

   If relationships are already established in your database, they appear in the Relationships window. In this window you can create additional table relationships.

② If necessary, click the Show Table button on the Relationship toolbar to display the Show Table dialog box.

③ Click the Tables tab.

④ Click the table you want.

⑤ Click Add.

   The table or query you selected appears in the Relationships window.

   Repeat steps 4 and 5 for each table you want to use in a relationship.

⑥ Click Close.

⑦ Drag the common field in the first table to the common field in the second table. When you release the mouse button, a line appears between the two tables, signifying that they are related. Also, the Edit Relationships dialog box opens, in which you can confirm or modify the relationship.

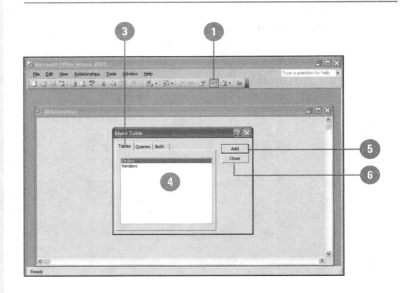

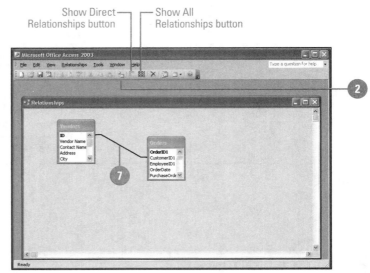

Show Direct Relationships button

Show All Relationships button

8 Click the Join Type button if you want to specify the join type. Click OK to return to the Edit Relationships dialog box.

9 Click Create to create the relationship.

Did You Know?

You can view the relationships you want to see. Click the Show Direct Relationships button on the Relationship toolbar to see tables that are directly related to each other. Click the Show All Relationships button on the Relationship toolbar to see all the relationships between all the tables and queries in your database.

You can print the Relationships window. Open the Relationships window you want to print, click the File menu, click Print Relationships, select the print settings you want, and then click OK.

You can delete a table relationship. In the Relationships window, select the line that joins the tables that you no longer want related to one another. Click the Edit menu, and then click Delete. In the message box, click Yes to confirm that you want to permanently delete this relationship. You will not be able to undo this change.

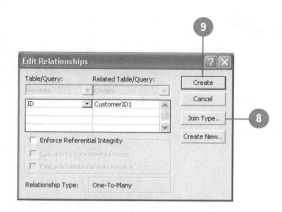

Join Types

Join Types	Description
Include rows only where the joined fields from both tables are equal	Choose this option if you want to see one record in the second table for every record that appears in the first table. The number of records you see in the two tables will be the same.
Include ALL records from "xxx" (the first table) and only those records from "yyy" (the second table) where the joined fields are equal	Choose this option if you want to see all the records in the first table (even if there is no corresponding record in the second table) as well as the records from the second table in which the joined fields are the same in both tables. The number of records you see in the first table might be greater than the number of records in the second table.
Include ALL records from "yyy" (the second table) and only those records from the "xxx" (the first table) where the joined fields are equal	Choose this option if you want to see all the records in the second table (even if there is no corresponding record in the first table) as well as the records from the first table in which the joined fields are the same in both tables. The number of records you see in the second table might be greater than the number of records in the first table.

3

Ensuring Referential Integrity

 AC03S-1-6

Referential integrity in table relationships keeps users from accidentally deleting or changing related data. If a primary table contains a list of employees and related tables contain additional information about those employees, and an employee quits, his record is removed from the primary table. His records should also be removed in all related tables. Access allows you to change or delete related data, but only if these changes are cascaded through the series of related tables. You can do this by selecting the Cascade Update Related Fields and Cascade Delete Related Records check boxes in the Edit Relationships dialog box.

Ensure Referential Integrity

① In the Database window, click the Relationships button on the Database toolbar.

② Double-click the join line for the relationship you want to work with.

③ Click to select the Enforce Referential Integrity check box to ensure that referential integrity always exists between related tables in the database.

④ If you want changes to the primary field of the primary table automatically copied to the related field of the related table, click to select the Cascade Update Related Fields check box.

⑤ If you want Access to delete records in the related tables whenever records in the primary table are deleted, click to select the Cascade Delete Related Records check box.

⑥ Click OK.

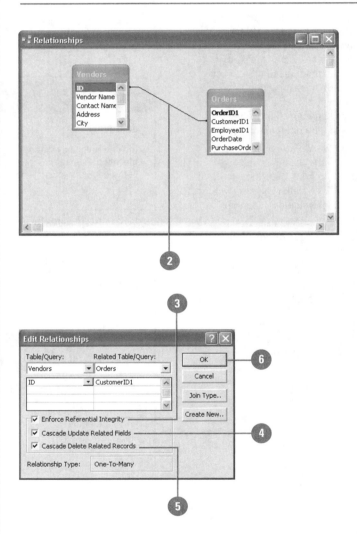

Identifying Object Dependencies

As you develop a database, you create a relationship between objects to share data and provide the information in forms and reports. When you make changes to one object, it might affect another object. For example, if you no longer need a field in a table, instead of deleting it right away and possibly creating problems, you can check object dependencies to make sure that the field you want to delete is not used in another table. Checking for object dependencies helps you save time and avoid mistakes. Access generates dependency information by searching name maps maintained by the Name AutoCorrect feature. If Track Name AutoCorrect Info is turned off on the General tab in the Options dialog box, you cannot view dependency information.

View Dependency Information

1. In the Database window, click the object in which you want to view dependencies.

2. Click the View menu, and then click Object Dependencies.

3. Click the Objects That Depend On Me option or the Objects That I Depend On option.

   The Object Dependencies task pane shows the list of objects that use the selected object.

4. To view dependency information for an object listed in the pane, click on the Expand icon (+) next to it.

5. When you're done, click the Close button on the task pane.

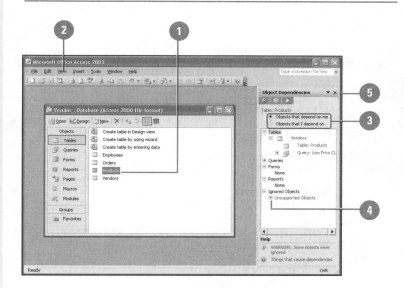

Did You Know?

You can view a list of database objects. Click the File menu, click Database Properties, and then click the Contents tab. When you're done, click OK.

Dependency Information

Object	Dependent	Description
Table	Table or query	A relationship is defined between the objects
Table	Form	Fields in the selected table look up values
Query	Table or query	Query is bound to the table or query
Form	Table or query	Form is bound to the table or query
Form	Form	Form includes the other form as a subform
Report	Table or query	Report is bound to the table or query
Report	Form	Report includes the form as a subform
Report	Report	Report include the other report as a subreport

3

Modifying Object Dependencies

ACO3S-4-1

Modify Dependency Information

1. In the Database window, click the object in which you want to view and modify dependencies.

2. Click the View menu, and then click Object Dependencies.

3. Click the Objects That Depend On Me option or the Objects That I Depend On option.

   The Object Dependencies task pane shows the list of objects that use the selected object.

4. Click the Expand icon (+) next to an object to view dependency information.

5. Click the object you want to open in Design view.

6. Modify the object in Design view, and then click the Close button in the Design view window.

7. When you're done, click the Close button on the task pane.

Did You Know?

Hidden objects don't appear unless you show them. Click the Tools menu, click Options, click the view tab, select the Hidden Objects check box, and then click OK.

As you view dependencies for an object in the Object Dependencies task pane and determine you can make changes without effecting other objects, you can open an object in Design view directly from the Object Dependencies task pane and modify it. If you need to look at other objects, you can open more than one from the Object Dependencies task pane. If you are having problems viewing dependency information, you need to turn on the Track Name AutoCorrect Info option on the General tab of the Options dialog box on the Tools menu.

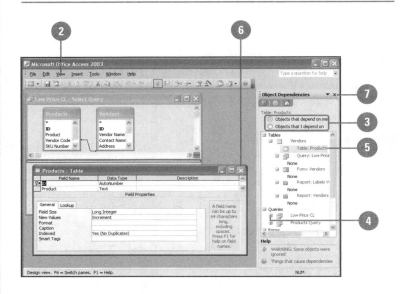

Working with Fields

4

Introduction

An important part of creating your own database is field design. How you design your fields determines how accurately they will be able to store data. Microsoft Office Access 2003 provides flexibility and control in field design. You can design fields so that they allow you to:

◆ Assign a data type so the field accepts and displays the data in the appropriate format.

◆ Include input masks that guide users during data entry.

◆ Specify whether data must be entered into certain fields.

◆ Include a default value for a field.

◆ Include validation checks to ensure that correct data is entered.

◆ Accommodate data whose values are taken from lookup lists.

By taking advantage of these tools during the database design stage, you can save yourself and your database users a lot of trouble later on. By properly designing your fields, you can remove many sources of data-entry error and make your database simpler to manage.

What You'll Do

Insert, Delete, and Reorder Fields

Specify Data Types and Field Properties

View Field Properties

Change Field Properties

Update Field Properties

Set Field Size

Format Text Values

Format Numbers and Currency Values

Format Date and Time Values

Create Input Masks

Specify Required Fields and Default Values

Add a Caption to a Field

Create Indexed Fields

Validate Field Values

Use Expression Builder

Create a Lookup Field

Set Lookup Properties

Inserting, Deleting, and Reordering Fields

You can insert, delete, and edit fields in your database tables in Design view. In Design view for tables, each row corresponds to a field. You can add a field by inserting a new row that contains the field name, data type, and other properties. You can delete a field by removing a row. You can also change field order by re-ordering the rows to better suit your data entry needs. Using Design view for tables makes these tasks easy.

Insert a New Field

1. In the Database window, click Tables on the Objects bar, click the table in which you want to insert a new field, and then click the Design button.

2. Click the row selector for the field that will be below the new field you want to insert.

3. Click the Insert Rows button on the Table Design toolbar.

   A new blank row appears above the row you selected.

4. Click the Field Name cell for the row you inserted, type the name of the new field (up to 64 characters), and then press Tab.

5. Click the list arrow in the Data Type column, click the data type you want to assign to the field, and then press Tab.

6. Type a brief description of the new field (up to 255 characters).

7. Set additional field properties in the property sheet, if appropriate.

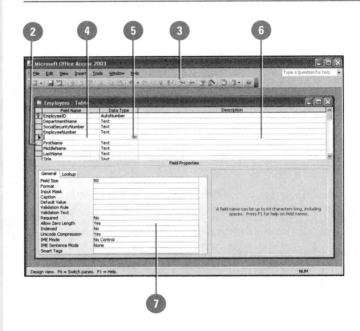

Did You Know?

Field descriptions appear in the status bar. Access displays the description in the status bar, giving your users more information during data entry.

Delete a Field

① Display the table in Design view, and then click the row selector for the row you want to delete.

② Click the Delete Rows button on the Table Design toolbar.

If any records in the table contain data for this field, a message informs you that deleting this field will also delete any data in the field.

③ Click Yes to confirm you want to continue, or click No to cancel the deletion.

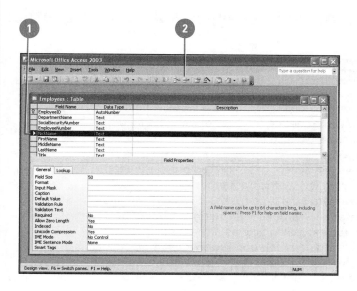

Change the Order of Fields in a Table

① Display the table in Design view, and then click to select the row selector for the field you want to move.

② Click the row selector again, and then press and hold the mouse button.

③ Drag the row to the new position where you want the field to appear, and then release the mouse button.

The dark line indicates the new position of the row.

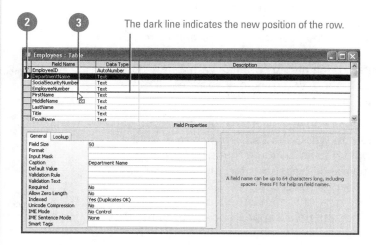

Specifying Data Types and Field Properties

 AC03S-1-3

Access provides different **data types**— field formats that define the kind of data the field can accept—which cover a wide variety of data. When you choose a data type for a field, Access will accept data entered only in the format specified by the data type. Selecting the appropriate data type makes it easier for users to enter and retrieve information in the database tables. It also acts as a check against incorrect data being entered. For example, a field formatted to accept only numbers removes the possibility that a user will erroneously enter text into the field.

You can change the data type for a field even after you have entered data in it. However, you might need to perform a potentially lengthy process of converting or retyping the field's data when you save the table. If the data type in a field conflicts with a new data type setting, you may lose some or all of the data in the field.

Once you've selected a data type, you can begin to work with field properties. A **field property** is an attribute that defines the field's appearance or behavior in the database. The number of decimal places displayed in a numeric field is an example of a property that defines the field's appearance. A property that forces the user to enter data into a field rather than leave it blank controls that field's behavior. In Design view for tables, Access provides a list of field properties, called the **properties list**, for each data type.

Data Types	
Data Type	**Description**
Text (default)	Text or combinations of text and numbers, as well as numbers that don't require calculations, such as phone numbers. Limited to 255 characters.
Number	Numeric data used in mathematical calculations.
Date/Time	Date and time values for the years 100 through 9999.
Currency	Currency values and numeric data used in mathematical calculations involving data with one to four decimal places. Values are accurate to 15 digits on the left side of the decimal separator.
AutoNumber	A unique sequential number (incremented by 1) or a random number Access assigns whenever you add a new record to a table. AutoNumber fields can't be changed.
Yes/No	A field containing only one of two values (for example, Yes/No, True/False, On/Off).
OLE Object	An object (such as a Microsoft Excel spreadsheet) linked to or embedded in an Access table.
Hyperlink	A link that, when clicked, takes the user to another file, a location in a file, or a site on the Web.
Lookup Wizard	A wizard that helps you to create a field whose values are chosen from the values in another table, query, or list of values.

Viewing Field Properties

Text Field Properties

Field	Action
Field Size	Specify the maximum number of characters (up to 255) that can be entered in the field.
Format	Specify how the data for the field will appear on the screen.
Input Mask	Specify a format or pattern in which data must be entered.
Caption	Enter a label for the field when used on a form. If you don't enter a caption, Access uses the field name as the label.
Default Value	Specify a value that Access enters automatically.
Validation Rule	Enter an expression that limits the values that can be entered in this field.
Validation Text	Enter an error message that appears when a value prohibited by the validation rule is entered.
Required	Indicate whether data entry is required.
Allow Zero Length	Specify if field allows zero length text strings.
Indexed	Indicate whether Access will keep an index of field values.
Unicode Compression	Indicate whether you want Access to save space if only plain text is entered.

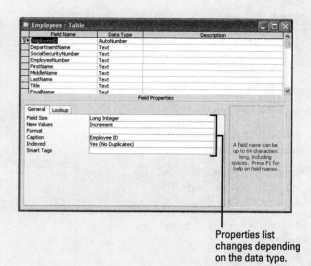

Properties list changes depending on the data type.

4

Changing Field Properties

AC03S-1-3, AC03S-1-4

After you create fields in a table, you can specify properties that define the field's appearance or behavior in the database. In Design view for tables, Access provides a list of field properties for each data type. The properties list changes depending on the data type. Some of the field text properties include Field Size, Format, Input Mask, Caption, Default Value, Validation Rule, Validation Text, Required, Allow Zero Length, and Smart Tags.

Change Field Properties

1. Display the table in Design view.

2. Click the field you want to change.

3. Click the field property box you want to change.

4. Type or change the value, or click the list arrow, and then select a value or option.

5. Click the Save button on the toolbar.

6. When you're done, click the Close button in the Table window.

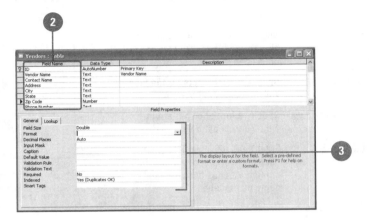

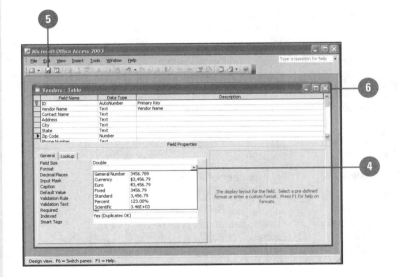

Updating Field Properties

When you make property changes to a field in Table Design view, you can choose to update the corresponding property of controls on forms and reports that are bound to the field. When a bound control inherits a field property change, the Property Update Options button appears in Table Design view, where you can choose the Update command. If a bound control doesn't inherit the field's property change, Access doesn't update the control's property.

Update Field Properties

1. Display the table in Design view.

2. Click the field property box you want to change.

3. Click the General or Lookup tab, and then change a property.

   If you changed the value of an inherited property, the Property Update Options button appears.

4. Click the Property Update Options button, and then click Update.

5. Select the forms or reports that contain the controls needed to be updated, and then click Yes.

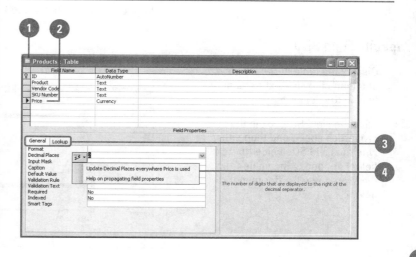

Turn Off Property Update

1. Click the Tools menu, and then click Options.

2. Click the Tables/Queries tab.

3. Clear the Show Property Update Options Buttons check box.

4. Click OK.

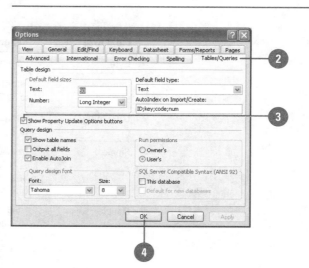

4

Setting Field Size

For Text, Number, and AutoNumber data types, you can use the Field Size property to set the maximum size of data stored in the field. In the case of text data, this property specifies the number of characters allowed (from 0 to 255). Numeric field sizes include Byte, Integer, and Long Integer options for integer values, and Single and Double options for decimals. The difference between these sizes lies in the amount of storage space they use and the range of possible values they cover. If your integers will cover only the range 0 to 255, you should use Byte, but for a larger range you should use Integer or Long Integer.

Specify Field Size

① Display the table in Design view, and then click the text or numeric field in the field list.

② Click the Field Size box in the properties sheet, and then either type the Field Size value (for text fields) or choose the value from the drop-down list (for numeric fields).

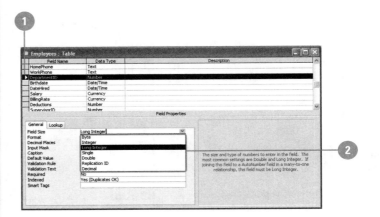

Numeric Field Sizes		
Field Size	**Range**	**Storage**
Byte	Integers from 0 to 255	1 byte
Integer	Integers from -32,768 to 32,767	2 bytes
Long Integer	Integers from -2,147,483,648 to 2,147,483,647	4 bytes
Single	from -3.402823E38 to -1.401298E-45 (negative values) and 1.401298E-45 to 3.402823E38 (positive values)	4 bytes
Double	from -1.797693E308 to -4.940656E-324 (negative values) and 1.797693E308 to 4.940656E324 (positive values)	8 bytes
Replication ID	Values used to establish unique identifiers	16 bytes

Formatting Text Values

A **format** is a property that determines how numbers, dates, times, and text are displayed and printed. Access provides custom formats for dates and times, but you can also create your own formats using formatting symbols. **Formatting symbols** are symbols that Access uses to control how it displays data values. For example, the formatting symbol "<" forces Access to display text characters in lowercase, while the symbol ">" displays those same characters in uppercase. Formatting may also include use of **literals**, which are text strings that are displayed exactly as they appear in format. Formatting only affects the way the data is displayed. It does not affect the data itself.

Format Text Data

1. Display the table in Design view, and then click a text field for which you want to set formatting values.

2. Click the Format box, and then enter a text format for all data values in the text field.

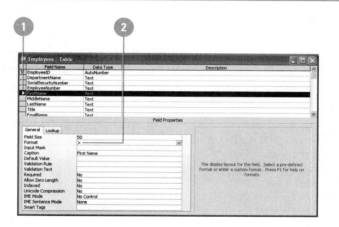

General and Text Formatting Symbols

Symbol	Data	Format	Display
!	321	!	321
<	Today	<	today
>	News	>	NEWS
"ABC"	20	&"lbs."	20lbs.
(space)	16	& "oz."	16 oz.
\	10	&\k	10k
@	5551234	@@@-@@@@	555-1234
&	Mr	&\.	Mr.
*	Hello	&*!	Hello!!!!!!
[*color*]	Alert	[gray]	Alert

4

Formatting Number and Currency Values

If a field has a Number or Currency data type, Access provides a list of predefined formats to display the data values. You can also create your own format using formatting symbols applicable to numeric values and currency.

Choose a Predefined Numeric or Currency Format

1. Display the table in Design view, and then click a numeric or currency field.

2. Click the Format list arrow.

3. Select a format from the predefined list of formats, or enter the appropriate formatting symbols.

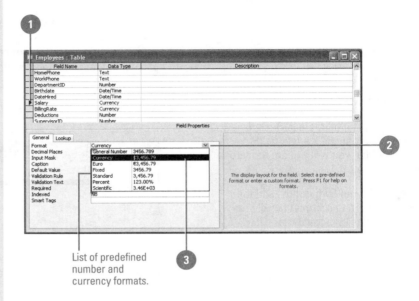

List of predefined number and currency formats.

Did You Know?

You can set the number of decimal places. Another way to set the number of decimal places for numeric fields is to specify the number of decimal places in the Decimal Places box in the list of field properties.

You can use different formats for different values. Access allows you to specify different formats for positive, negative, zero, and null values within a single field. Use online Help for more information.

Numeric and Currency Formatting Symbols

Symbol	Data	Format	Display
#	15	#	15
0	20.1	#.00	20.10
.	15	#.	15.
,	92395	#,###	92,395
$	19.3	$#.00	$19.30
%	0.75	#%	75%
E-,E+,e-,e+	625971	#.00E+00	625E+05

Formatting Date and Time Values

Access provides formatting symbols and predefined formats for date and time values that allow you to display different combinations of the time, date, and day. The predefined formats include a general form, which displays the date and time, as well as short, medium, and long forms of the date and time.

Specify a Date and Time Format

1. Display the table in Design view, and then click a date and time field.

2. Click the Format list arrow.

3. Select a format from the predefined list of formats, or enter the appropriate formatting symbols.

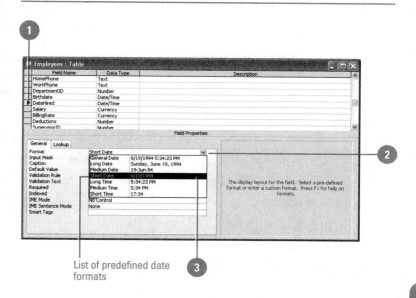

List of predefined date formats

Predefined Date Formats

Format	Display
General Date	1/1/05 12:35:15 PM
Long Date	Saturday, January 1, 2005
Medium Date	01-Jan-05
Short Date	1/1/05
Long Time	12:35:15 PM
Medium Time	12:35 PM
Short Time	12:35

4

Creating Input Masks

AC03S-1-4

An **input mask** allows you to control what values a database user can enter into a field. Input masks consist of literal characters, such as spaces, dots, parentheses, and placeholders. A **placeholder** is a text character, such as the underline symbol (_), that indicates where the user should insert values. An input mask for a phone number field might appear as follows: (_ _ _) _ _ _ - _ _ _ _ . The parenthesis and dash characters act as literal characters, and the underscore character acts as a placeholder for the phone number values. Access provides several predefined input masks, which cover most situations, but you can create your own customized masks, if necessary. The **Input Mask Wizard** is available only for text and date fields. If you want to create an input mask for numeric fields, you must enter the formatting symbols yourself.

Specify an Input Mask

1. Display the table in Design view, and then click a field for which you want to specify an input mask.

2. Click the Input Mask box.

3. Click the Build button to start the Input Mask Wizard.

4. Scroll thru the predefined list to find an input mask form.

5. Type some sample values to see how the input mask affects your sample values, and then click Next.

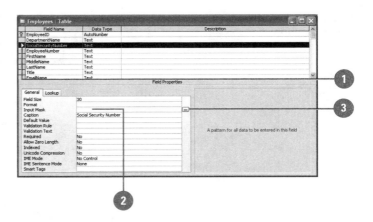

Click to modify or add input masks to Access' predefined list.

6 If you change the input mask, type new formatting codes.

7 If you want to display a different placeholder, click the Placeholder list arrow, and select the placeholder you want to use.

8 Enter values to test the final version of your input mask, and then click Next.

9 Indicate whether you want to store the input mask symbols along with the data values.

10 Click Next, and then click Finish.

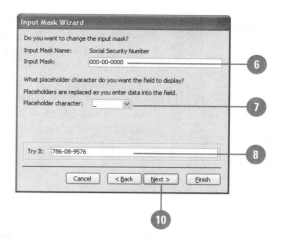

Input Mask Wizard

Do you want to change the input mask?

Input Mask Name: Social Security Number
Input Mask: 000-00-0000 **6**

What placeholder character do you want the field to display?
Placeholders are replaced as you enter data into the field.
Placeholder character: _ **7**

Try It: 786-08-9576 **8**

Cancel | < Back | Next > | Finish

10

Did You Know?

You can use the Input Mask Wizard. The Input Mask Wizard is available only for text and date fields. If you want to create an input mask for numeric fields, you must enter the formatting symbols yourself.

You can create a password mask. For sensitive data, choose the password input mask from the Input Mask Wizard. Any text the user types will be saved as the text, but displayed as an asterisk (*).

Input Mask Symbols

Symbol	Description
0	Digit 0 to 9 (required)
9	Digit 0 to 9 (optional)
A	Letter or digit (required)
a	Letter or digit (optional)
#	Digit or space
&	Any character or space (required)
C	Any character or space (optional)
L	Letter A-Z (required)
?	Letter A-Z (optional)
>	Make following characters uppercase
<	Make following characters lowercase

4

Specifying Required Fields and Default Values

Some fields contain essential information. For example, social security numbers are required for employees in order to process payroll and other reports. You set fields like these as **required fields**, which means that Access refuses to accept a record until you enter an acceptable value for that field. You can also set a **default value** for a field, a value Access uses unless a user enters a different one. If a field usually has the same value, such as a city or state if most contacts are local, you could assign that value as the default in order to speed up data entry.

Create a Required Field

① Display the table in Design view, and then click a field that you want to be a required field.

② Click the Required box.

③ Click the list arrow, and then click Yes.

Specify a Default Value

① Display the table in Design view, and then click a field for which you want to set a default value.

② Click the Default Value box.

③ Enter the default value for the field in the box.

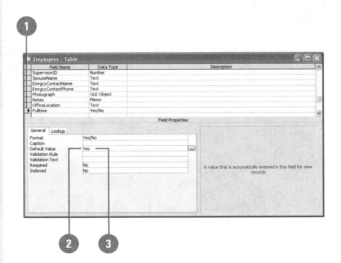

Adding a Caption to a Field

A field **caption** is text displayed alongside a field to better describe its purpose and content. You can add a caption to a field, and later when you create forms and reports that use this field, Access automatically displays the caption you specify. Captions can contain up to 2,048 characters, including spaces. If you don't specify a caption, Access uses the field name as the field caption in any forms or reports you create.

Set the Caption Property

1. Display the table in Design view, and then click a field for which you want to set a caption.

2. Click the Caption box.

3. Type text you want to appear as the field's caption.

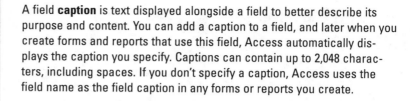
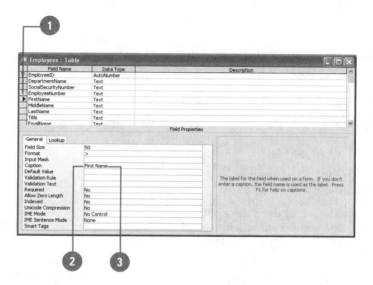

Did You Know?

You can set zero-length strings. Text and Memo data type fields allow you to control whether or not a user can leave a field blank. To ensure that some text is entered, set the Required property to Yes.

Creating Indexed Fields

Just like an index in a book, an index in Access helps you locate and sort information quickly, especially in a very large table. An **index** in Access is an invisible data structure that stores the sort order of a table based on the indexed field or fields. When you sort a large table by an indexed field, Access consults the index and is able to sort the table very quickly. It can be helpful to index fields you frequently search or sort or fields you join to fields in other tables in queries. If a field contains many different values, rather than many values that are the same, indexing can significantly speed up queries. After indexing a field, you can view and then modify indexes as necessary.

Create a Field Index

1. Display the table in Design view, and then click a field you want as an index.

2. Click the Indexed box.

3. Click the list arrow, and then select one of the following.

   ◆ Yes (Duplicates OK) if you want to allow multiple records to have the same data in this field.

   ◆ Yes (No Duplicates) option if you want to ensure that no two records have the same data in this field.

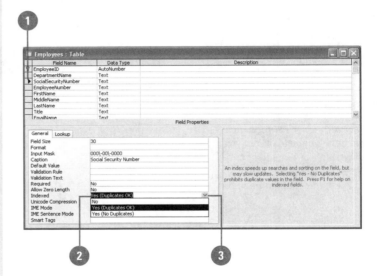

View or Edit Indexes

1. Display the table in Design view.

2. Click the Indexes button on the Table Design toolbar.

3. Type a name for the index.

4. Select a field to act as an index.

5. Click the list arrow, and then select Ascending or Descending to indicate the index sort order.

6. Click the Close button.

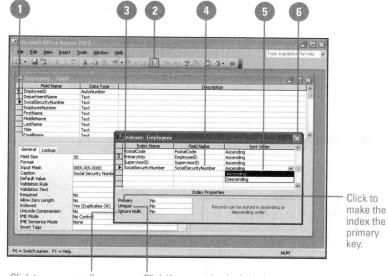

Click to make the index the primary key.

Click to remove null values from the index.

Click if every value in the index must be unique.

Did You Know?

You can index data types. You don't have to index all data types, and there are some data types you cannot index. For example, you do not need to index the primary key of a table, because it is automatically indexed. You can index a field only if the data type is Text, Number, Currency, or Date/Time. You cannot index a field whose data type is Memo or OLE Object.

You can create a multiple-field index. If you think you'll often search or sort by two or more fields, create a multiple-field index by adding additional fields in the Field Name column for each index name.

4

Validating Field Values

When you need explicit control over data entered in a field, such as a range of numbers or dates, you can enforce a **validation rule**, which causes Access to test values a user enters in a field. If the value doesn't satisfy the validation rules criteria, Access refuses to enter the value and displays an error message. You can specify the text of the error message yourself. You can use the Expression Builder to create a validation rule by selecting the functions, constants, and operators you need for your rule from a list of options.

Create a Validation Rule

1. Display the table in Design view, and then click a field that you intend to validate.

2. Click the Validation Rule box, and then click the Build button to open the Expression Builder.

3. Create an expression by clicking the appropriate elements in the Expression Builder dialog box.

4. Click OK.

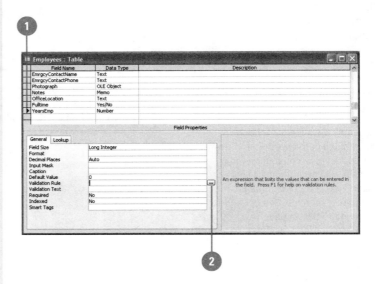

Specify Validation Text

1. Display the table in Design view, and then click a field.

2. Click the Validation Text box.

3. Type the text that Access will display when the user tries to enter incorrect data for the field.

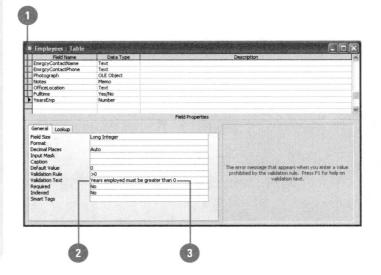

Using Expression Builder

Click a button to insert one of these frequently used functions, constants, and operators.

As you select options and type variables, the expression appears in this pane.

Double-click to display a list of Access functions.

Click to display a list of Access constants.

Click to display a list of Access operators.

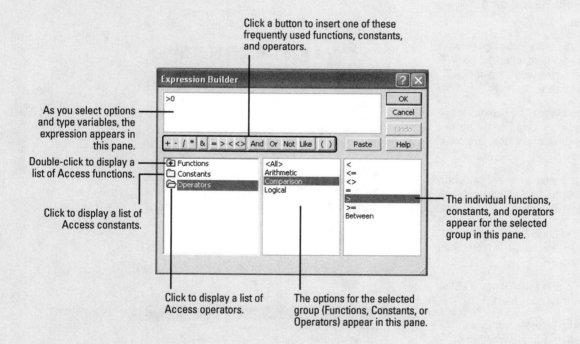

The individual functions, constants, and operators appear for the selected group in this pane.

The options for the selected group (Functions, Constants, or Operators) appear in this pane.

4

Creating a Lookup Field

AC03S-1-3

The **Lookup Wizard** helps you create a field that displays either of two kinds of lists during data entry: a **Lookup** list that displays values looked up from an existing table or query, or a **Value** list that displays a fixed set of values you enter when you create the field. Because values are limited to a predefined list, using Lookup fields helps you avoid data entry errors in situations where only a limited number of possible values are allowed. The lists are not limited to a single column. You can include additional columns that could include descriptive information for the various choices in the list. However, only a single column, called the **bound column**, contains the data that is extracted from the list and placed into the Lookup field.

Create a Field Based on a Lookup List

1. Display the table in Design view, enter a new field, click the Data Type list arrow, and then click Lookup Wizard.

2. Click the I Want The Lookup Column To Look Up The Values In A Table Or Query option, and then click Next.

3. Select the table or query you want to use for the Lookup list, and then click Next.

4. Select the fields that you want to appear in the Lookup list, and then click Next.

5. Choose a sort order for the Lookup list, and then click Next.

6. Resize the column widths in the Lookup list, indicate whether or not to include the primary key column, and then click Next.

   If the table or query lacks a primary key, you will be prompted for the column that will act as the bound column. Otherwise the primary key will be the bound column.

7. Enter a label for the Lookup column, and then click Finish.

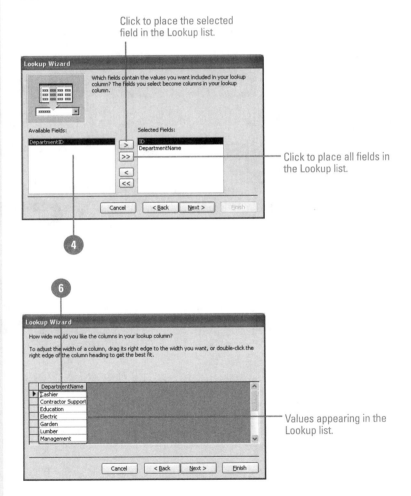

Click to place the selected field in the Lookup list.

Click to place all fields in the Lookup list.

Values appearing in the Lookup list.

Create a Field Based on a Value List

1. Display the table in Design view, enter a new field, click the Data Type list arrow, and then click Lookup Wizard.

2. Click the I Will Type In The Values That I Want option, and then click Next.

3. Specify the number of columns you want in the Value list.

4. Enter the values in the list. If necessary, resize the column widths. Click Next to continue.

5. Choose which column will act as the bound column, and then click Next.

6. Enter a label for the Lookup column.

7. Click Finish.

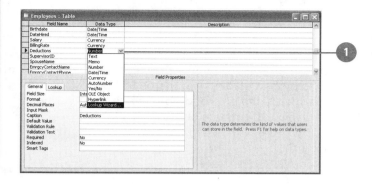

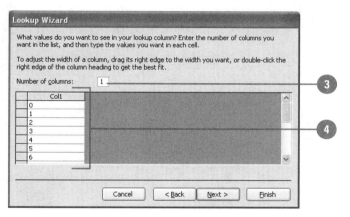

Setting Lookup Properties

If you want to create a Lookup field manually or make changes to the field created by the wizard, you can do so by changing the values in the Lookup properties. These properties allow you to specify the type of drop-down list Access will display, the source of the values in the list, the appearance of the list, and the column that will act as the bound column. You can also indicate whether the user is limited to the choices in the list or can enter other values during data entry.

Specify the type of source for the Lookup data.

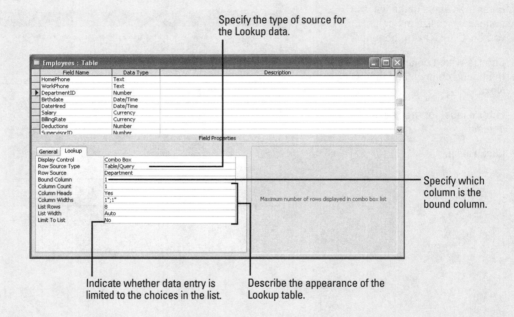

Specify which column is the bound column.

Indicate whether data entry is limited to the choices in the list.

Describe the appearance of the Lookup table.

Working with Tables

Introduction

Tables are the storage containers of your data. To help you work effectively with tables, Microsoft Office Access 2003 provides features that assist you not only in entering and editing the data in your tables but also in locating the information you need.

- You can locate records based on the text they contain with the Find feature.

- You can enter and edit data more accurately with features like AutoCorrect, copy, collect, paste, and language features.

- You can display records in either ascending or descending order based on the contents of a specific field.

- You can arrange records and columns so your information is listed in the order you want, and adjust the size of your rows and columns to show more or less of the information displayed in any of the fields. You can also view subdatasheets that show groups of data related to the records in your tables.

- To focus on certain records in a table, you can apply a filter to change which records are displayed. With a filter, you describe characteristics or contents of the records you want to view.

What You'll Do

Work with a Table

Move to a Specific Record in a Table

Search for and Replace Text

Enter Data Accurately with AutoCorrect

Use Smart Tags

Edit Text

Work with the Clipboard

Check Spelling

Arrange Columns

Change the Size of Rows and Columns

Manage Columns in Datasheet View

Format a Datasheet

Repair Renaming Errors

Sort, Copy and Paste Records

View a Subdatasheet

Filter Out Records

Create Complex Filters Using Forms

Working with a Table

AC03S-2-1

A **database** is made up of groups of fields organized into tables. A **field** is a specific category of information, such as a name or a product. Related fields are grouped in tables. You usually enter data into fields one entity at a time (one customer at a time, one product at a time, and so on). Access stores all the data for a single entity in a record. You can view a table in Datasheet or Design view. Design view allows you to work with your table's fields. Datasheet view shows a grid of fields and records. The fields appear as columns and the records as rows. The first field in a table is often an **AutoNumber** field, which Access uses to assign a unique number to each record. You can't select or change this value.

Enter a New Record and Move Around in a Table

1. In the Database window, click Tables on the Objects bar, and then double-click the table.

2. Click the New Record button.

3. Press Tab to accept the AutoNumber entry.

4. Enter the data. If you make a typing mistake, press Backspace.

5. Press Tab to move to the next field or Shift+Tab to move to the previous field.

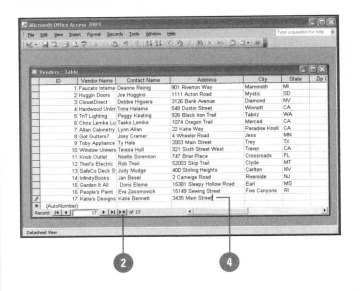

Delete a Record from a Table

1. In the Database window, click Tables on the Objects bar, and then double-click the table.

2. Right-click the row selector.

3. Click Delete Record.

4. Click Yes.

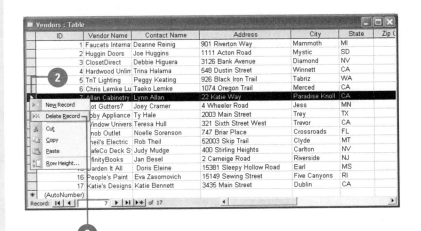

Moving to a Specific Record in a Table

 AC03S-2-2

When you scroll through a table in Datasheet view, you are simply viewing different parts of the table; the insertion point (cursor) stays in its original location in the first record. If you type any text, it appears in the first record, regardless of which record is currently visible. To move the insertion point to a specific record, you must click the record (or a field in the record). If the record you want to select is not visible, you can use the navigation buttons to move to the next, previous, first, or last record. Or you can type the number of the record (if you know it) in the Specific Record box to display that record.

Move to a Record

◆ Current Record icon:

Indicates the current record.

◆ Specific Record box:

To move to a new record, select the current record number, type the new record number, and then press Enter.

◆ New Record button:

Click to create a new, blank row at the end of the table.

◆ Selection bar:

Click the row selector to the left of a record to select it.

◆ First Record button:

Click to move to the first record in the table.

◆ Previous Record button:

Click to move to the previous record in the table.

◆ Next Record button:

Click to move to the next record in the table.

◆ Last Record button:

Click to move to the last record in the table.

Current Record icon   Specific Record box   New Record button

ID	Vendor Name	Vendor ID	Contact Name	Address	City
1	Faucets International	FI	Deanne Reinig	901 Riverton Way	Mammoth
2	Huggin Doors	HD	Joe Huggins	1111 Acton Road	Mystic
3	ClosetDirect	CL	Debbie Higuera	3126 Bank Avenue	Diamond
4	Hardwood Unlimited	HU	Trina Halama	548 Dustin Street	Winnett
5	TnT Lighting	LT	Peggy Keating	926 Black Iron Trail	Tabriz
6	Chris Lemke Lumber	LB	Taeko Lemke	1074 Oregon Trail	Merced
7	Allan Cabinetry	AC	Lynn Allan	22 Katie Way	Paradise K
8	Got Gutters?	GG	Joey Cramer	4 Wheeler Road	Jess
9	Toby Appliance	TA	Ty Hale	2003 Main Street	Trey
10	Window Universe	WU	Teresa Hull	321 Sixth Street West	Trevor
11	Knob Outlet	KO	Noelle Sorenson	747 Briar Place	Crossroads
12	Theil's Electric	EL	Rob Theil	52003 Skip Trail	Clyde
13	SafeCo Deck Systems	SD	Judy Mudge	400 Stirling Heights	Carlton
14	InfinityBooks	IB	Jan Besel	2 Carneige Road	Riverside
15	Garden It All	GI	Doris Eleine	15381 Sleepy Hollow Road	Earl
16	People's Paint	PP	Eva Zasomovich	15149 Sewing Street	Five Canyo
17	Katie's Designs	KD	Katie Bennett	3435 Main Street	Dublin

First Record button   Previous Record button   Last Record button   Next Record button

5

Searching for and Replacing Text

AC03S-2-2

To locate one or more records in which you expect to find specific text, you can use the Find feature. In the Find dialog box, you enter the text you want to find, and specify whether Access should search the current field or the entire table, and whether the text you enter should match part of the field or the whole field. You can also indicate whether Access should look for matching capitalization. When Access finds the first record that contains the specified text, it selects that record. You can then move to the next matching record or cancel the search. You can also use the Find and Replace feature to automatically replace specified text with new text. You can review and change each occurrence individually, or replace all occurrences at once.

Search for Text in the Current Field

1. Display the table in Datasheet view.

2. Click the insertion point anywhere in the field (column) where you expect to find the text for which you want to search.

3. Click the Find button on the Table Datasheet toolbar.

4. Type the text you want to find in either uppercase or lowercase letters.

5. Click the Look In list arrow to specify whether Find should search the current field or the entire table.

6. Click the Match list arrow, and indicate whether you want the text you typed to match the whole field or part of the field.

7. Click Find Next as many times as necessary to view all the records that contain the specified text.

8. When you're done, click the Close button.

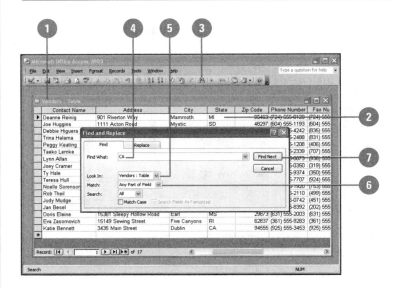

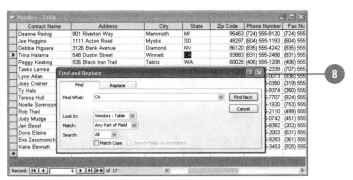

Find and Replace Text

1. In the Find And Replace dialog box, click the Replace tab.

2. Type the text you want to find, and then press Tab.

3. Type the replacement text.

4. Click Find Next.

5. Click Replace to replace the first occurrence with the replacement text, or click Replace All to replace all occurrences with the replacement text, or click Find Next to skip to the next occurrence.

6. Click the Close button.

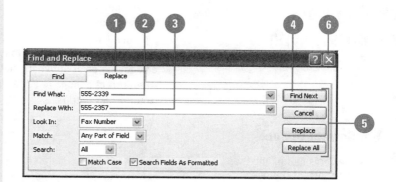

Did You Know?

You can search for formatted text. To search for records matching the case of the text you type, select the Match Case check box.

You can search for formatted text. You might need to find information that has been assigned a specific data format, such as a date format, without entering the information in the specified format. For example, if dates are displayed in the format 05-Jan-04, you can locate that number by typing 1/5/04. Select the Search Fields As Formatted check box to only search for the text as formatted. Be aware that searching this way can be slow.

5

Entering Data Accurately with AutoCorrect

As you enter data in tables, you might occasionally make typing mistakes. For certain errors, Access will correct the errors as soon as you type them and then press the Spacebar or Enter. For example, if you type *compnay* when you meant to type *company*, the AutoCorrect feature will correct the error automatically. You can easily customize the preset AutoCorrect options or add errors that you commonly make to the list of AutoCorrect entries.

Set AutoCorrect Options

1. Click the Tools menu, and then click AutoCorrect Options.

2. Select the Replace Text As You Type check box to enable AutoCorrect.

3. Select or clear the Show AutoCorrect Options Buttons check box to show or hide it.

4. Select the check boxes with the additional options you want.

   ◆ Correct two initial capital letters so that only the first letter is capitalized.

   ◆ Always capitalize the first word in a sentence.

   ◆ Capitalize the names of days.

   ◆ Correct accidental use of the Caps Lock key.

5. Click OK.

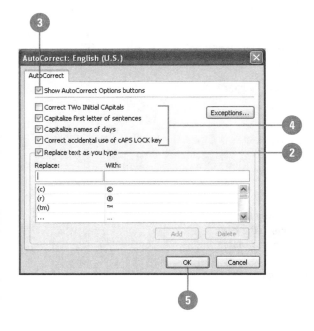

Replace Text as You Type

◆ To correct incorrect capitalization or spelling errors automatically, simply continue to type and AutoCorrect will make the required correction.

Examples of AutoCorrect Changes

Type of Correction	If You Type	AutoCorrect Inserts
Capitalization	CAlifornia	California
Capitalization	thursday	Thursday
Common typos	accommodate	accommodate
Common typos	can;t	can't
Common typos	windows	windows

Change Correction as You Type

1. After an AutoCorrect correction, point to the AutoCorrect Options button.

2. Click the AutoCorrect Options button.

3. Click any of the following options:

   ◆ Change Back To.

   ◆ Stop Automatically Correcting.

   ◆ Control AutoCorrect Options to change the AutoCorrect settings.

Add or Edit an AutoCorrect Entry

1. Click the Tools menu, and then click AutoCorrect Options.

2. To edit an entry, select the entry you want to change.

3. To add an entry, type a word or phrase that you often mistype or misspell.

4. Type the correct spelling of the word.

5. Click Add or Replace.

6. Click OK.

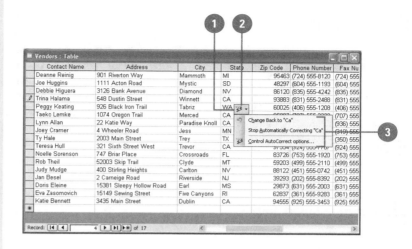

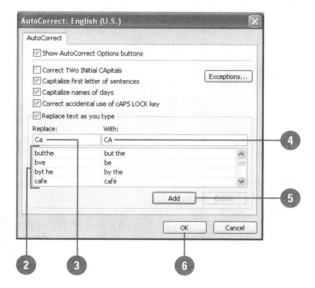

Using Smart Tags

Smart Tags help you integrate actions typically performed in other programs directly in Access. For example, you can add a person's name and address in a database to the contacts list in Microsoft Outlook, or copy and paste information with added control. Access analyzes the data you type and recognizes certain types that it marks with Smart Tags. You can add a smart tag to a field or control by setting the Smart Tag property. Once you have added a smart tag and activate the cell, the Smart Tag Actions button appears, where you can click the button to perform actions. The AutoCorrect Options button is a smart tag. Another smart tag is the Error Indicator button, which helps you correct common errors.

Show or Hide Smart Tags

1. Click the Tools menu, and then click Options.

2. Click the Forms/Reports tab.

3. Select or clear the Show Smart Tags On Forms check box.

4. Click the Datasheet tab.

5. Select or clear the Show Smart Tags On Datasheets check box.

6. Click OK.

Did You Know?

You can find new smart tags on the Web. In the Smart Tags dialog box, click More Smart Tags to access the Web where you can find information about the latest smart tags.

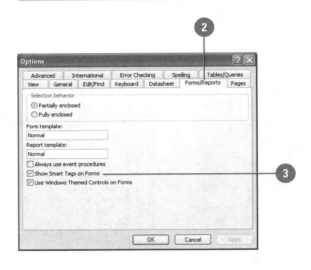

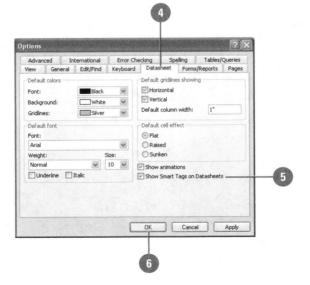

Add a Smart Tag

1. Select a location where you want to add a smart tag.

   - Open the table or query, and then select the field you want to add a smart tag.

   - Open the form or report, add or select a text box, and then click the Properties button on the toolbar.

2. Click the Build button in the Smart Tags property box.

3. Select the smart tag you want.

4. Click OK, and then save your changes.

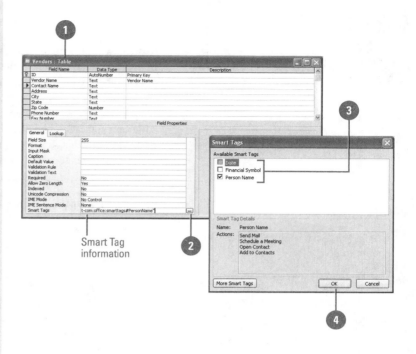

Smart Tag information

Use a Smart Tag

1. Open the table, query, form, or report with the smart tag.

2. Point to the purple triangle in the cell or text box to display the Smart Tag button.

3. Click the Smart Tag Options button, and then click the list arrow next to the button.

4. Click the smart tag option you want; options vary depending on the data.

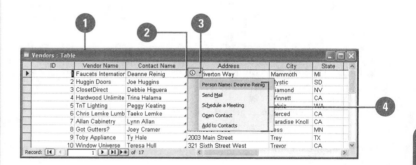

5

Editing Text

Microsoft® Office Specialist Approved Courseware AC03S-2-1

Before you can edit text, you need to highlight, or select, the text you want to modify. You can edit text you enter in a record by selecting the text you want to change and then performing an action. When you want to insert or delete text one character at a time, you point between two characters or words and then click to place the **insertion point**, a vertical cursor that indicates your location in a section of text. When you want to change the entire contents of a table cell, you select the cell. After you select the items you want, you can delete, replace, move (cut), or copy text within Access objects or between different programs. In either case, the steps are the same.

Select and Edit Text and Cell Contents

1. Select the text or cell contents you want to edit.

   ◆ Double-click a word.

   ◆ Drag to select multiple words.

   ◆ Click the border of a table cell to select its entire contents in Datasheet view.

   ◆ Point to the border of a table cell, and then drag to select multiple cells in Datasheet view.

2. Perform one of the following editing commands:

   ◆ To replace text, type your text.

   ◆ To delete text, press the Backspace key or the Delete key.

Pointer when you click a cell border to select all text in the cell.

Pressing Delete removes selected text.

Did You Know?

You can undo a mistake. If you insert or delete something by mistake, you can click the Undo button on the toolbar to reverse the action.

Insert and Delete Text and Cell Contents

1. Click in the field to place the insertion point where you want to make the change.

   ◆ To insert text, type your text.

   ◆ To delete text, press the Backspace key or the Delete key.

Insertion point

Move or Copy Text and Cell Contents

1. Select the text you want to move or copy.

2. Click the Cut or Copy button on the Standard toolbar.

3. Click where you want to insert the text.

4. Click the Paste button on the Standard toolbar.

   To paste the text with another format, click the Edit menu, click Paste Special, click a format option, and then click OK.

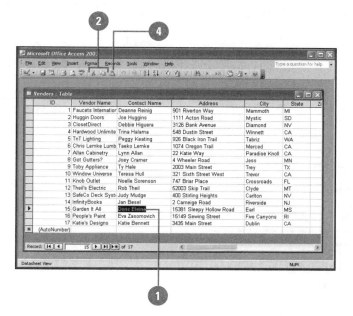

5

Working with the Clipboard

The **Office Clipboard** is available from within any Office program and holds up to 24 pieces of copied information, any or all of which you can paste to a new location. As you cut or copy information, Office collects it in the Office Clipboard. You can use the Office Clipboard task pane to manage the information and use it in Office documents. The Office Clipboard allows you to collect multiple items and paste them quickly. When you paste an item, the Paste Options button appears below it. When you click the button, a menu appears with options to specify how Office pastes the information. The available options differ depending on the content you are pasting.

Paste Items from the Office Clipboard

① Click the Edit menu, and then click Office Clipboard.

   TIMESAVER *Press Ctrl+C twice to access the Office Clipboard.*

② Click where you want to insert the text.

③ Click any icon on the Clipboard task pane to paste that selection. If there is more than one selection you can paste all the selections at once, by clicking Paste All.

④ When you're done, click the Close button on the task pane.

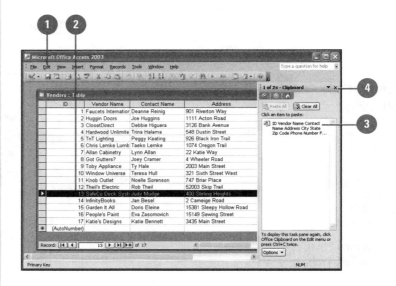

Did You Know?

You can paste information in a different format. Select the object or text, click the Copy button on the Standard toolbar, click to indicate where you want to paste the object, click the Edit menu, click Paste Special, click the object type you want, and then click OK.

Delete Items from the Office Clipboard

1. Click the Edit menu, and then click Office Clipboard.

2. Click the list arrow of the item you want to paste, and then click Delete.

3. To erase all items in the Office Clipboard, click Clear All.

4. When you're done, click the Close button on the task pane.

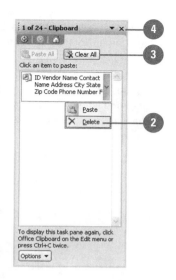

Change Clipboard Options

1. Click the Edit menu, and then click Office Clipboard.

2. Click Options, and then click to select any of the following options:

   ◆ Show Office Clipboard Automatically

   ◆ Show Office Clipboard When Ctrl+C Pressed Twice

   ◆ Collect Without Showing Office Clipboard

   ◆ Show Office Clipboard Icon On Taskbar

   ◆ Show Status Near Taskbar When Copying

3. When you're done, click the Close button on the task pane.

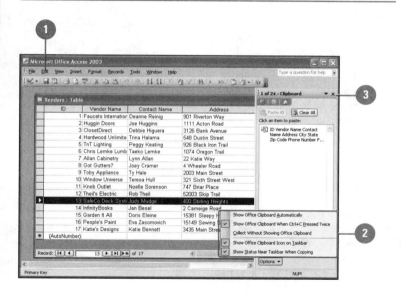

Checking Spelling

The Spelling feature helps you proofread your data by identifying potentially misspelled words and suggesting possible spellings to use instead. You can correct the spelling, ignore the word, add the word to the dictionary, or create an AutoCorrect entry. In addition, you can control the kinds of spelling errors Access identifies by specifying the spelling options you want in effect. If the text in your database is written in more than one language, you can automatically detect languages or designate the language of selected text so the spelling checker uses the right dictionary.

Check the Spelling in a Table

1. Display the table in Datasheet view, click the row selector for the record or select the field you want to check. Drag to select additional rows.

2. Click the Spelling button on the Table Datasheet toolbar. If Access identifies any misspelled words, it opens the Spelling dialog box.

3. Correct or ignore the identified words, as appropriate.

   ◆ Click Ignore to ignore the word and retain its spelling. Click Ignore All to ignore all instances of the word.

   ◆ Click Add to add the word to the dictionary so the spelling checker won't identify it as a misspelled word.

   ◆ Click a word in the Suggestions list, and then click Change to spell the word with the selected spelling. Click Change All to change all instances of the word to the selected spelling.

   ◆ Click AutoCorrect to add the word to the AutoCorrect list.

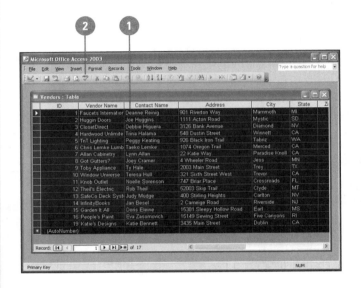

List of possible corrections

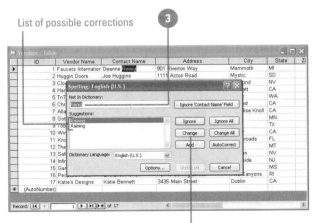

Click to replace the misspelled word with the selected word, which is spelled correctly.

Customize Spelling Options

1. In the Spelling dialog box, click Options.

2. Select the options you want to change.

   ◆ Clear the Suggest From Main Dictionary Only check box if you want to omit the list of suggested spellings or to check spelling from both the Custom and Main dictionaries.

   ◆ Clear the Ignore check box if you don't want to ignore words in uppercase, words with numbers, or Internet and file addresses.

3. Click OK.

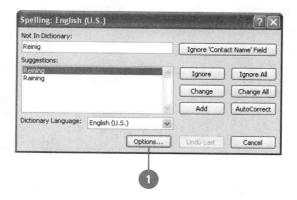

Did You Know?

You can proofread in different languages. The Microsoft Proofing Tools Kit provides fonts, templates, and spelling and grammar checkers to help you create and edit databases in different languages.

See Also

See "Using Multiple Languages" on page 300 for information on using different languages in Access.

Arranging Columns

The order in which columns appear in the Table window in Datasheet view is initially determined by the order established when you first designed the table. If you want to temporarily rearrange the order of the columns in a table, you can do so without changing the table design. You can arrange columns in the order you want by selecting and then dragging columns to a new location. You can also hide columns you do not want to view. The **freeze column** feature allows you to "freeze" one or more of the columns on a datasheet so that they are visible regardless of where you scroll.

Move a Column

1. In Datasheet view, click the column selector of the column you want to move.

2. Drag the selected column to its new location.

Pointer when you drag a column

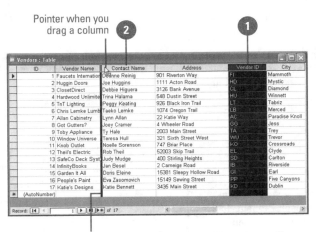

A vertical bar indicates where the column will appear.

Hide a Column

1. In Datasheet view, right-click the column or columns you want to hide.

2. Click Hide Columns.

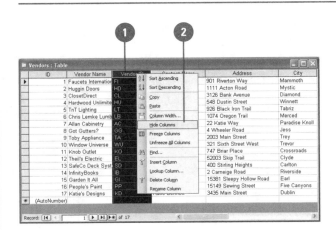

Display a Hidden Column

1. In Datasheet view, click the Format menu, and then click Unhide Columns.

2. Select the names of the columns that you want to show.

3. Click Close.

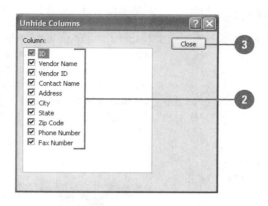

Freeze or Unfreeze Columns

1. In Datasheet view, select the column(s) you want to freeze or unfreeze. (To freeze or unfreeze just one column, skip step 1.)

2. Right-click a column or the selected columns, and then click Freeze Columns or Unfreeze All Columns.

Did You Know?

You can control a datasheet's appearance. Control the appearance of a datasheet by clicking Format, and then clicking Datasheet. In the Datasheet Formatting dialog box, you can control background and gridline colors and styles. You can control font appearance in the datasheet by clicking Format, and then clicking Font.

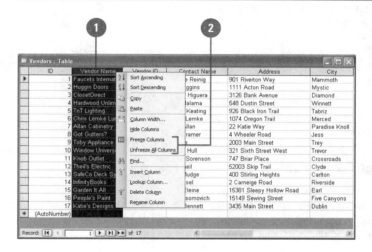

5

Changing the Size of Rows and Columns

If some of the text in a column is hidden because the column is too narrow, you can increase the width of the column. You can also change the height of the rows to provide more space for the text. Unlike changing the column width, which affects only the selected column or columns, changing the row height affects all the rows in the table. You can adjust the size of columns and rows by using commands or by dragging the borders between columns or rows.

Change Column Width

◆ Point to the border between two field selectors, and then drag the border left or right.

◆ Right-click a field selector, and then click Column Width. Click Best Fit, or enter a new width, and then click OK.

Number of characters that can be displayed with current column width.

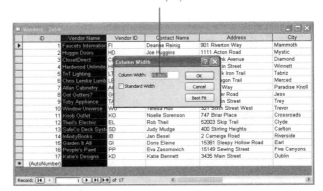

Change Row Height

◆ Point to the border between two row selectors, and then drag the border up or down to adjust the height of all the rows in the table.

◆ Right-click a row selector, and then click Row Height. Enter a new height, and then click OK.

Pointer when you change row height

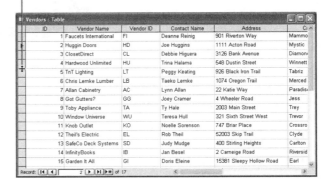

> **Did You Know?**
>
> **You can format columns in other Access objects.** These formatting steps also work for columns in queries, forms, views, or stored procedures.

Managing Columns in Datasheet View

You can quickly add, remove, and rename columns from within Datasheet view. If you remove a column, Access deletes all the data it contains, so delete a column only if you are sure you no longer require its data. If other database objects contain references to a deleted field, such as a query, Microsoft automatically updates those references.

Insert a Column

① In Datasheet view, right-click the column selector to the right of where you want to add the new column.

② Click Insert Column.

The column is inserted with the name Field1, which you can rename.

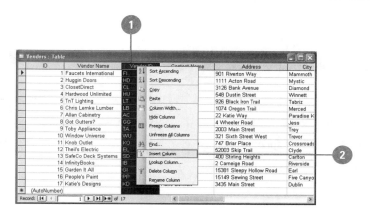

Delete a Column

① In Datasheet view, right-click the column selector(s) for the column(s) you want to delete.

② Click Delete Column.

③ Click Yes to confirm the deletion.

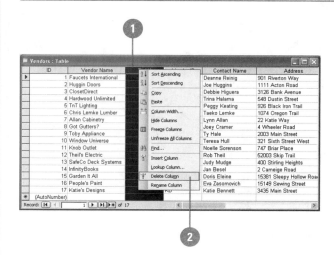

Did You Know?

You can rename a column. In Datasheet view, right-click the selector for the column you want to rename, click Rename Column, type the name you want, and then press Enter.

You can't delete a column in a relationship. You must delete the relationship first before you can delete a column.

5

Formatting a Datasheet

AC03S-3-4

Format a Datasheet

1. Open the datasheet you want to format.

2. Click the Format menu, and then click Datasheet.

3. Click a cell effect option.

4. Select or clear the Horizontal or Vertical check box to show or hide gridlines.

5. Click the Background Color or Gridline Color list arrow, and then select a color.

6. Click the Border And Line Styles list arrow, and then select the styles you want.

7. Click a display direction option.

8. Click OK.

Did You Know?

You can change the font and font style in a datasheet. Open the datasheet you want to format, click the Format menu, click Font, select the font and style settings you want, and then click OK.

If you want to print a datasheet, you can use formatting tools to make it look better than the standard display. You can apply special effects to cells, change the background and gridline color, and modify border and line styles. If you don't want to show the gridlines, you can hide either the horizontal or vertical gridlines, or both. The default display for a datasheet is to display the columns from left to right. If you prefer, you can change the column display to appear from right to left.

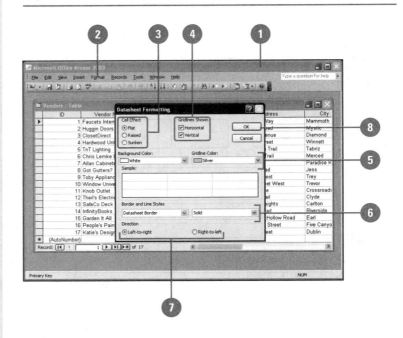

Repairing Renaming Errors

Access can correct errors that commonly occur when you rename forms, reports, tables, queries, text boxes, or other controls in a database. When Access detects a change in the name of one of these objects, it automatically corrects all the other objects that use that name. You can set Access to track renaming without taking action, to apply changes if you rename an object, and to log any changes it makes. Although Name AutoCorrect eliminates errors for database objects that don't employ Visual Basic for Applications (VBA) code, it doesn't repair renaming errors under some circumstances, such as in replicated databases and OBDC linked tables.

Enable and Log Name AutoCorrect

1. Click the Tools menu, click Options, and then click the General tab.

2. Select the Track Name AutoCorrect Info check box to allow Access to maintain the information it needs to perform Name AutoCorrect but not take any action.

3. Select the Perform Name AutoCorrect check box to perform Name AutoCorrect as changes are applied to the database.

4. To log name AutoCorrect changes, you need to select all three Name AutoCorrect check boxes: Track Name AutoCorrect Info, Perform Name AutoCorrect, and Log Name AutoCorrect Changes.

   You can view the name changes in a table called AutoCorrect Log.

5. Click OK.

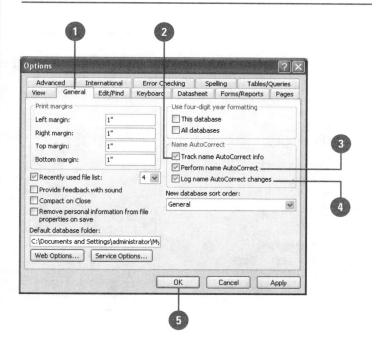

5

Sorting Records

AC03S-3-5

You can change the order in which records appear in a table, query results, forms, or reports by sorting the records. You can select a field and then sort the records by the values in that field in either ascending or descending order. Ascending order means that records appear in alphabetical order (for text fields), from most recent to later, (for date fields), or from smallest to largest (for numeric fields). In Descending order, the order is reversed. You might also want to sort records by more than one field; this is referred to as a **secondary sort**. For example, in a table containing information about products, you might need to view information about specific prices for each product. You can sort the records first by product and then, in records with the same product, sort the records by price.

Sort Records

1. In the Datasheet view, display the table, query results, form, or report in which you want to sort records.

2. To sort multiple columns, rearrange them to be adjacent.

3. Click the column selector of the column you want to sort. To select another column, press and hold Shift, and then click the column selector.

4. Click the Sort Ascending button on the Table Datasheet toolbar (A to Z), or click the Sort Descending button on the Table Datasheet toolbar (Z to A).

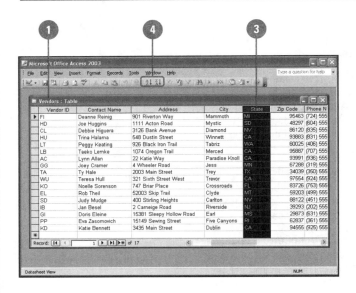

Sorted results

Change the Order of Records Based on Multiple Fields

1. Display the table in Datasheet view.

2. Because multiple fields that you want to sort must be adjacent and in the order of sort priority, rearrange columns if necessary.

3. Click the column selector of the first column you want to sort, and then before you release the mouse button, drag the mouse to the right to select the adjacent columns fields.

4. Click the Sort Ascending button on the Table Datasheet toolbar to sort the records in ascending order, or click the Sort Descending button on the Table Datasheet toolbar to sort the records in descending order.

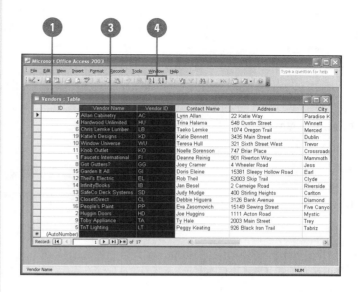

Sorted results

Did You Know?

You can specify a sort order when designing a table. Changing the order of records displayed in a table is not the same as specifying the sort order when you first design the table. Use the Sort feature when designing a table to display records in the order that you are likely to use most often, and then use the Sort Ascending and Sort Descending buttons to handle the exceptions when you display the table in Datasheet view.

Copying and Pasting Records

When you are entering a lot of records in Datasheet view that are nearly identical, you can use the Windows Clipboard to copy and paste existing records to create new records quickly. After copying and pasting, you can edit individual records to make a few changes. If only part of the record is similar, you can still use the Windows Clipboard to copy and paste the data in a single table cell.

Copy and Paste a New Record

1. In Datasheet view, right-click the row selector for the row you want to copy.

2. Click Copy.

3. Right-click an empty row selector for the new record row.

4. Click Paste.

5. Edit the new record as required.

> **Did You Know?**
>
> **You can select data to copy.** When you select data to copy, you can select an entire row or a single cell, but not multiple cells within a single row.

Viewing a Subdatasheet

In a table that has a one-to-many relationship with another table, a given record might have multiple related items. For example, a customer in a Customers table might have many products in a Products table. Access allows you to view the products related to that customer from the Customers table. You can open a **subdatasheet**, a list of the records from the "many" table that relate to a single record from the "one" table in a one-to-one or one-to-many relationship. Subdatasheets help you browse related data in tables, queries, forms, and subform datasheets. For any related tables, Access automatically creates subdatasheets. You can also insert a sub-datasheet in a table or query to view related data.

Display or Hide a Subdatasheet

1. In Datasheet view of the table, click the plus sign next to the record for which you want to see related information.

2. To hide the subdatasheet, click the minus sign next to the record whose subdatasheet you want to hide.

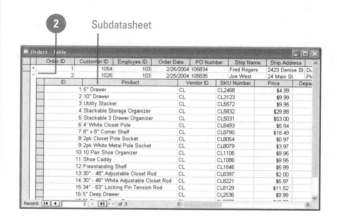

Subdatasheet

Insert a Subdatasheet in a Table

1. Display the table or query in Datasheet view.

2. Click the Insert menu, and then click Subdatasheet.

3. Click the tab corresponding to the object you want to insert as a subdatasheet.

4. Click a table or query in the list.

5. Select the field you want to use as a foreign key.

6. Select the field you want to use as a primary key.

7. Click OK.

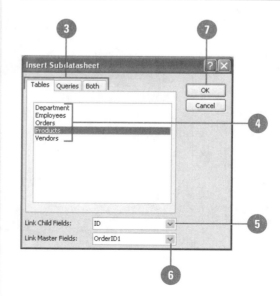

5

Filtering Out Records

AC03S-3-6

Instead of displaying all the records in a table, you can use a **filter** to display only those records that you want to see. You can display records based on a specific value in one field or based on multiple values in multiple fields. You can filter by selecting the field value on which to base the filter in Datasheet view or by using Filter By Form to help you create more complex filters involving multiple field values. After you apply a filter, Access displays only those records that match your specifications. You can remove a filter to return the datasheet to its original display.

Filter a Table by Selection

1. Display the table in Datasheet view.

2. Right-click the field value on which you want to base the filter.

3. Click Filter By Selection. Notice that the bottom of the Table window tells you the number of records matching your filter criteria. Also, the notation FLTR in the status bar indicates that a filter is currently in effect.

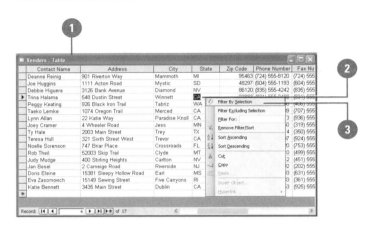

Clear a Filter from a Table

1. Display the table with the filter in Datasheet view.

2. Click the filtered table, and then click the Remove Filter button on the Table Database toolbar.

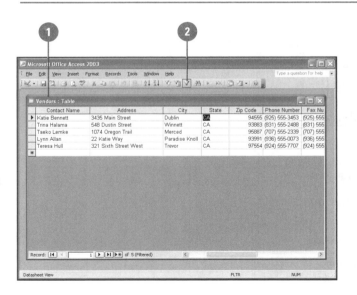

Did You Know?

You can save a filter as a query.
Display the filtered table in Datasheet view, click the Records menu, point to Filter, and then click Advanced Filter/Sort. Click the Save As Query button on the Filter/Sort toolbar, type a name, and then click OK.

Save a Filter as a Query

1. Display the filtered table in Datasheet view.

2. Click the Records menu, point to Filter, and then click Advanced Filter/Sort.

   The details of the filter appear in Design view.

3. Click the Save As Query button on the Filter/Sort toolbar.

4. Type the name you want to assign to the query. If you enter the name of an existing query, Access will ask if you want to overwrite the existing query. Be sure to answer "No" if you want to retain the original query, so you can give the new query a different name.

5. Click OK to save the filter as a query.

   The query you have just saved appears in the Queries list in the Database window.

6. Click OK.

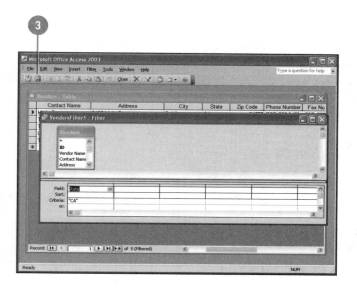

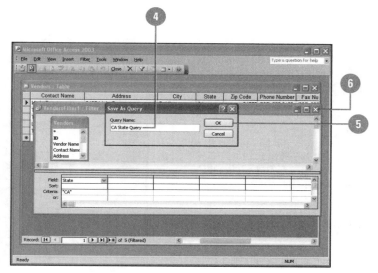

5

Creating Complex Filters Using Forms

AC03S-3-6

The Filter By Form feature allows you to create a more complex filter. Adding criteria on a particular tab in the form restricts the filter so that records must match all the criteria on the form for the records to be displayed; this is called an AND filter. To expand the filter to include more records, you can create an OR filter by specifying criteria on the subsequent Or tab in the Filter By Form grid. To be displayed, a record needs to match only the criteria specified on the Look For tab or the criteria specified on any one of the Or tabs.

Create an AND or OR Filter

1. In Datasheet view, click the Filter By Form button on the Table Datasheet toolbar.

2. Click in the empty text box below the field you want to filter.

3. Click the list arrow, and then click the field value by which you want to filter the records.

4. For each field by which you want to filter, click the list arrow, and then select the entry for your filter. Each new field in which you make a selection adds additional criteria that a record must match to be included.

5. If you want to establish Or criteria, click the Or tab at the bottom of the form to specify the additional criteria for the filter. If not, proceed to step 6.

6. Click the Apply Filter button on the Filter/Sort toolbar.

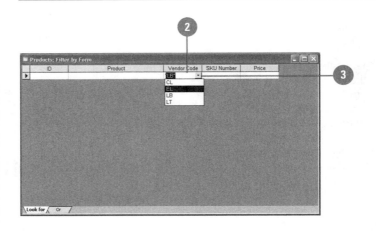

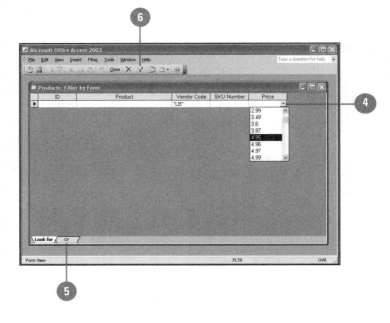

> **Did You Know?**
>
> **You can clear previous filters.** If necessary, click the Clear Grid button on the Filter/Sort toolbar to clear the previous filter.

Locating Specific Information Using a Query

6

Introduction

A **query** is a description of the records you want to retrieve from a database. As the name implies, a query helps answer specific questions about the information in your database—for example, "Which customers have placed orders in the last six months?" or "Who sent us greeting cards over the holidays in the last two years?" The description of the records you want to retrieve identifies the names of the fields and the values they should contain; this description is called the **selection criteria**. With a Microsoft Office Access 2003 query you can:

◆ Focus on only the information you need by displaying only a few fields from a large table.

◆ Apply functions and other expressions to fields to arrive at calculated results.

◆ Add, update, or delete records in tables; or create entirely new tables.

◆ Summarize and group values from one table and display the result in a table.

◆ Save a query definition that Access will treat as a table for the purpose of creating forms and reports.

◆ Retrieve information stored in multiple tables, even if the tables are not open.

What You'll Do

Understand Types of Queries

Create and Modify a Query in Design View

Get Information with a Query

Create a Query Using a Wizard

Change the Query Fields

Specify Criteria for a Single or Multiple Fields

Create Queries with Comparison and Logical Operators

Perform Calculations in Queries

Create a Parameter Query

Find Duplicate Fields and Unmatched Records

Create New Tables with a Query

Add Records with a Query

Delete Records with a Query

Update Records with a Query

Summarize Values with a Crosstab Query

Create SQL-Specific Queries

Understanding Types of Queries

Access offers several types of queries that help you retrieve the information you need—select queries, crosstab queries, action queries, and parameter queries.

♦ A **select query** retrieves and displays records in the Table window in Datasheet view.

♦ A **crosstab query** displays summarized values (sums, counts, and averages) from one field in a table, and groups them by one set of fields listed down the left side of the datasheet and by another set of fields listed across the top of the datasheet.

♦ An **action query** performs operations on the records that match your criteria. There are four kinds of action queries that you can perform on one or more tables: delete queries delete matching records; update queries make changes to matching records; append queries add new records to the end of a table; and make-table queries create new tables based on matching records.

♦ A **parameter query** allows you to prompt for a single piece of information to use as selection criteria in the query. For example, instead of creating separate queries to retrieve customer information for each state in which you do business, you could create a parameter query that prompts the user to enter the name of a state, and then continues to retrieve those specific records from that state.

Creating Queries in Access

As with most database objects you create in Access, there are several ways to create a query. You can create a query from scratch or use a wizard to guide you through the process of creating a query.

With the Query Wizard, Access helps you create a simple query to retrieve the records you want. All queries you create and save are listed on the Queries tab in the Database window. You can then double-click a query to run it and display the results. When you run a select query, the query results show only the selected fields for each record in the table that matches your selection criteria. Of course, once you have completed a query, you can further customize it in Design view. As always, you can begin creating your query in Design view without using the wizard at all. Queries are not limited to a single table. Your queries can encompass multiple tables as long as the database includes a field or fields that relate the tables to each other.

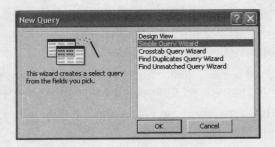

Creating a Query in Design View

Although a wizard can be a big help when you are first learning to create a query, you do not need to use a wizard. If you prefer, you can create a query without the help of a wizard. Instead of answering questions in a series of dialog boxes, you can start working in Design view right away. As you create a query, you can include more than one table or even another query in Design view. You can use comparison operators, such as >, <, or =, to compare field values to constants and other field values in the Criteria box. You can also use logical operators to create criteria combining several expressions, such as >1 AND <5.

Create a Query in Design View

1. In the Database window, click Queries on the Objects bar.

2. Click New, click Design View, and then click OK.

3. Select the table or query you want to use.

4. Click Add.

5. Repeat steps 3 and 4 for additional tables or queries, and then click Close.

6. Double-click each field you want to include in the query from the field list.

7. In the design grid, enter any desired search criteria in the Criteria box.

8. Click the Sort box, click the list arrow, and then specify a sort order.

9. Click the Save button, type a name for the query, and then click OK.

See Also

See "Performing Calculations in Queries" on page 128 for information on using the expression builder to add search criteria.

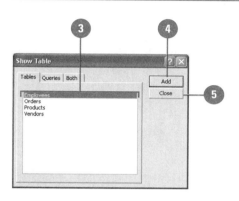

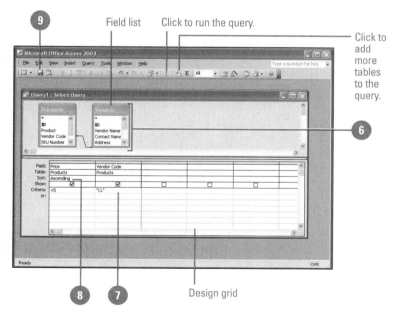

Field list   Click to run the query.

Click to add more tables to the query.

Design grid

Getting Information with a Query

Open and Run a Query

1. In the Database window, click Queries on the Objects bar.

2. Click the query you want to run.

3. Click the Open button.

   The query opens in a table called a dynaset. The dynaset displays the records that meet the specifications set forth in the query.

Access saves and lists the queries you create on the Queries tab in the Database window. You can double-click a query to run it and display the results. When you run a query, the query results show only the selected fields for each record in the table that matches your selection criteria.

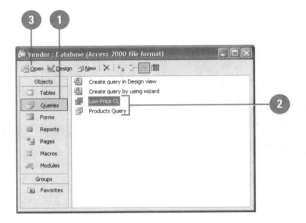

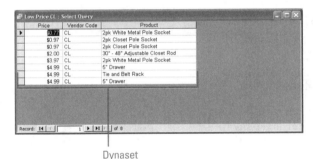

Dynaset

Modifying a Query
in Design View

 AC03S-1-7

Once you have completed a query, you can further customize it in Design view. However, you can also create a query in Design view without using the wizard. Queries are not limited to a single table. Your queries can encompass multiple tables as long as the database includes a field or fields that relate the tables to each other. You can create a query using specific criteria and sort the results. If you no longer want to include a table or field, you can remove it from the query. In some cases you might want to hide a field from the query results while keeping it part of the query design for selection design purposes.

Modify a Query in Design View

1 In the Database window, click Queries on the Objects bar.

2 Click the query you want to modify, and then click the Design button.

3 Double-click or drag each field you want to include in the query from the field list.

4 In the design grid, enter any search criteria in the Criteria box.

5 Click the Sort box, click the list arrow, and then specify a sort order.

6 To hide a field, clear the Show check box.

7 To delete a field, select the field, and then press Delete.

8 Click the Save button on the Query Design toolbar.

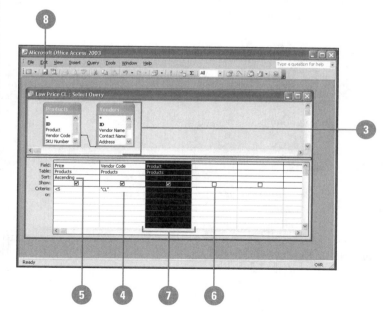

Did You Know?

You can sort the retrieved records. Display the query in Datasheet view, select the field in which you want to sort, and then click the Sort Ascending or Sort Descending button on the Table Datasheet toolbar.

You can remove a table. In the query, right-click the table, and then click Remove Table.

Creating a Query Using a Wizard

A query is a simple question you ask a database to help you locate specific information within the database. When you create a query with the **Query Wizard**, you can specify the kind of query you want to create and type of records from a table or existing query you want to retrieve. The Query Wizard guides you through each step; all you do is answer a series of questions, and Access creates a query based on your responses. All queries you create are listed on the Queries tab in the Database window.

Create a Simple Query Using the Query Wizard

1. In the Database window, click Queries on the Objects bar, and then double-click the Create Query By Using Wizard icon.

2. Select a table or existing query.

3. Click to select the fields that you want included in the query.

4. Click Next to continue.

5. If you selected numeric or date fields in step 3, indicate whether you want to see detail or summary information.

6. If you choose Summary, click Summary Options to specify the calculation for each field, and then click OK.

7. Click Next to continue.

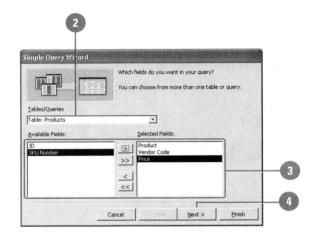

Did You Know?

You can include fields from another source. Click the Tables/Queries list arrow if you want to include a field from another source.

You can use the New button to create a query. In the Database window, click Queries on the Objects bar, click New, click the wizard you want to use, click OK, and then follow the wizard instructions.

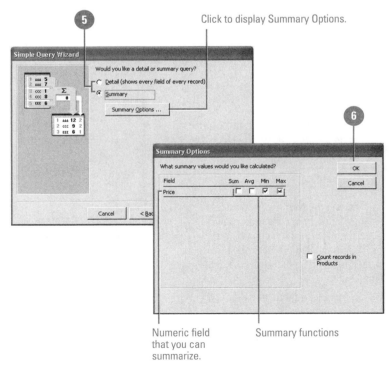

Click to display Summary Options.

Numeric field that you can summarize.

Summary functions

8 In the final wizard dialog box, type the name of the query.

9 Choose whether you want to view the results of the query or modify the query design in Design view.

10 For more help on queries, select the Display Help On Working With The Query? check box.

11 Click Finish.

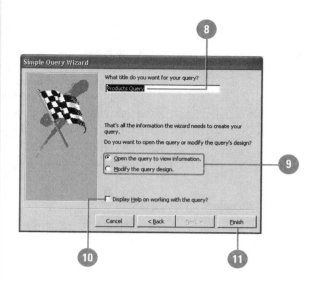

Name of query   Type of query

Records retrieved by the query

Changing the Query Fields

In Design view, you can add or remove fields in your query design to produce different results. You can also include fields from other tables in your database. In some cases you might want to hide a field from the query results while keeping it part of the query design for selection criteria purposes. When you remove a field from the query design grid, you're only removing it from the query specifications. You're not deleting the field and its data from the underlying table. When you hide a field by clearing the Show check box, the field remains part of the query; it just won't be displayed to the user.

Add a Field to a Query

1. Display the query in Design view.

2. Double-click a field name from the field list to place the field in the next available column in the design grid, or drag a field to a specific column in the design grid.

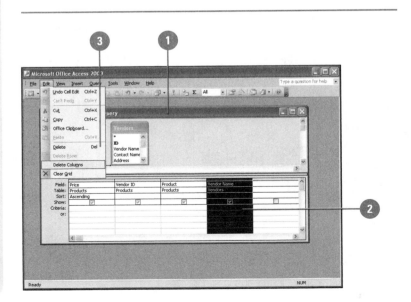

Fields from the Products table

Field from the Vendors table

Remove a Field from a Query

1. Display the query in Design view.

2. Select the field you want to remove from the query.

3. Press Delete, or click the Edit menu, and then click Delete or Delete Columns.

Add a Field from Another Table to a Query

1. Display the query in Design view.

2. Click the Show Table button on the Query Design toolbar.

3. Select the table that contains the fields you want to include in the query.

4. Click Add.

5. Repeat steps 3 and 4 for each table you want to include.

6. Click Close.

7. Double-click or drag the fields you want to include to the design grid.

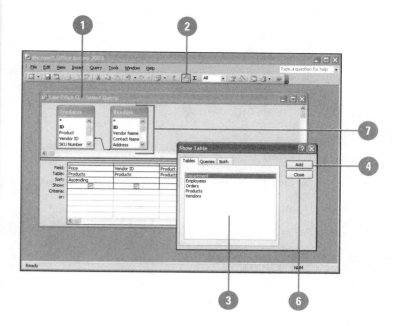

Did You Know?

You can format a query field. To modify the appearance of a query field, click anywhere within the query field's column, and then click the Properties button on the toolbar. You can then specify the format, caption, input mask, and other features of the query field.

You can change the order of fields in a query. In the design grid, point at the column selector for the column you want to move. (The column selector is the thin gray box at the top of a column.) When the pointer changes to a small black arrow, click to select the column. When the black arrow changes back, use the mouse pointer to drag the selected column to a new position.

You can remove a table from the Query design grid. To remove a table, right-click its field list in the top portion of the Query Design View window, and then click Remove Table.

6

Specifying Criteria for a Single Field

For each field you include in a query, you can specify criteria that a record must match to be selected when you run the query. For example, you can create a query to retrieve toys of a certain type, such as infant toys, from a toys database. You do this by entering a criterion's value in the Query Design window. Access allows you to add multiple criteria values for a single field so that the query retrieves records that meet either (or both) of the criteria you specify.

Specify Criteria for a Single Field in a Query

1. Display the query in Design view.

2. Click the field's Criteria box.

3. Enter a criterion value for the field.

4. If additional values of the field are allowed, enter them into the Or box listed below the Criteria box.

5. Click the Run button on the Query Design toolbar.

Did You Know?

You can specify text to search for in your selection criteria. When the criterion is a text value, it must be enclosed in quotation marks. Access inserts quotation marks after you type the value and press Tab or Enter.

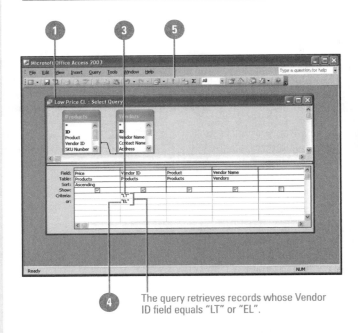

The query retrieves records whose Vendor ID field equals "LT" or "EL".

The query retrieves products by vendor LT and EL.

Specifying Criteria for Multiple Fields

You can specify several query fields. If the criteria for the fields occupy the same row in the Query Design window, Access retrieves records for which **all** of the criteria are satisfied. For example, if you specify the vendor ID as "LT" (TnT Lighting) and the product price equal to "9.99," only products equal to $9.99 by LT will be retrieved. On the other hand, if the criteria are entered into different rows, Access retrieves records for which **any** of the criteria are satisfied. For example, placing "LT" and "9.99" in different rows will cause Access to retrieve either LT products or products with the price $9.99.

Specify Criteria for Multiple Fields in a Query

1 Display the query in Design view.

2 Enter the criteria value or values for the first field.

3 Enter a criteria value or values for additional fields.

4 Click the Run button on the Query Design toolbar.

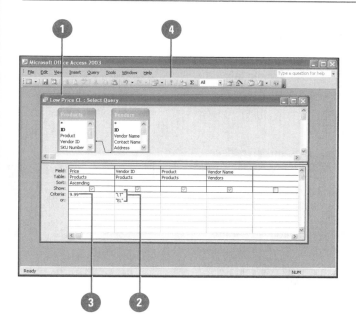

The query retrieves products with a price of $9.99 for LT or any price for EL.

6

Creating Queries with Comparison and Logical Operators

You can use the Expression Builder to create more complicated queries. For example, you can use **comparison operators**, such as >, <, or =, to compare field values to constants and other field values. For example, you can use the greater-than operator (>) to create a query that retrieves records in which more than 1 toy is ordered. You can also use logical operators to create criteria combining several expressions. For example, you can use the AND operator to retrieve records in which the number of toys ordered is greater than 1 AND less than 5. You can also use **logical operators** to negate expressions. For example, you could run a query that retrieves toy records that are NOT infant toys.

Use a Comparison Operator

1. Display the query in Design View, and then click the Criteria box for the field.

2. Click the Build button on the Query Design toolbar.

3. Click the appropriate comparison operator button.

   To see additional comparison operators, click the Operators folder, click Comparison, and then choose the comparison operator you want from the list on the right.

4. Enter a value or click a field whose value you want to compare.

5. Click OK.

6. Click the Run button on the Query Design toolbar.

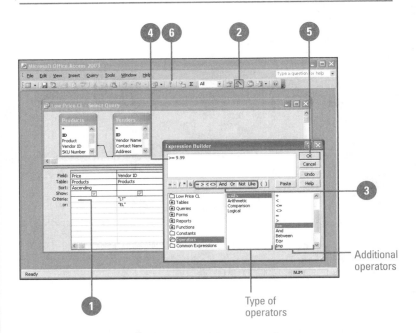

Type of operators

Additional operators

Access retrieves only those records whose price is greater than or equal to $9.99 for LT or any price for EL.

Use a Logical Operator

1. Display the query in Design view, and then click the Criteria box.

2. Click the Build button on the Query Design toolbar.

3. Click the appropriate logical operator button.

   To see additional comparison operators, click the Operators folder, click Logical, and then choose the logical operator you want from the list on the right.

4. Enter any values needed to complete the expression.

5. Click OK.

6. Click the Run button on the Query Design toolbar.

Did You Know?

You can fine-tune selection criteria. To fine-tune your selection criteria, combine logical and comparison operators in the same expression.

You can compare one field with another. To create an expression that compares one field with another, use the Expression Builder and look within the Tables folder to locate the table and field of interest. Double-click the field name to add it to the expression. The expression should contain the table name and field name in brackets, separated by an exclamation point. For example, to choose records where the value of the OnOrder field in the Orders table is greater than the value of the InStock field, the expression is: *[Orders]![OnOrder]>[Orders]![InStock]*.

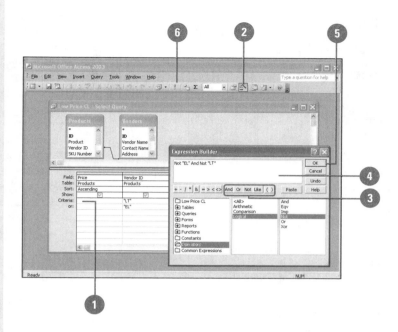

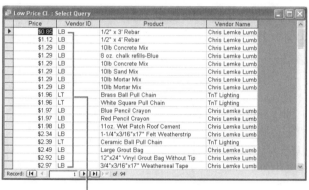

Access retrieves only those records in which the vendor is not EL and LT.

Performing Calculations in Queries

AC03S-3-1

In addition to the built-in functions you can use to compare values in a query, you can use the **Expression Builder** to create your own calculations using arithmetic operators. By clicking the operator buttons you want to use and entering constant values as needed, you can use the Expression Builder to include expressions in a query. For example, to determine fees based on a contract amount, you can create an arithmetic expression in your query to compute the results. When you run the query, Access performs the required calculations and displays the results. You can also insert functions, such as AVG and Count, to perform other operations. When you insert a function, <<expr>> appears in parentheses, which represents an expression. Select <<expr>> and replace it with a field name, which you can select in Expression Builder.

Create a Calculated Field

1. Within Query Design view, position the insertion point in the Field row of a blank column in the design grid.

2. Click the Build button on the Query Design toolbar.

3. Double-click the field (or fields) you want to use in the calculation.

4. Build an expression using the operator buttons and elements area.

   ◆ Click the button corresponding to the calculation you want.

   ◆ Click the Operators folder, click the Arithmetic folder, and then click the operator you want to use.

   ◆ Click the Functions folder, click Built-In Functions, and then click the function you want to use.

5. Type any other values (constants) you want to include in the expression.

6. Click OK.

7. Click the Run button on the Query Design toolbar.

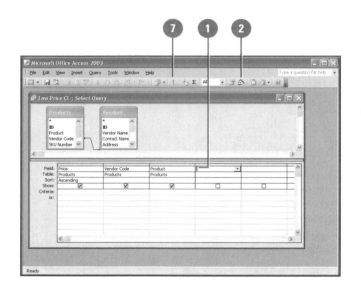

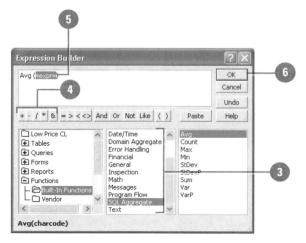

Creating a Parameter Query

ACO3S-1-7

When you need to change the criterion value for a query, you either must edit the old query or create a new one. However, if the change involves simply altering a value, you might consider using a parameter query. A **parameter query** prompts the user for the value of a particular query field, rather than having the value built into the query itself. For example, if you want to display the records for particular toy types, a parameter query can prompt you for the type, saving you from creating a separate query for each type.

Create a Parameter Query

1. In Query Design view, click the Criteria box.

2. Enter the text of the prompt surrounded by square brackets.

3. Click the Run button on the Query Design toolbar.

4. Enter a criteria name in response to the prompt.

5. Click OK.

Did You Know?

You can rename a field. Access assigns a name to a calculated field. If you want a different name, click the field in the design grid, and then click the Properties button on the Query Design toolbar. Enter a new name in the Caption box, and then click OK.

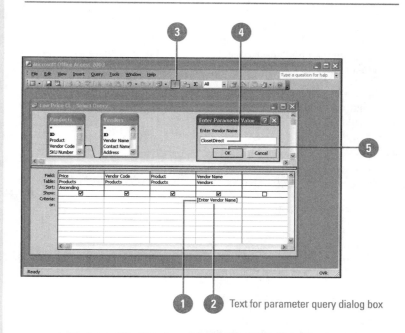

Text for parameter query dialog box

Access retrieves records with the ClosetDirect vendor.

6

Finding Duplicate Fields

AC03S-1-7

Find Duplicate Records

1 In the Database window, click Queries on the Objects bar, click New, and then double-click Find Duplicates Query Wizard.

2 Choose the table or query that you want to search for duplicate records.

3 Click Next to continue.

4 Select the field or fields that might contain duplicate information.

5 Click Next to continue.

6 Select any other fields that you want displayed in the query.

7 Click Next to continue.

8 Enter a name for the new query.

9 Specify whether you want to view the query results or further modify the query design.

10 Click Finish.

In some tables, you need to find records that have duplicate values in particular fields. For example, in a table of employees, you might want to discover which employees work at the same location. You can create a query that retrieves all the records from the Employees table that have duplicate values for the Office Location field. Access provides the Find Duplicate Query Wizard to guide you through each step to help you create the query.

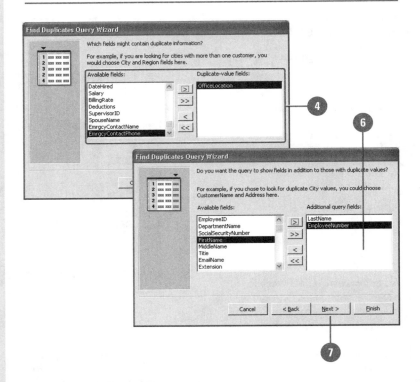

Access retrieves only those records with duplicate office locations.

Finding Unmatched Records

AC03S-1-7

When you have related tables, you might want to find which records in one table have no match in the other table. For example, if you have a table of products and a table of customer orders, you might need to know whether there are products that have no match in the Orders table. In other words, are there some products that no customer has yet purchased? Access provides a query wizard to help you answer questions of this type.

Find Unmatched Records

1. In the Database window, click Queries on the Objects bar, click New, and then double-click Find Unmatched Query Wizard.

2. Choose the table or query whose values you want displayed in the query. Click Next to continue.

3. Choose the related table or query. Click Next to continue.

4. Specify the field that matches records in the first table to records in the second. Click Next to continue.

5. Choose which fields from the first table to display in the query results. Click Next to continue.

6. Enter a name for the new query.

7. Specify whether you want to view the query results or further modify the query design.

8. Click Finish.

Table displayed in the query results

Related links

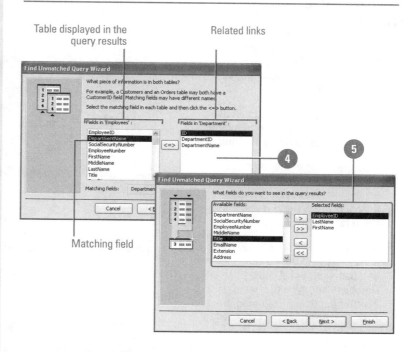

Matching field

Access retrieves only those records that are not matched in related Department table.

Creating New Tables with a Query

The data that appears after you run a query appears in table form and Access allows you to work with those results like tables. However, query results are not tables. If you want to place the results of a query into a separate table, you can use the **make-table query**. This query directs Access to save the results of your query to a new table in either the current database or a different database.

Create a New Table with a Query

1. In Query Design view, create a select query, including any combination of fields, calculated fields, or criteria.

2. Click the Query Type button list arrow on the Query Design toolbar, and then click Make-Table Query.

3. Type the name of the table you want to create, or click the list arrow, and then select a table from the list if you want to replace the existing one.

4. Click the Current Database option if the table is in the currently open database, or click Another Database and type the name of another database (including the path, if necessary).

5. Click OK.

6. Click the Run button on the Query Design toolbar.

7. Click Yes when Access asks if you're sure you want to create the new table.

8. Open the new table to view the records resulting from the query.

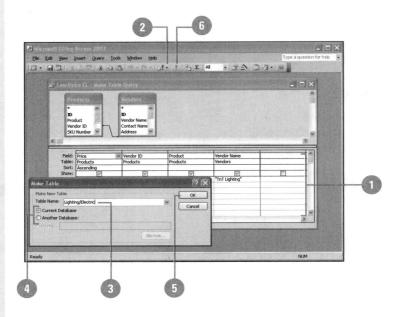

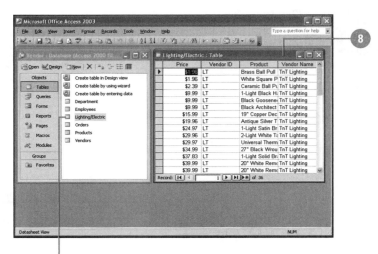

Access adds a new table to the database.

Adding Records with a Query

You can use a query to add records to a table by creating an **append query**. If the fields you've selected have the same name in both tables, Access automatically fills the matching name in the Append To row in the design grid. If the fields in the two tables don't have the same name, enter the names of the fields in the Append To row in the design grid. If the table you are appending records to includes a primary key field, the records you are appending must have the same field or an equivalent field of the same data type. Access won't append any of the records if either duplicate or empty values would appear in the primary key field.

Add Records with a Query

1. In Query Design view, create a select query.

2. Click the Query Type button list arrow on the Query Design toolbar, and then click Append Query.

3. Type the name of the table to which you want to append the records, or click the list arrow, and then choose one.

4. Click the Current Database option, or click Another Database and type the name of another database (including the path, if necessary).

5. Click OK.

6. Specify which fields will contain the appended values by entering the field names in the Append To row of the design grid.

7. Click the Run button on the Query Design toolbar.

8. Click Yes when Access asks if you're sure you want to append records to the table.

9. Open the table to view the appended records.

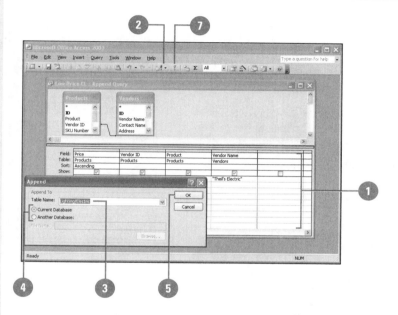

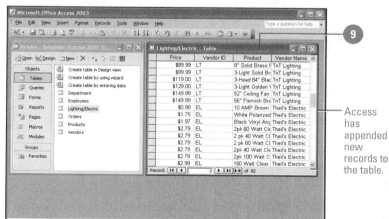

Access has appended new records to the table.

6

Deleting Records with a Query

If you want to remove records from a table based on a criterion or criteria, you can do so with a **delete query**. The delete query searches the table you specify and removes all records that match your criteria. Because Access permanently deletes these records, use caution before you run a delete query. You can preview the results before you actually run the query. By clicking the Datasheet View button, you can see which records will be deleted before you actually run the query.

Create a Query to Delete Records

① In Query Design view, create a select query.

② Click the Query Type button list arrow on the Query Design toolbar, and then click Delete Query.

③ Click the Datasheet View button on the Query Design toolbar to preview the list of deleted records.

④ If you're satisfied that the appropriate records would be deleted, click the Design View button to return to Query Design view.

⑤ Click the Run button on the Query Design toolbar.

⑥ Click Yes when Access asks if you're sure you want to delete records from the table.

⑦ Open the table to view the remaining records.

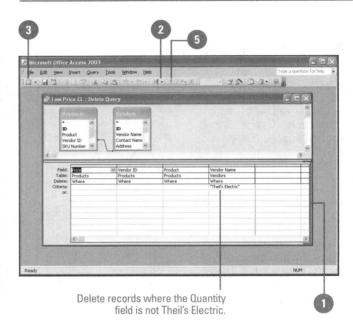

Delete records where the Quantity field is not Theil's Electric.

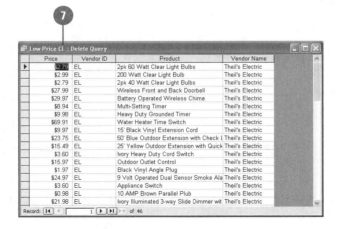

Updating Records with a Query

An **update query** allows you to make changes to a set of records that match your query's criteria. For example, if you want to increase the unit price of board games in a toy product table by $3, you can construct a query that will locate those records and update them to the new value. Make sure you preview the changes to the records before you run the query, because once the records are changed you can't easily change them back.

Create a Query to Update Records

1. Display a new query in Query Design view. Add the fields or fields you intend to update and any fields that you want to use for the selection criteria.

2. Click the Query Type button list arrow on the Query Design toolbar, and then click Update Query.

3. Enter an expression to update the selected field.

4. Enter a criterion, if needed, to indicate which records should be updated.

5. Click the Datasheet View button on the Query Design toolbar.

6. If you're satisfied that the appropriate records would be updated, click the Design View button to return to Query Design view.

7. Click the Run button on the Query Design toolbar.

8. Click Yes when Access asks if you're sure you want to update the records.

9. Open the table to view the remaining records.

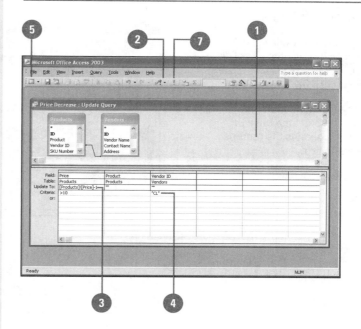

Access decreases the price by $1 for every product by CL over $10.

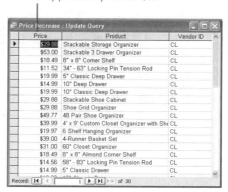

Summarizing Values with a Crosstab Query

AC03S-1-7

A **crosstab query** allows you to summarize the contents of fields that contain numeric values, such as Date fields or Number fields. In this type of query, the results of the summary calculations are shown at the intersection of rows and columns. Crosstab queries can also involve other functions such as the average, sum, maximum, minimum, and count. You cannot update crosstab queries. The value in a crosstab query cannot be changed in order to change the source data.

Create a Crosstab Query

1. In the Database window, click Queries on the Objects bar, click New, click Crosstab Query Wizard, and then click OK.

2. From the list at the top of the dialog box, select the table or query that contains the records you want to retrieve.

3. Click Next to continue.

4. Double-click the field(s) you want to use in the crosstab query.

5. Click Next to continue.

6. Select the field for the columns in the crosstab query.

7. Click Next to continue.

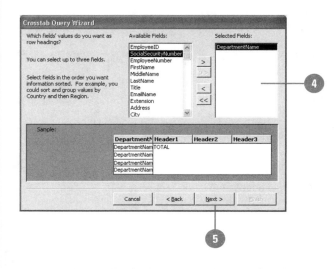

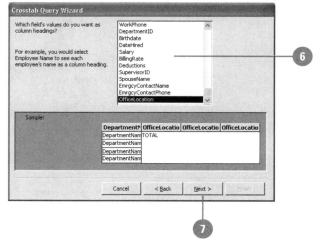

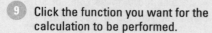

⑧ Click the field whose values you want to be calculated and displayed for each row and column intersection.

⑨ Click the function you want for the calculation to be performed.

⑩ Select the Yes, Include Row Sums check box if you want to see a total for each row, or clear the check box if you do not want to see a total for each row.

⑪ Click Next to continue.

⑫ Enter a name for your query.

⑬ Indicate whether you want to immediately view the query or modify the design.

⑭ Click Finish.

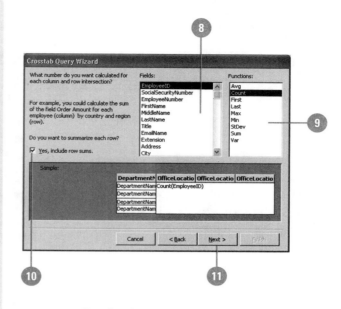

Did You Know?

You can use a PivotTable instead of a crosstab query. Display crosstab data without creating a separate query in your database either by using the PivotTable Wizard in a form, or by creating a PivotTable list in a data access page.

You can change column headings in a crosstab query. If you want to change the column headings, open the query in Design view, and then open the Properties dialog box for the query. Enter the column headings you want to display in the Column Headings property box, separated by commas.

Overall total

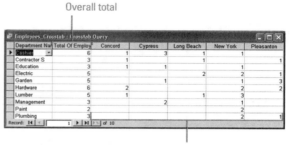

Total broken down by office location

6

Creating SQL-Specific Queries

SQL (Structured Query Language) is a powerful database language used in querying, updating, and managing relational databases. For each query, Access automatically creates an equivalent SQL statement. If you know SQL, you can edit this statement, or write an entirely new one, to create new, more powerful queries. Access supports three kinds of SQL-specific queries: union, pass-through, and data-definition. Each of these query types fulfills a different need.

Create a SQL-Specific Query

1. In Query Design view, click the Query menu, and then point to SQL Specific.

2. Click Union, Pass-Through, or Data Definition.

3. Enter SQL commands to create the query.

4. Save and view the query.

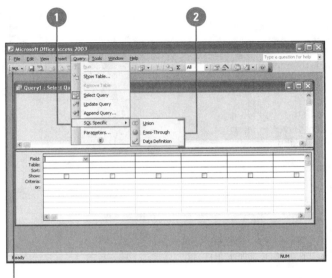

Click to view the SQL commands used in constructing an Access query.

> ### Did You Know?
>
> *You can view a query in SQL.* To see what your query looks like in SQL, click the View button and then click SQL View.

Types of SQL-Specific Queries

Type	Definition
Union	A query that combines related fields from multiple tables into one field, thus combining the data from several tables.
Pass-Through	A query that sends SQL commands directly to an SQL database server. This allows you to work with tables on the server instead of linking the tables to your Access database.
Data Definition	A query that deletes an index, or creates, alters, or deletes a table.

Simplifying Data Entry with Forms

7

Introduction

Forms allow a database designer to create a user-friendly method of data entry in Microsoft Office Access 2003. Instead of entering records in the grid of rows and columns in Datasheet view, you can use a form that can represent a paper form. Such a form can minimize data-entry errors because it closely resembles the paper-based form containing the information you want to enter in your table. A form can include fields from multiple tables, so you don't have to switch from one table to another when entering data.

If your table contains fields that include graphics, documents, or objects from other programs, you can see the actual objects in Form view. (In Datasheet view, the object is identified with text or with an icon.) To make it even easier to enter and maintain data, you can also include instructions and guidance on the form so that a user of the form knows how to complete it. You can add borders and graphics to the form to enhance its appearance.

The Windows XP operating system offers you several themes. If you have chosen a theme other than the default, Access will apply the chosen theme to views, dialog boxes, and controls. You can prevent form controls from inheriting themes from the operating system by setting an option in the database or project.

What You'll Do

Create Forms

Work with Form Controls

Create a Form Using AutoForm

Create a Form Using a Wizard

Create a Form in Design View

Edit an Existing Form

Add and Modify Controls

Use the Control Wizards

Create a Subform

Edit in Form View

Enter and Edit Data in a Form

Use Windows XP Themes in Forms

Creating Forms

As with most objects you create in a database, you have several choices when creating a form.

- You can use the AutoForm command to create a simple form that contains all the fields in the currently selected table or query.

- With the AutoForm Wizards, Access creates a simple form (columnar, tabular, or datasheet) based on the table or query you specify.

- With the Form Wizard, you can specify the kind of form you want to create and the wizard guides you through each step of the process. You answer a series of questions about your form, and Access creates a form using your formatting preferences.

Of course, once you have completed a form, you can further customize it in Design view. As always, you can begin creating your form in Design view without using the wizard at all.

Click to create a form in Design view.

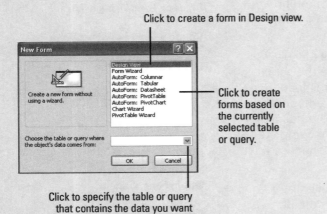

Click to create forms based on the currently selected table or query.

Click to specify the table or query that contains the data you want displayed in a form.

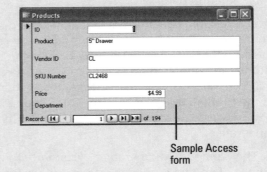

Sample Access form

Working with Form Controls

Each item on a form, such as a field name, a field value, and the form title, is called a control. When you create a form with a wizard, the wizard takes care of arranging and sizing the controls to make a form according to the selections you provided to the wizard. If you want to modify a form, you can do so in Design view by:

- Moving and sizing controls.

- Changing control properties.

- Changing the appearance of controls with borders, shading, and text effects such as bold and italics.

- Inserting new controls.

- Organizing controls using group boxes.

Types of Form Controls

There are three kinds of controls you can use in a form:

- **Bound controls** are fields of data from a table or query. A form must contain a bound control for each field that you want to appear on the form. You cannot create a calculation in a bound control.

- **Unbound controls** are controls that contain a label or a text box. Typically, you use unbound controls to identify other controls or areas on the form. You can create calculations from an unbound control.

- **Calculated controls** are any values calculated in the form, including totals, subtotals, averages, percentages, and so on.

To create a control, you click the control button for the kind of control you want to create and then drag the pointer over the area where you want the control to appear. The control buttons are available on the Toolbox in Design view.

In Design view, you see two parts for every control: the control itself and its corresponding label. When you drag a control to position it, its corresponding label moves with it (and visa versa). You cannot separate a label from its control.

If you are unsure of how to create controls, you can click the Control Wizard button on the toolbox to activate the Control Wizards. With the Control Wizards active, a wizard guides you through the process of creating certain types of controls. For example, if you create a list box control with the Control Wizards button active, the wizard appears, providing information about this type of control. It also prompts you to enter a name for the control label. To turn off the Control Wizards, click the Control Wizards button again (so that it is no longer indented).

Each type of form control has specific characteristics you can change using the Properties feature. You simply select the control you want to modify and then click the Properties button on the Form Design toolbar. In the control property sheet, you can specify the characteristics you want to change.

Creating a Form
Using AutoForm

AC03S-1-8

To create a simple form in Access, you can use one of the AutoForm wizards. These wizards quickly arrange the fields from the selected table or query into an attractive form. In a form created with the AutoForm: Columnar Wizard, you see each record's data displayed vertically, and with the AutoForm: Tabular Wizard, you see each record's data horizontally. With the AutoForm: Datasheet Wizard, the form displays the records in Datasheet view. After you create a form, you can save and name it so that you can use it again. If you need a more custom form, you can use the Form Wizard to select the information you want to include from a variety of places.

Create a Form Using the AutoForm Wizard

1. In the Database window, click Forms on the Objects bar, and then click the New button.

2. Click the AutoForm you want to create.

   ◆ AutoForm: Columnar to display records in a column.

   ◆ AutoForm: Tabular to display records in rows.

   ◆ AutoForm: Datasheet to display records in Datasheet view.

   ◆ AutoForm: PivotTable to display records in a PivotTable.

   ◆ AutoForm: PivotChart to display records in a PivotChart.

3. Click the list arrow, and then click the name of a table or query on which to base the form.

4. Click OK.

   After a moment, Access creates a form and displays it in Form view.

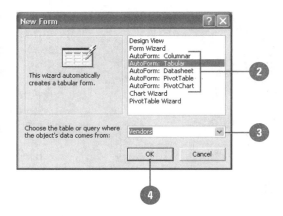

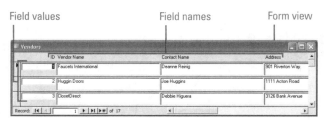

Save a New Form

1. Display the new form in Form view, and then click the Save button on the Form View toolbar.

2. Type the name of your form.

3. Click OK.

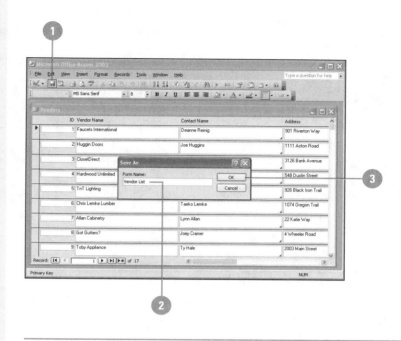

Create an AutoForm

1. In the Database window, click Tables or Queries on the Objects bar.

2. Click the table or query in which you want to create an AutoForm.

3. Click the New Object button list arrow on the Database toolbar.

4. Click AutoForm.

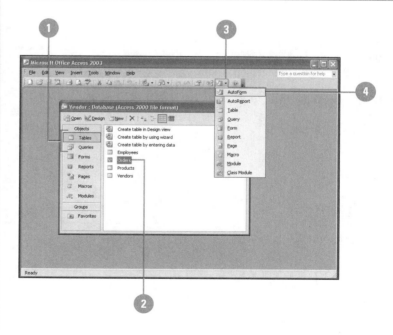

Creating a Form Using a Wizard

 AC03S-1-8

Access makes it easy to create forms with the Form Wizard. The Form Wizard lets you select the information you want to include in your form and choose from a variety of formatting options to determine how you want the form to look. You can choose the specific fields (including fields from multiple tables or queries) you want to see in the form. When you enter information in a form, the new data will be stored in the correct tables.

Create a Custom Form Using the Form Wizard

1. In the Database window, click Forms on the Objects bar, and then double-click the Create Form By Using Wizard icon.

2. Click the list arrow for choosing a table or query on which to base the form, and then click the name of the table or query you want.

3. Specify the fields that you want included in the form by double-clicking the fields.

4. Click Next to continue.

5. Determine the arrangement and position of the information on the form (Columnar, Tabular, Datasheet, or Justified).

6. Click Next to continue.

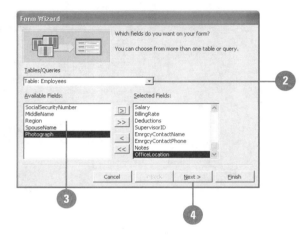

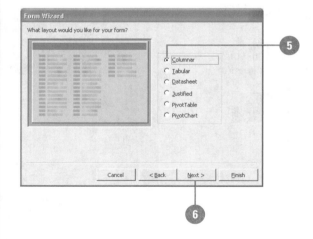

7 Specify the style of the form, which affects its formatting and final appearance. In the preview area of the dialog box, you can see a preview of the selected style.

8 Click Next to continue.

9 Enter a name for your form.

10 Indicate whether you want to open the form or display it in Design view.

11 Click Finish.

Did You Know?

You can save a new form. While the new form is displayed, click the Save button on the Form View toolbar. Type the name of your form in the Save As dialog box, and then click OK.

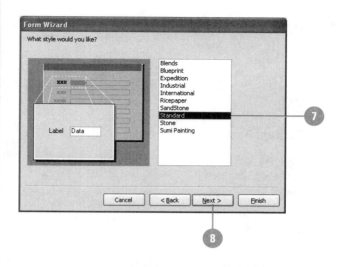

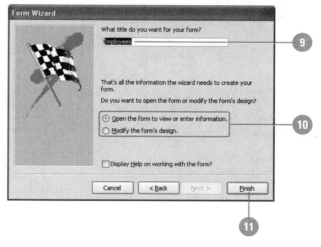

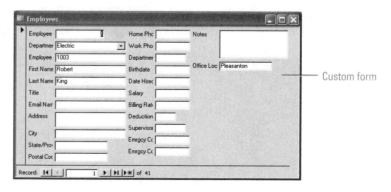

Custom form

Creating a Form in Design View

Although a wizard can be a big help when you are first learning to create a form, you can create a form without the help of a wizard if you have a good idea of how you want it to look. Instead of answering questions in a series of dialog boxes, you can start working in Design view right away. You can create and modify controls, and move and format the controls, to create the exact form you want.

Create a Form in Design View

1. In the Database window, click Forms on the Objects bar, and then click the New button.

2. Click Design View, select the table or query from which the data will come, and then click OK.

3. If necessary, click the Field List button on the Form Design toolbar to add a bound control.

4. Select the field you want to add to the form.

5. Drag the field to the location in the form where you want the field to appear, and then release the mouse button to position the field.

6. Create new controls as needed by clicking the appropriate toolbox button.

7. Format the text in the form, as needed.

8. Click the Save button on the Form Design toolbar to name the form and save it in the database.

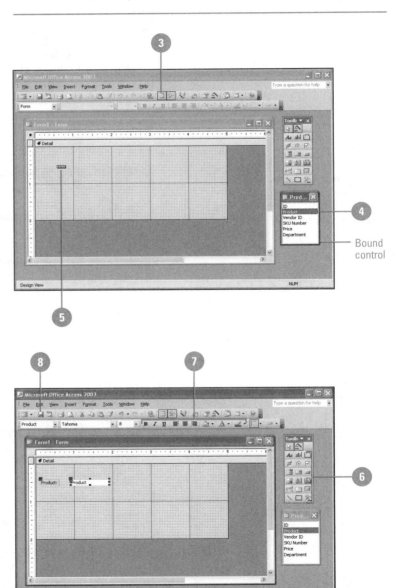

Bound control

Editing an Existing Form

After you create a form, you might decide to modify certain features to make the form easier to use. For example, you might want more descriptive labels to identify each field. Or you might create a box around a group of fields to help the user identify and complete related fields. To modify a form, you display the form in Design view, which you can do from the Forms option on the Objects bar in the Database window or from Form view. The View button lets you switch between Form view and Design view so that you can easily modify a form and view the results.

Edit a Form

1. In the Database window, click Forms on the Objects bar.

2. Click the form you want to use.

3. Click the Design button, and then make the modifications you want.

Did You Know?

You can insert fields quickly. To insert a block of fields, click the first field, press and hold Shift, and then click the last field. To insert nonadjacent fields, press and hold Ctrl, and then click the fields you want. To insert all fields, double-click the Field List title bar.

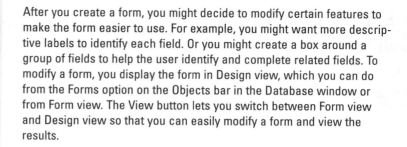

Switch Between Views

1. In Design or Form view, click the View button list arrow.

   The View button changes according to the view you are in.

2. Click the view name (Form View or Design View) of the view to which you want to switch.

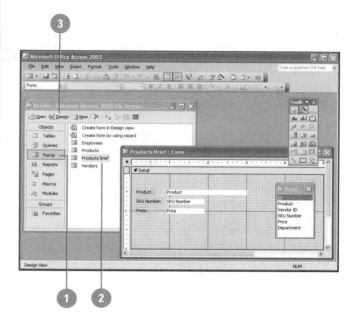

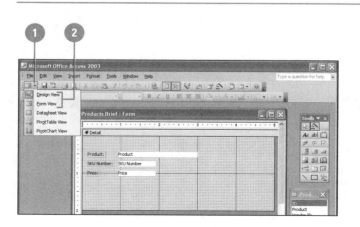

Adding and Modifying Controls

AC03S-1-9

Controls can make a form easier to use and improve its appearance. Controls also allow you to display additional information on your forms. To create a control on a form, you click the appropriate control button on the Toolbox. The Toolbox appears by default in Design view; however, if the Toolbox was closed for some reason, you need to redisplay it when you want to create new controls on a form. With the control pointer, drag in the form where you want the control to appear. You can also edit controls to change text and delete controls that you no longer want.

Add Controls to a Form

1. Open the form in which you want to add controls in Design view.

2. Click the button on the Toolbox for the type of control you want to create.

3. In the Form window, drag the pointer to draw a box in the location where you want the control to appear.

4. Select the field you want to add to the form.

5. Drag the field to the location in the form where you want the field to appear, and then release the mouse button to position the field.

6. If a smart tag appears indicating an error, click the Smart Tag Options button, and then click an option.

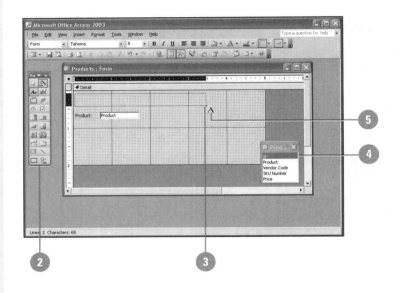

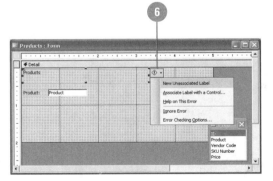

Did You Know?

You can change the tab order in a form. Tab order determines the sequence when move between fields using the Tab key. To change the tab order, open the form you want to change in Design view, click the View menu, click Tab Order, click a section option, drag selected row to a new tab order, and then click OK.

Edit Controls in a Form

1. Open the form in which you want to edit controls in Design view.

2. Click the Select Objects button on the Toolbox.

3. Click the control you want to edit.

   Small black boxes, called handles, appear around the control to indicate it is selected. You can use them to resize the control.

4. To remove the control, press Delete.

5. To edit the control, click the control to place the insertion point, and then use the Backspace or Delete key to remove text or type to insert text.

Modify Control Properties

1. Open the form or report in which you want to modify controls in Design view.

2. Double-click the object (control, section, or form) to open the object's property sheet.

   TROUBLE? *If the property sheet doesn't open, double-click the edge of the object.*

3. Enter the property information you want to add or change.

4. Click the Close button.

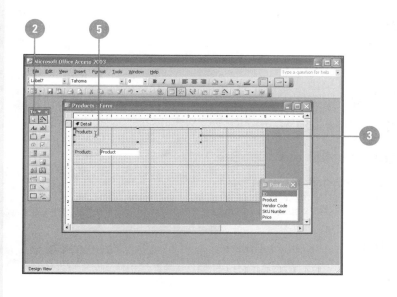

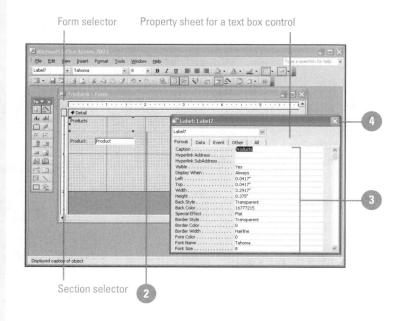

Form selector   Property sheet for a text box control

Section selector

Using the Control Wizards

AC03S-1-9

Create a List Box or Combo Box

1 Display the form in Design view, and then, if necessary, click the Control Wizards button on the Toolbox.

2 Click the Combo Box or List Box button on the Toolbox.

3 In the Form window, drag a rectangle in the location where you want the control to appear. When you release the mouse button, the wizard dialog box for the selected control appears.

4 Specify whether you want the control to get its values from a table or query, from what you type in the box, or from what value is selected in the list or combo box. Click Next to continue.

5 If applicable, select the table that contains the values you want displayed in the list or combo box. Click Next to continue.

6 Select the field that contains the values you want displayed in control. Click Next to continue.

7 Select the first sort list arrow, select a table to sort, and then click the Sort button. If you want, select additional sorts. Click Next to continue.

8 Adjust the width of the columns for the list box as necessary. Click Next to continue.

The **Control Wizards** help you create controls on your form. Although there are many controls you can create, the procedures for creating each control are quite similar, with minor variations depending on the type of control. For example, when you want to include a list of valid options for a field on a form, you can create either a **combo box** or **list box** control. Both controls provide a list from which a user can choose when entering data. The easiest way to create either of these controls is with a Control Wizard, which includes additional sorting options.

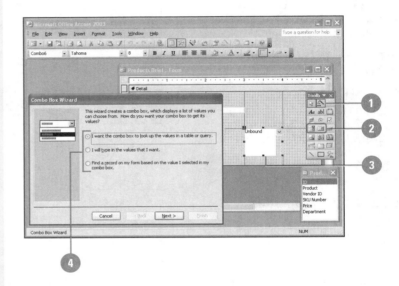

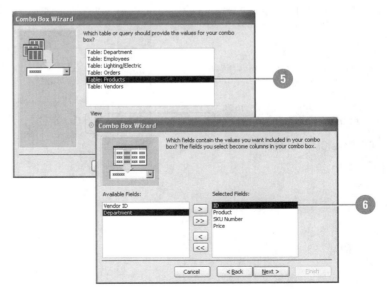

9. If necessary, specify which column contains the value that will be stored in the list box control. Click Next to continue.

10. Specify whether you want Access merely to display the column value (for later use to perform a task) or to store the value in a field in a table.

11. If you choose to store the value in a field, specify the field.

12. Click Next to continue.

13. Enter a label for the new control, and then click Finish.

Did You Know?

You can create a list box with custom values. If you want specific values (rather than values from a table) to populate the list box, click the I Will Type In The Values That I Want option in the wizard's first step, and then enter the values manually when you are prompted by the wizard.

You can create a list box to display a specific record. If you want your list box to cause Access to retrieve records, click the Find A Record On My Form Based On The Value I Selected In My List Box option in the wizard's first step. The wizard then prompts you for the field from which the list box will receive its values. When the list box is added to the form, choosing a specific value causes Access to retrieve the matching record.

You can display Help on customizing the combo box. Click to select the check box at the bottom of the wizard dialog box, where you label your list or combo box.

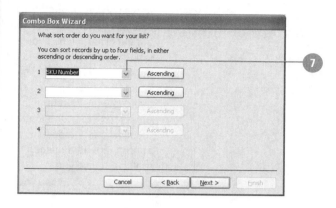

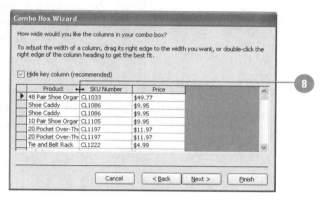

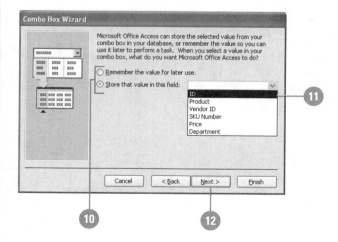

Creating a Subform

Some forms use fields from multiple tables. One of the most common forms involves a one-to-many relationship between two tables. For example, an order form would include a single order date and customer, but the order might involve several different products. Thus there are two tables involved: an orders table with information about the order and a detailed orders table with data about the products purchased. The user should not have to enter the order date for each product. This can be avoided with a **subform**, a form embedded within a **main form**. The user enters the order date and other general information in the main form, and the individual products are listed in the subform. Access then stores the appropriate data in each table without the user being aware that multiple tables are involved.

Create a Subform

1. In the Database window, click Forms on the Objects bar, and then double-click the Create Form By Using Wizard icon.

2. Click the Tables/Queries list arrow, and then select the table that will appear in the main form.

   The table contains general information (the *one* table).

3. Select the fields from the table that will appear in the main form. Make sure you include the common field that links the one table to the many table.

4. Click the Tables/Queries list arrow, and then select the table that will appear in the subform.

   The table contains detailed information (the *many* table).

5. Select the fields from the table that will appear in the subform. Do not include the common field you entered in the previous step, since this will appear in the main form.

6. Click Next to continue.

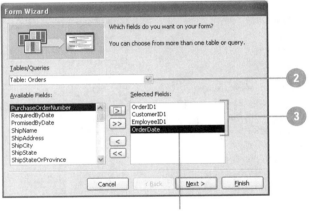

Common field between tables

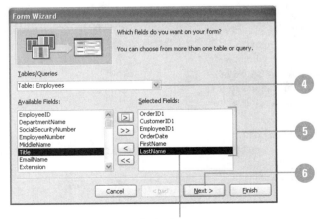

Do not include the common field twice.

⑦ Click the option to view the data by the one table.

⑧ Click the Form With Subform(s) option.

⑨ Click Next to continue.

⑩ Specify whether you want the subform to be laid out in tabular or datasheet format. Click Next to continue.

⑪ Specify a style for the form. Click Next to continue.

⑫ Enter a name for the form and subform. Specify whether to open the form for viewing or to modify the form's design in Design view.

⑬ Click Finish.

The form and subform are ready for data entry or further editing.

Did You Know?

You can create a form with tables in a one-to-one relationship. If the tables have a one-to-one relationship, use the Form Wizard to create the form, including the common field only once in the field list. The wizard will create a single form, combining the fields from both tables.

You can create a linked form. If you want a linked form instead of a sub-form (so that the form appears in response to the user clicking a button), click the Linked Forms option when the Form Wizard asks you how you want to view your data.

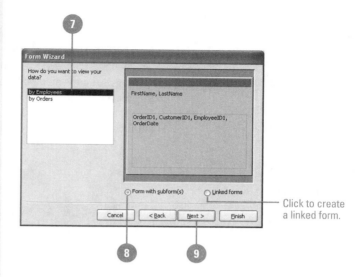

Click to create a linked form.

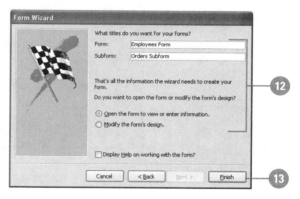

Form with subform

Editing in Form View

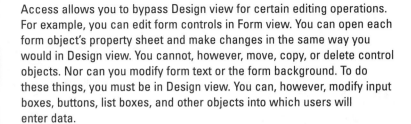

Access allows you to bypass Design view for certain editing operations. For example, you can edit form controls in Form view. You can open each form object's property sheet and make changes in the same way you would in Design view. You cannot, however, move, copy, or delete control objects. Nor can you modify form text or the form background. To do these things, you must be in Design view. You can, however, modify input boxes, buttons, list boxes, and other objects into which users will enter data.

Edit a Form in Form View

① Display the form in Form view.

② Right-click a control object.

③ Click Properties on the shortcut menu.

④ Edit the object's properties in the property sheet.

⑤ Click the Close button.

Did You Know?

You can format input boxes in Form view. You can format the text in an input box using the buttons on the Formatting toolbar. For example you can change the color, alignment, or style of the text within each input box.

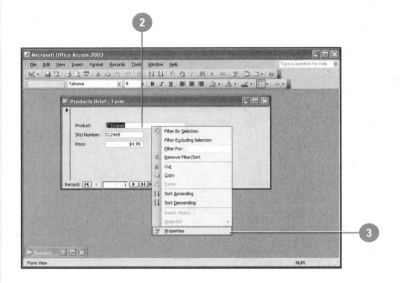

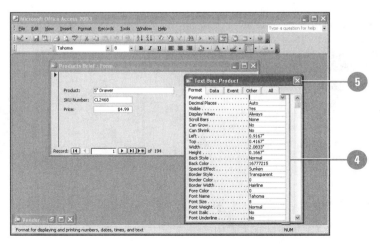

Entering and Editing Data in a Form

Database designers often display data in forms that mimic the paper forms used to record data. Forms facilitate data entry and record viewing. They can also contain buttons that allow you to perform other actions, such as running macros, printing reports, or creating labels. The options that appear on a form depend on what features the database designer included. A form directs you to enter the correct information and can automatically check your entries for errors. Access places the data you've entered in the form into the proper table. You can open a form in Form view or Design view. Form view allows you to view all the information associated with a record; Design view allows you to modify the form's design.

7

Enter a New Record in a Form

1. In the Database window, click Forms on the Objects bar.

2. Click the form you want to use.

3. Click the Open button.

4. Click the New Record button.

5. Enter the data for the first field.

6. Press Tab to move to the next field or Shift+Tab to move to the previous field.

   When you have finished entering the data, you can close the form, click the New Record button to enter another record, or view a different record.

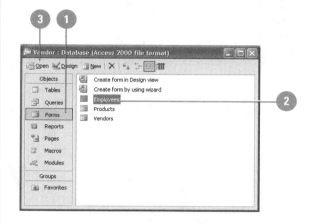

Did You Know?

You can delete a record from a form. In Forms view, display the record you want to delete, click the Delete Record button on the Form View toolbar, and then click Yes.

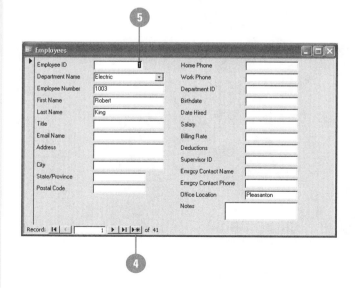

Using Windows XP Themes in Forms

The Microsoft Windows XP operating system offers you several themes. If you have chosen a theme other than the default, Access applies the selected theme to views, dialog boxes, and controls. However, you can prevent form controls from taking on themes from the operating system by setting an option on the database or project.

Enable or Disable Windows XP Themes in Forms

1 Click the Tools menu, and then click Options.

2 Click the Forms/Reports tab.

3 Select or clear the Use Windows Themed Controls On Forms check box.

4 Click OK.

Creating Reports to Convey Information

8

Introduction

To print a simple list of the records in your table, you can click the Print button. But if you want to include calculations, graphics, or a customized header or footer, you can create a report. A report is a summary of information in one or more Microsoft Office Access 2003 tables. Reports allow you to include enhancements that a simple printout of records in a table would not provide. In many cases a report answers important questions about the contents of your database. For example, a report might tell you how many movies in several different categories (such as drama, comedy, and western) have been rented each month or the amount of catalog sales made to customers in Canada in the last quarter. In addition to providing detailed and summary information that can include calculations, reports also provide these features:

- ◆ Attractive formatting to help make your report easier to read and understand.

- ◆ Headers and footers that print identifying information at the top and bottom of every page.

- ◆ Grouping and sorting that organize your information.

- ◆ Graphics to enhance the appearance of a report with clip art, photos, or scanned images.

What You'll Do

Explore Different Ways to Create a Report

Create a Report Using a Wizard

Use Sections in Design View

Work with Controls

Create a Report in Design View

Use Toolbox Buttons and Controls

Arrange Information

Create Mailing Labels

Set Properties

Perform Calculations in Reports

Group Records

Insert a Header or Footer

Assign a Shortcut Key to a Control

Check for Errors in Reports and Forms

Change the Page Setup

Preview and Print Information

Exploring Different Ways to Create a Report

As with most objects you create in a database, you have several ways to create a report—by using Access wizards or by creating it from scratch in Design view.

Click to create a report with the aid of the wizard.

Click to create a report from scratch in Design view.

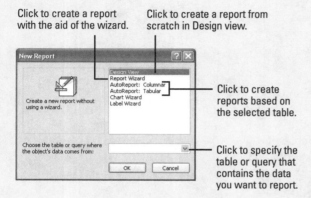

Click to create reports based on the selected table.

Click to specify the table or query that contains the data you want to report.

Report Wizard

With the Report Wizard you can specify the kind of report you want to create, and the Report Wizard guides you through each step of the process. All you do is answer a series of questions about your report, and Access builds a report with your data, using your formatting preferences. Creating a report with the Report Wizard allows you to select the fields you want to include from available tables and queries.

Opens list of available tables and queries.

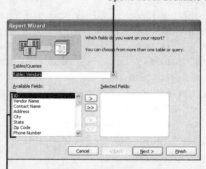

Fields from selected table or query; you can select fields from multiple tables and queries.

AutoReport Wizards

With the AutoReport Wizards, Access creates a simple report based on the data in the currently selected table or query. You can create a report using an AutoReport Wizard in two formats: Columnar, where each field appears on a separate line with a label to its left, or Tabular, where the fields in each record appear on one line with the labels at the top of the page.

Design View

Once you have completed a report, you can further customize it in Design view. As always, you can also begin creating your report in Design view without using a wizard.

When you work with a report in Design view, Access displays not the report data, but rather the individual parts, or controls, that make up the report, including titles, fields whose data appear in the report, labels that clarify the report contents, and objects such as headers and footers.

Previewing a Report

Once you have created your report and finalized its design, you can preview it using two views: Print Preview and Layout Preview. Print Preview displays the report as it will print, in a "what you see is what you get" format. Layout Preview displays a sample of the report as it will print, with just a few rows of data, so you can get a feel for the report's appearance without having to view all the data in the report.

8

Report in Design view.

Same report in Print Preview.

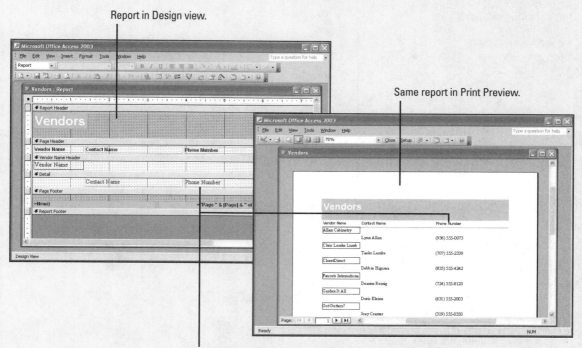

Objects in Design view correspond to objects in the printed report.

Creating a Report Using a Wizard

AC03S-1-10

One of the features you can use to create a simple report in Access is the **AutoReport Wizard**, which arranges data in a selected table or query as a formatted report. The AutoReport: Columnar Wizard displays each record's data vertically, while the AutoReport: Tabular Wizard displays the data for each record horizontally. You can also create a report using the **Report Wizard**, which allows you to select the fields and information you want presented and to choose from available formatting options that determine how the report will look.

Create and Save a Report Using the AutoReport Wizard

1. In the Database window, click Reports on the Objects bar, and then click New.

2. Click AutoReport: Columnar (to display records in a column), or click AutoReport: Tabular (to display records in rows).

3. Click the list arrow, and then click a table or query on which to base the report.

4. Click OK.

   Access displays the form in Print Preview, but you can switch to Design view, save, print, or close the report.

5. Click the Save button, type a name for your report, and then click OK.

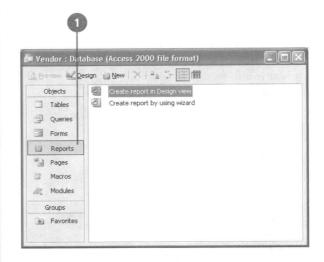

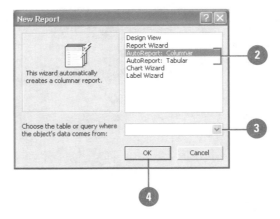

> ### Did You Know?
>
> **You can create an instant report with the AutoReport command.** In the Database window, select the table or query that contains the data you want formatted as a report. Click the Insert menu, and then click AutoReport. After a moment, Access generates a simple columnar report without headers or footers.

Create and Save a Report Using the Report Wizard

1. In the Database window, click Reports on the Objects bar, and then double-click the Create Report By Using Wizard icon.

2. Click the list arrow for choosing a table or query on which to base the form, and then click the name of the table or query you want.

3. Select the fields you want to include, indicating the source of any fields you want to include from other tables or queries. Click Next to continue.

4. If necessary, specify any groupings of the records, choosing any or all of the selected fields (up to ten). Click Next to continue.

5. Specify the order of records within each group, sorting by up to four fields at a time, and then specify ascending or descending order. Click Next to continue.

6. Determine the layout and orientation of your report. Click Next to continue.

7. Specify the style of the report, which affects its formatting and final appearance. Click Next to continue.

8. In the final wizard dialog box, name your report, and then indicate whether you want to preview the report or display it in Design view. Click Finish.

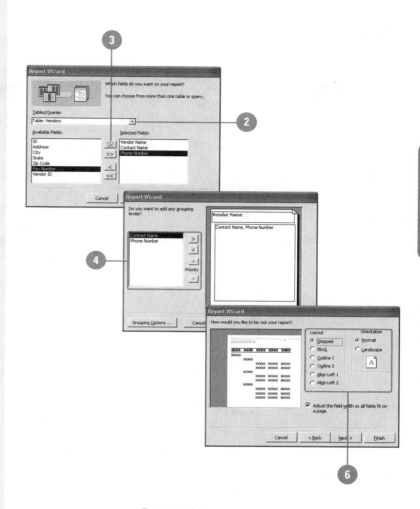

Report preview

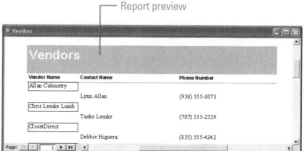

Using Sections in Design View

When Access displays a report or a form in Design view, it divides the report or form into sections, individual parts that control what elements appear and how they are formatted.

Each section has a **selector**, a box to the left of its heading, that you can click to select the section. Any formatting changes you make then affect just that section. Clicking the selector in the upper-left corner selects the entire report or form.

Header and footer sections come in pairs. **Headers** in a report display text at the top of each page or at the top of the report. **Footers** appear at the bottom of the page. Headers and footers can also appear at the start and end of records you have grouped together. As with other sections in a report, you can add controls to headers and footers that include text, expressions, page numbers, and date and time information.

Design View Sections

Section	Description
Report Header	Text that appears at the top of the first page of a report, such as a title, company logo, or introduction.
Page Header	Text that appears at the top of each page of a report, such as page numbers or report date.
Group Header	Text that appears before each group of records, such as a vendor name.
Detail	Contains the main body of the report, the fields that display values.
Group Footer	Text that appears at the end of a group of records, such as totals.
Page Footer	Text that appears at the bottom of each page of a report, such as explanations of symbols or page numbers.
Report Footer	Text that appears at the end of the report, such as report totals or other summary information.

Report Header selector

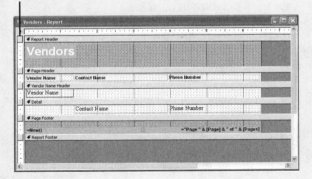

Working with Controls

Each item in a report or form—such as a field name, a field value, and the report title—is represented in Design view by a control. When you create a report or form with a wizard, the wizard arranges and sizes the controls to make the report according to the selections you provided. If you want to modify a report, you can do so in Design view by:

- Creating and deleting controls
- Moving and sizing controls
- Changing control properties
- Formatting the contents and appearance of controls

Types of Report Controls

There are three kinds of controls you can use in a report:

- **Bound controls** are fields of data from the table or query. You cannot create a calculation in a bound control.

- **Unbound controls** are controls that contain a label or a text box. You can create calculations in an unbound control.

- **Calculated controls** are any values calculated in the report, including totals, subtotals, averages, percentages, and so on.

Each type of control has specific characteristics you can change using the Properties feature. You can modify properties by right-clicking the control you want to modify, and then clicking Properties. In the controls property sheet, you can specify the characteristics you want to change. Although there are menu commands and buttons you can use to change a specific characteristic, using the Properties button is a fast way to see all of the characteristics for a control and make several changes at once.

8

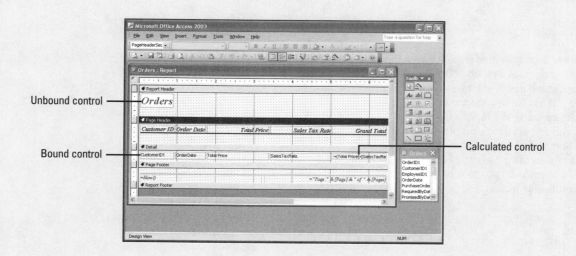

Unbound control

Bound control

Calculated control

Creating a Report in Design View

AC03S-1-10, AC03S-3-3

Create or Modify a Report in Design View

1. In the Database window, click Reports on the Objects bar, and then click New, or click a report, and then click Design; skip step 2.

2. In the New Report dialog box, click Design View, select the table or query on which to base the report, and then click OK.

3. Use the Toolbox and Field List to create or modify a report in Design view.

4. To view or hide headers and footers, click the View menu, and then click Report Header/Footer or Page Header/Footer.

Did You Know?

You can display or hide display boxes. When you create a report in Design view, three boxes might appear: the Field List box (where you can add bound controls), the Toolbox (where you can add unbound controls), and the Sorting And Grouping box. You can hide or view these boxes by clicking their corresponding buttons on the Report Design toolbar.

When you create a report from scratch in Design view, three sections appear: Page Header, Detail, and Page Footer. Once you create the report, you need to populate it with data. You can add **bound controls**—fields of data from a table or query—directly from the Field List, or you can add other types of **unbound controls**—text boxes, labels, pictures, buttons, and so on—from the Toolbox. In Design view, you can see two parts for every control: the control itself and its corresponding label. When you move a control, its corresponding label moves with it.

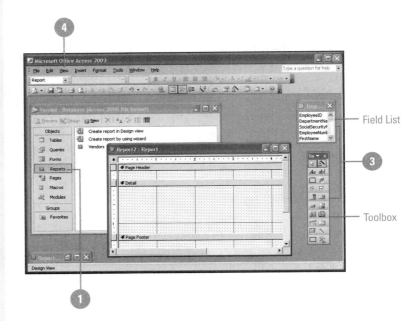

Field List

Toolbox

Add a Bound Control

1. Display the report in Design view.

2. Select the fields you want to include from the Field List; press Shift or Ctrl while you click to select multiple fields.

3. Drag the selected field or fields to the section in which you want the field to appear. Two boxes appear for each field: one containing the label and one for the field values.

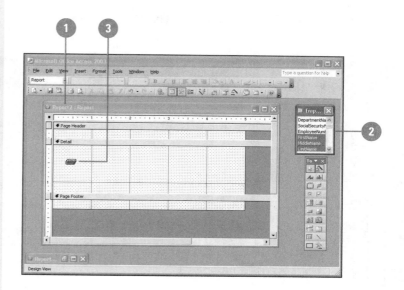

Add an Unbound Control

1. Display the report in Design view, and then click the Toolbox button for the control you want to add, such as a text box, a horizontal line, or a shape.

2. Drag to draw a box in the location where you want the control to appear.

Did You Know?

You can display or hide the ruler and grid. The ruler and grid provide guides to help you arrange your controls. Click the View menu, and then click to select Ruler or Grid.

You can create an unbound report. Create a report without choosing a table or query on which it is based. Such reports are called unbound reports. A dialog box is an example of an unbound report.

The ruler shows the size of the control as you drag.

The grid provides dots that help you align controls.

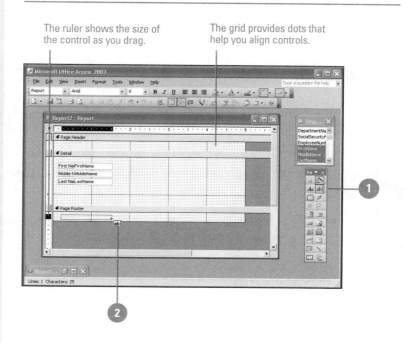

Using Toolbox Buttons and Controls

Toolbox Buttons

Button	Name	Description
	Select Objects	Click this button, and then click the control you want to select. To select multiple controls that are grouped together, click this button, and then drag a rectangle shape around all the controls you want to select.
	Control Wizards	Click to use control wizards when they are available.
	Text Box	This button creates a text box in which the user can enter text (or numbers) for the selected field in the record. Use this control for fields assigned to a text or number data type.
	Label	This button creates a text label. Because the other controls already include a corresponding label, use this button to create labels that are independent of other controls, such as text needed for user instructions or the name of the form in a heading.
	Option Group	This button creates a box around a group of option buttons. The user is only allowed to make one selection from the buttons enclosed by a group box.
	Toggle Button	This button creates a button that allows the user to make a yes or no selection by clicking the toggle button. Use this control for fields assigned to the yes/no data type.
	Option Button	This button creates an option button (also known as a radio button) that allows the user to make a single selection from at least two choices. Use this control for fields assigned to the yes/no data type.
	Check Box	This button creates a check box that allows a user to make multiple yes or no selections. Use this control for fields assigned to the yes/no data type.
	List Box	This button creates a list box that allows a user to select from a list of options. You can enter your own options in the list, or can have another table provide a list of options.

Toolbox Buttons Continued

Button	Name	Description
	Combo Box	This button creates a combo box in which the user has the option to enter text or select from a list of options. You can enter your own options in the list, or you can display options stored in another table.
	Command Button	This button creates a button that runs a macro or Microsoft Visual Basic function when the user clicks the button in the form.
	Image	This button inserts a frame, in which you can insert a graphic in your form. Use this control when you want to insert a graphic that remains the same in all the records displayed in a form, such as clip art or a logo.
	Unbound Object Frame	This button inserts an OLE object from another source. Use this button to insert an object that is linked to another program and needs to be updated to reflect recent changes.
	Bound Object Frame	This button inserts an OLE object from another source within the same database. Use this button to insert an object that is linked to another source in the database and needs to be updated to reflect recent changes.
	Page Break	This button forces the fields that start at the insertion point to appear on the next screen.
	Tab Control	This button creates a tab in your form. Creating tabs in a form gives your form the appearance of a dialog box in a program so that related controls can appear together on their own tab.
	Subform/Subreport	This button inserts another form within the current form at the insertion point.
	Line	This button creates a line that you draw on the form.
	Rectangle	This button creates a rectangle or border that you draw on the form.
	More Controls	Click to display other toolboxes.

Arranging Information

The information in a form or report is arranged according to the arrangement of the sections and controls in Design view. You can modify that arrangement by changing section heights and by moving and resizing controls. When you select a control on a form, sizing handles appear on the sides and at the corners of the control. You can drag the sizing handles to adjust the size of the control. You can also drag inside a selected control to move the control to a new location.

Change the Size of a Control

1. In Design view, click the control you want to resize.

2. Position the pointer over a sizing handle until the pointer shape changes to a two-headed arrow.

3. With the sizing pointer, drag to resize the control.

   For example, to make the control wider, drag the sizing handle on the center- right area of the control further to the right.

Sizing handles indicate control is selected

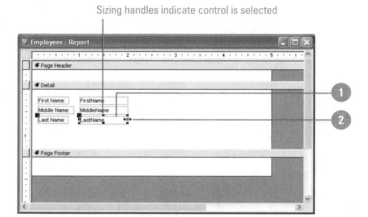

Move a Control

1. Display the form in Design view, and then display the Toolbox.

2. Select the control you want to format.

3. To move a control without a label, position the pointer over the large sizing handle in the upper-left corner of the control, and then drag to a new location.

   Only the label or control will move, not both.

4. To move a control, position the pointer over an edge of a control until the pointer changes to a black hand, and then drag to a new location.

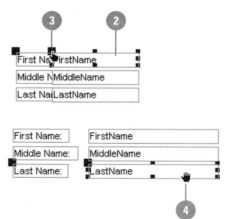

Adjust Page or Section Spacing

1. Display the report or form in Design view whose page or section size you want to change.

2. Position the pointer (which changes to a two-headed arrow) over the bottom of the section whose height you want to change.

3. Drag the border up or down in the appropriate direction to change the spacing. You can drag the border all the way to the previous or next section to hide that section.

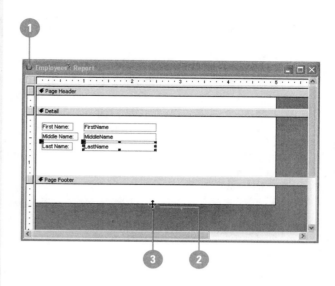

Working With Controls

To	Do This
Change control font	Select a control, click the Font list arrow on the Formatting toolbar, and then click the font name you want, or click the Bold, Italic, or Underline button on the Formatting toolbar.
Remove formatting	Select the control, and then click the button that corresponds to the formatting you want to remove.
Change the position of text within a control	Select the control, and then click the Align Left, Center, or Align Right button on the Formatting toolbar. If the control is in a header or footer, the control is aligned within the page margins.
Keep labels aligned with controls in the Detail section	When you adjust bound controls in the Detail section, be sure to make the same adjustments in the Header sections so that the headings appear directly over the data.

8

Creating Mailing Labels

Access provides a **Label Wizard** to help you create mailing labels quickly. The wizard supports a large variety of label brands and sizes. You can also create customized labels for brands and sizes not listed by the wizard, provided you know the dimensions of your labels and label sheets. You can create labels by drawing data from any of your tables or queries. In addition to data values, labels can also include customized text that you specify.

Create Mailing Labels

1. In the Database window, click Reports on the Objects bar, and then click the New button.

2. Click Label Wizard, select the table or query to be used in the mailing labels, and then click OK.

3. Select the type of mailing label you're using. Click Next to continue.

4. Specify the font style and color for the label text. Click Next to continue.

5. Double-click the field names in the Available Fields list to place them on your mailing labels. Type any text that you want to accompany the field values. Click Next to continue.

6. If necessary, select a field to sort your labels by. Click Next to continue.

7. Enter a name for your mailing labels report, and then choose whether to preview the printout or modify the label design.

8. Click Finish.

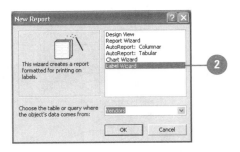

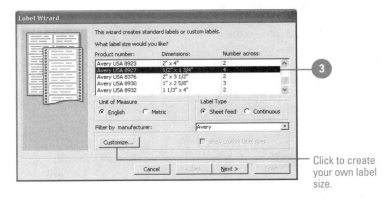

Click to create your own label size.

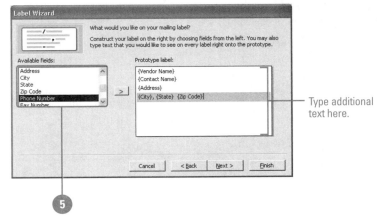

Type additional text here.

Setting Properties

Set Properties

1. In Design view, select the control, section, form, or report whose properties you want to modify.

2. Click the Properties button on the toolbar.

3. Click the tab that contains the property you want to modify.

4. Click the property box for the property you want to modify, and then do one of the following.

   ◆ Type the information or expression you want to use.

   ◆ If the property box contains a list arrow, click the arrow and then click a value in the list.

   ◆ If a Build button appears to the right of the property box, click it to display a builder or a dialog box giving you a choice of builders.

5. When you're done, click the Close button.

> **Did You Know?**
>
> **You can enter long settings.** When you are entering long information in a property box, right-click the box, and then click Zoom to open a Zoom box that allows you to see the entire setting you are modifying.

Every object has **properties**, or settings, that control its appearance and function. A form or report has properties; each section in a form or report has properties, and each control in a section has properties. When you work with a control in a form or report, you can open a property sheet that displays all the settings for that control.

Control whose property sheet is open

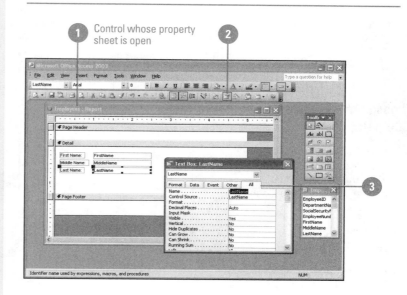

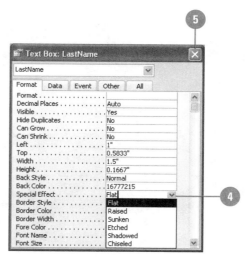

8

Performing Calculations in Reports

AC03S-1-11

When you create a report, you might want to include summary information or other calculations. The wizards often include built-in functions, but you can use the **Expression Builder** to create your own by clicking buttons for the arithmetic operators you want to use and including constant values as needed. For example, if you want to determine bonuses based on a percentage of sales, you can create an arithmetic expression to compute the results. When you generate the report, Access will perform the required calculations and display the results in the report. To display the calculations in the appropriate format, you can also use the Properties feature to specify formats for dates, currency, and other numeric data.

Choose Fields to Use in a Calculation

1. In Design view, create a text box control and position it where you want the calculated field to appear, or select an existing unbound control.

2. Click the Properties button on the Report Design toolbar.

3. Click the Control Source property box, which specifies what data appears in a control, and then click the Expression Builder button.

4. Click the equal sign (=) button.

5. Enter the values and operators you want to use.

   ◆ Click operator buttons to supply the most common operations.

   ◆ Double-click folders in the left pane to open lists of objects you can use in your expression, including existing fields, constants, operators, and common expressions.

   ◆ Manually type an expression.

6. Click OK to insert the calculation.

7. Click the Close button.

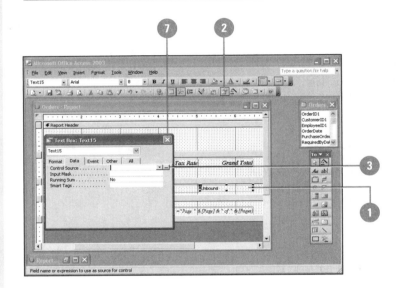

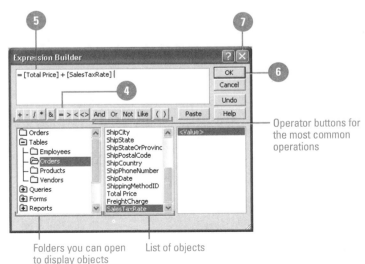

Folders you can open to display objects

List of objects

Operator buttons for the most common operations

Format Values in a Report

1. In Design view, position the insertion point in the field whose format you want to change, and then click the Properties button on the Report Design toolbar.

2. On either the All tab or the Format tab of the property sheet, click the Format property box, click the list arrow that appears, and then click the format you want to use.

   The names of the formats appear on the left side of the drop-down list, and examples of the corresponding formats appear on the right side.

3. If you are formatting a number (rather than a date), and you do not want to accept the default, "Auto", click the Decimal Places property box, click the list arrow, and then click the number of decimal places you want.

4. Click the Close button.

Did You Know?

You can use a builder. Access makes it easy to change many types of settings by providing builders, or tools that simplify tasks. The Expression Builder is just one of many builders in Access. You know a builder is available for a task when you click a property box and a Build button appears.

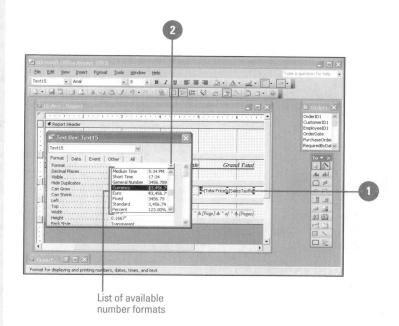

List of available
number formats

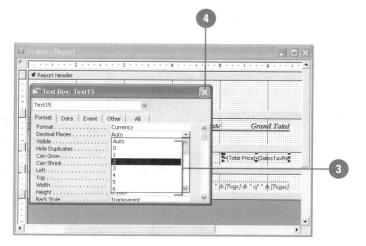

Grouping Records

When you create a report with the Report Wizard, you can choose to group like records together to obtain subtotals and other calculations for each group. For example, in a report of sales representative sales figures for a year, you might group the representatives' sales by month. In this way, you can easily determine who was the top achiever each month. In another report, you could group all the sales representatives' results together to see trends for the representatives' performance over a whole year. Even if you create your report from scratch or decide to group records later, you can use the Sorting And Grouping feature to further organize information in your report.

Group Records

1. In Design view, click the Sorting And Grouping button on the Report Design toolbar.

2. Click the Field/Expression box, and then click the list arrow that appears. Choose a field for grouping records, or type an expression.

3. Click the corresponding Sort Order box, click the list arrow that appears, and then click Ascending or Descending, depending on what sort order you want to use.

4. Select the Group Properties settings you want to use.

5. Repeat steps 2 through 4 for each Field/Expression you want to create to group and sort your data.

6. When you're done, click the Close button.

When you group data, you can insert a group header for each group.

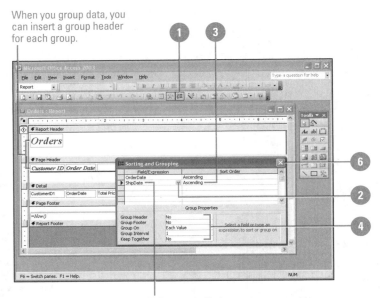

This report will show sales grouped by quarter and then sorted by shipping date.

Select Group Properties

If you want to change the default Group Properties settings, you can do so from within the Group Properties dialog box.

1. Click the Group Header property box, and then choose Yes, if you want to include a header that will separate the start of each group of records.

2. Click the Group Footer property box, and then choose Yes, if you want to include a footer that will separate the end of each group of records. Choose this option if you want to include a subtotal or summary calculation for each group of records.

3. Click the Group On property box, click the list arrow, and then indicate whether you want to start a different group with each value or in a different manner.

4. Click the Group Interval property box, and then indicate the number of characters to group on.

5. Click the Keep Together property box, and then indicate whether you want to keep each group together on one page.

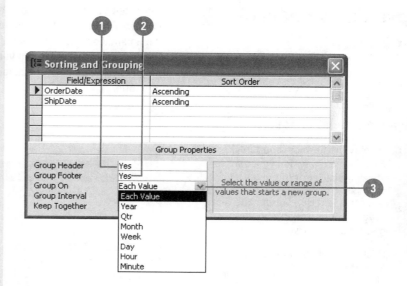

Did You Know?

You can use a second field to further sort the records within each group.
Click the right side of the first blank field in the Field/Expression column, and then choose a second field for sorting records. You can also click the right side of the Sort Order column, and then choose either ascending or descending order for sorting records in each group.

8

Inserting a Header or Footer

Most reports use headers and footers to help you keep track of where you are. A **header** is text printed in the top section of every page within a document. **Footer** text is printed in the bottom section. Commonly used headers and footers contain your name, the document title, the file name, the print date, and page numbers. You can also add a header and footer to a form.

Insert a Header or Footer

1. Display the form or report in Design view in which you want to insert a header or footer.

2. Click the Text Box button, and then drag a text box control in the header or footer section.

3. Click the Build button on the Report Design toolbar.

4. Click Expression Builder.

5. Double-click the Common Expressions folder.

6. Double-click the expression you want to use, such as Page Number, Total Pages, Page N of M, Current Date/Time, and so on.

7. Click OK to insert the expression.

8. When you're done, click the Close button.

See Also

See "Formatting a Form or Report" on page 184 for information on showing and hiding headers or footers.

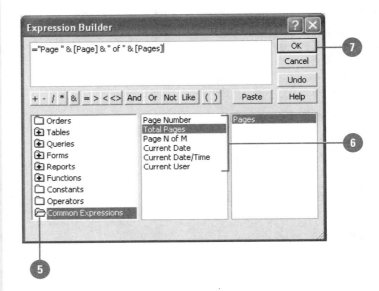

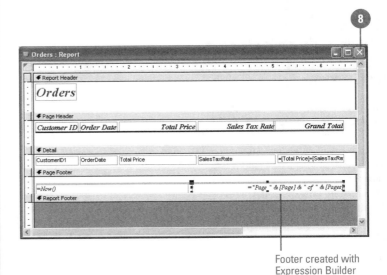

Footer created with Expression Builder

Assigning a Shortcut Key to a Control

You can make selecting a control easier in a form or report by assigning it a shortcut key (also known as an **access key**). When you assign an access key to a label or button on a form or report, you can press ALT + an underline character to move the focus to the control. In a data access page—a Web page published by Access—you can assign the access key to the control instead of the label attached to the control.

Assign an Access Key to a Control

① Display the form or report with the label or button you want to assign an access key.

② Select the label or button.

③ Click the Properties button on the toolbar.

④ In the Caption property box, type an ampersand (&) immediately before the character you want to use as the access key.

⑤ Click the Close button in the Properties dialog box.

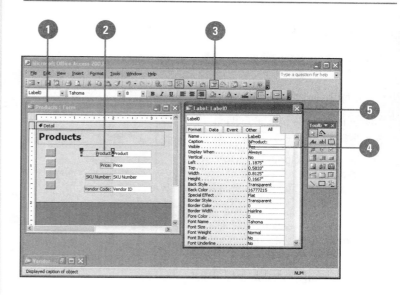

Did You Know?

You can assign an access key to a control on a data access page. In a data access page, select the control in which you want to assign a key, type the character you want in the Access Key property box.

Checking for Errors in Reports and Forms

As you create reports and forms, Access helps you by catching common errors, such as controls being positioned outside the page size, as they happen. Error checking points out errors in a report or form, and provides you with options using a smart tag button for correcting them. When an error occurs, the Error Checking Options button appears, indicating a problem. Click the button to display a list of options to correct or ignore the problem.

Enable Error Checking

1. Click the Tools menu, and then click Options.

2. Click the Error Checking tab.

3. Select the Enable Error Checking check box.

4. To change the color of the error indicator, click the Error Indicator Color list arrow, and then select a color.

5. Select or clear check boxes for the specific errors in which you want to check.

   ◆ Unassociated Label And Control

   ◆ New Unassociated Labels

   ◆ Keyboard Shortcut Errors

   ◆ Invalid Control Properties

   ◆ Common Report Errors

6. Click OK.

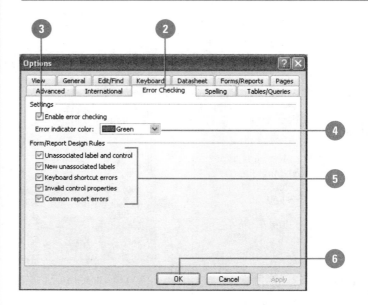

Error Checking Types

Type	Description
Unassociated label and control	A label and a control, such as a text box or list box, are not associated with each other. The Trace Error button appears instead of the Error Checking Options button.
New unassociated labels	A label to a form or report is not associated with any other control.
Keyboard shortcut errors	A control with an invalid shortcut key; either an unassociated label has a shortcut key, or a label or button has a duplicated shortcut key or a space character as its shortcut key.
Invalid control properties	A control with one or more properties is set to an invalid value.

Correct Errors in Reports and Forms

1. When an error indicator (small triangle) appears in a control, select the control.

2. Click the Error Checking Options button.

3. Click the option you want (options vary depending on the type of error found). Some of the common options include:

   ◆ Help On This Error

   ◆ Ignore Error or Dismiss Error

   ◆ Error Checking Options

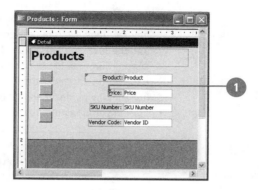

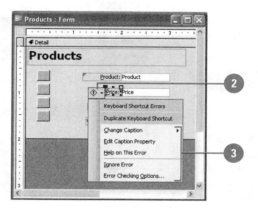

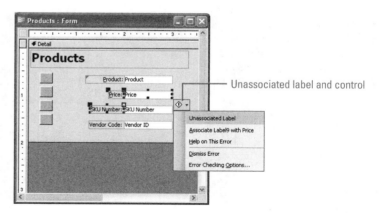

Unassociated label and control

Changing the Page Setup

AC03S-3-3

Change Page Setup Options

1. In the Database window, click the report, form, table, query, or any data you want to preview.

2. Click the File menu, and then click Page Setup.

3. To change margin settings, click the Margins tab, and then change the top, bottom, left, or right margins you want.

4. To change paper settings, click the Page tab, and then select the orientation (portrait or landscape), paper size and source, and printer for vendor labels you want.

5. To change column settings, click the Columns tab, and then change or select the column and row grid settings, column size, and column layout (Down, Then Across or Across, Then Down) you want.

6. Click OK.

Once you have created a report or form, you can change the page setup, which includes the margin, paper size and orientation, and grid and column settings. Margins are the blank space between the edge of a page and the text. You can also select the page orientation (portrait or landscape) that best fits the entire page or any section. Portrait orients the page vertically (taller than it is wide), and landscape orients the page horizontally (wider than it is tall). When you shift between the two, the margin settings automatically change.

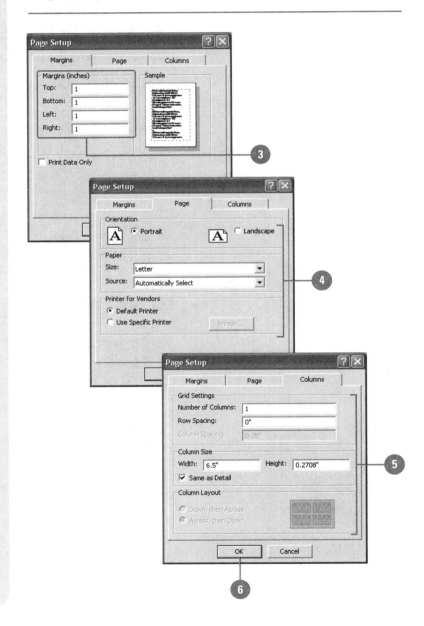

Previewing Information

AC03S-4-2

Preview Data

1. In the Database window, click the report, form, table, query, or any data you want to preview.

2. Click the Print Preview button on the Database toolbar.

3. Use the One Page, Two Pages, or Multiple Pages buttons on the Print Preview toolbar to view the data.

4. Use the record navigation buttons (First, Previous, Record Selection box, Next, and Last) to display pages.

5. To print from the Print Preview window, click the Print button on the Print Preview toolbar.

6. When you're done, click the Close button on the Print Preview toolbar.

Before printing, you should verify that the data you want to print looks the way you want. You save time, money, and paper by avoiding duplicate printing. Print Preview shows you exactly how your data will look on each printed page. This is especially helpful when you have a multi-page report. The Print Preview toolbar provides the tools, such as the One Page, Two Pages, Multiple Pages, Previous, and Next buttons, you need to proof the look of each page.

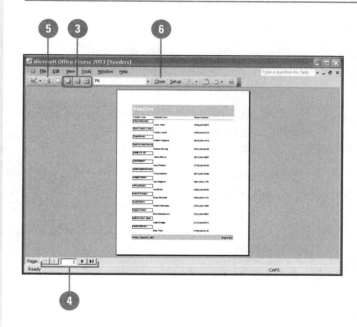

Printing Information

AC03S-4-3

Printing a paper copy is one of the most common ways to share your data from Access. You can print a report, a table, a query, or any data in a single step using the Print button, in which case Access prints a single copy of all pages. If you want to print only selected pages or if you want to specify other printing options, use the Print command on the File menu.

Print Data

1. Display the report, form, table, query, or any data you want to format in Design View.

2. Click the File menu, and then click Print.

3. If necessary, click the Name list arrow, and then select the printer you want to use.

4. Select the print range you want.

   ◆ To print all pages, click the All option.

   ◆ To print selected pages, click the Pages option, and then type the first page in the From box and the ending page in the To box.

   ◆ To print selected record, click the Selected Record(s) option.

5. Click OK.

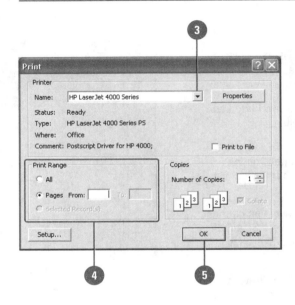

Improving the Appearance of Forms and Reports

Introduction

The objects in a database most "on display" are the forms and reports designed for those individuals responsible for data entry and those who receive reports from the database. For this reason, database designers often give extra attention to the visual appearance and clarity of those objects.

Microsoft Office Access 2003 offers database designers many aids in creating attractive data entry and display objects. The wizards that create databases, forms, and reports format those objects attractively, but if you want to go beyond the design provided by a wizard, Access provides numerous formatting, layout, and style options. You can enhance the appearance of your forms and reports with different fonts and font styles, borders and lines, and judicious use of color. You can also add special effects to certain objects, giving them an embossed or 3-D effect. Access formatting features help you give your customized reports and forms the exact look you want. Although most design changes take place within Design view, you can make color, line, and special effect formatting changes from within a form or report without having to switch to Design view.

You can also insert pictures, charts, and graphs to enhance the appearance of database forms and reports. Access allows you to insert Microsoft Excel charts and objects such as graphs created with other software programs that display data from database tables or queries. When you insert an object, you can edit the inserted information without having to leave Access.

What You'll Do

Format a Form or Report

Add Lines and Rectangles

Change Line or Border Thickness

Change Colors

Apply Special Effects to Controls

Apply Conditional Formatting

Align and Group Controls

Share Information Among Documents

Copy and Paste Objects

Insert a New Object

Insert an Object from a File

Insert a Picture

Insert Excel Charts and Worksheets

Insert a Graph Chart

Format Chart Objects

Move and Resize an Object

Formatting a Form or Report

 AC03S-1-9, AC03S-3-2

A fast way to format a form or report is with the **AutoFormat** button, available in Design view. When you click this button on the Form Design toolbar, you can select and preview a variety of layouts and styles. After you make your selections, Access formats the entire report or form consistently for you. After using AutoFormat, you can always make additional changes to the formatting using buttons on the Formatting (Form/Report) toolbar. If you don't see the header and footer sections, you can display them to add controls. When you select a control, sizing handles appear around the control, which you can drag to size it. You can also drag inside a selected control to move it to a new location.

Format a Form or Report with AutoFormat

1. Display the report or form you want to format in Design view.

2. Click the AutoFormat button on the Report Or Form Design toolbar.

3. Click the style option you want.

4. To apply attributes (Font, Color, or Border), click Options, and then select or clear the options you want to apply with AutoFormat.

5. Click OK.

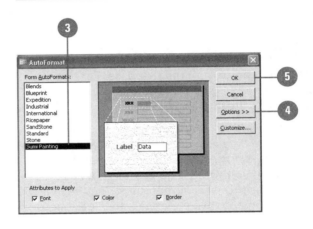

Format a Form or Report Using Formatting Tools

1. Display the report or form you want to format in Design view.

2. Select the item you want to format.

3. Use formatting buttons on the Formatting (Form/Report) toolbar to apply the following:

   ◆ Text style, color, and alignment.

   ◆ Box fill and line/border color, line/border width, and special effects, such as shadowed, etched, and raised.

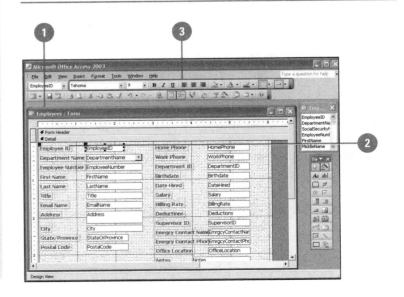

Show and Hide Headers and Footers

1. Display the form in Design view, and then display the Toolbox.

2. Click the View menu.

3. Click the Header/Footer you want to show or hide:

   - Page Header/Footer displays a header and footer for each page.

   - Form Header/Footer displays a header and footer for the form.

Did You Know?

Access inherits the theme from Windows XP. If the operating system is Windows XP SP1 or later, and you have chosen a theme other than Windows Classic, Access inherits the theme (color scheme, fonts, lines, etc.). Most of the views, controls, and dialog boxes will match the Windows theme.

See Also

See "Inserting a Header or Footer" on page 176 for information on working with headers or footers.

9

Adding Lines and Rectangles

You can make forms and reports that contain a lot of information easier to read by adding lines between sections or by adding rectangles around groups of controls. Lines and rectangles help organize the information so that reports are easier to read and forms are easier to fill out.

Add a Line to a Form or Report

1. Display the form or report in Design view.

2. Click the Line button on the Toolbox.

3. With the Line pointer, drag a line where you want the line to appear.

    Sizing handles appear.

4. To adjust the line length or angle, drag a sizing handle left, right, up, or down.

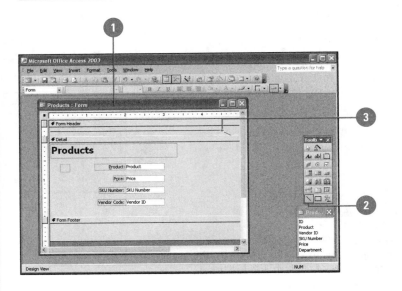

Add a Rectangle to a Form or Report

1. Display the form or report in Design view.

2. Click the Rectangle button on the Toolbox.

3. Drag a rectangle where you want the border to appear.

    Sizing handles appear at each corner and on each side of the border.

Did You Know?

You can adjust the position of the line or rectangle. Position the pointer over the line or rectangle (not a sizing handle), and then drag the line or rectangle to the new position.

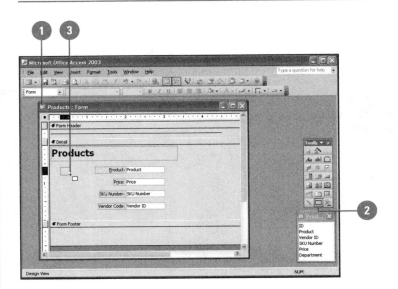

Changing Line or Border Thickness

You can adjust the thickness of any line, shape, or field border with the Line/Border Width button. You can modify field border thickness from Form or Report view, but to modify lines or rectangles, you must work in Design view. After you choose one of the many Formatting toolbar buttons, such as Line/Border Width, any similar objects you subsequently create will be formatted with the currently selected formatting, as indicated on the toolbar button.

Change the Thickness of a Line or Border

1. Display the form or report in Design view, or, if you are modifying a field border, display the form or report in Form or Report view.

2. Select the line or border whose line thickness you want to adjust.

3. Click the Line/Border Width button list arrow on the Formatting toolbar, and then select the thickness you want.

   If you want to format an existing object with the currently selected formatting, you can simply select the object, and then click the appropriate button on the Formatting toolbar—you don't need to click the button's list arrow and repeat your selection from the menu.

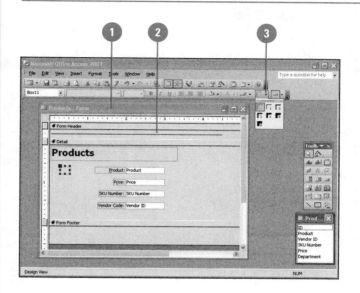

Did You Know?

You can set control defaults. When you create a control, you can set the initial formatting. Create a control, format the control the way you want, click the Format menu, and then click Set Control Defaults.

9

Changing Colors

Choosing appropriate colors for your form or report is an important formatting decision. For example, colors on forms can be used to assist users in correctly filling them out. Also, if you have a color printer available, you can significantly enhance the appearance of a report or form by adding color to lines or text. Other elements you can add color to include rectangles, backgrounds, headers, footers, or detail areas of a report or form.

Change Line or Border Color

1. Display the form or report in Design view, or for a field border, in Form or Report view.

2. Select the line or border whose color you want to change.

3. Click the Line/Border Color button list arrow on the Formatting toolbar, and then select the color you want. You can also select Transparent to make the border around a colored object disappear.

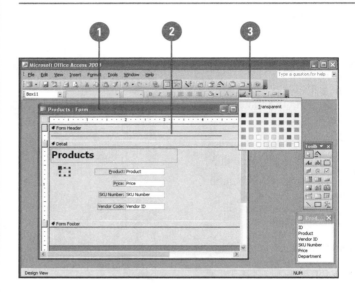

Change Fill Color

1. Select the object whose color you want to change.

2. Click the Fill/Back Color button list arrow on the Formatting toolbar.

3. Select the color you want.

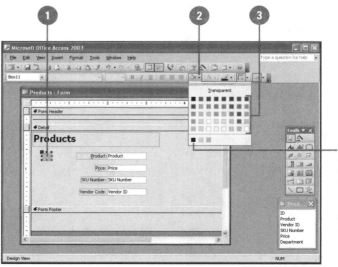

Colors you've worked with recently appear at the bottom of the palette.

Change Text Color

1. Display the form or report in Design view.

2. Select the text box with the text whose color you want to change.

3. Click the Font Color button list arrow on the Formatting toolbar, and then select the color you want.

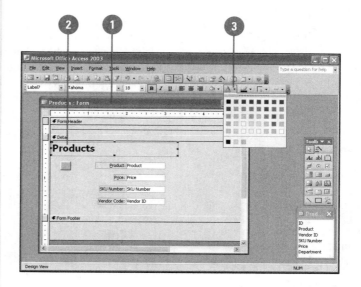

Applying Special Effects to Controls

You can apply special effects to one or more controls in a form or report to enhance the appearance of the form or report. For example, you can create three-dimensional effects, including flat (the default effect), raised, sunken, etched, shadowed, and chiseled. Use the effect that seems most appropriate for the tone of the form or report. For example, in a more formal financial report, you might choose the simple flat effect. In a report outlining future technology needs, consider using a high-tech shadowed effect.

Apply a Special Effect to a Control

1. Display the form or report in Design view.

2. Select the control to which you want to apply a special effect.

3. Click the Special Effect button list arrow on the Formatting toolbar, and then select the effect you want to use.

   Note that only the control's line or border is affected. Any text in the control is not affected by applying a special effect.

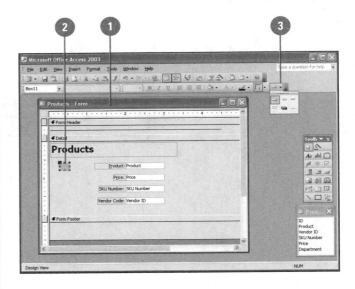

Applying Conditional Formatting

You can make your reports and forms more powerful by setting up conditional formatting. **Conditional formatting** allows you to format a field based on values the user enters. For example, you can use a conditional format to make negative values appear in red and positive values appear in black.

Apply Conditional Formatting to a Field

① Display the form or report in Design view, and then click the field to which you want to apply conditional formatting.

② Click the Format menu, and then click Conditional Formatting.

③ Specify the default format for the field.

④ Click the Condition 1 list arrow, and then select Field Value Is.

⑤ Click the second list arrow, and then select a condition type.

⑥ Enter values for the condition.

⑦ Specify the format when this condition is true.

⑧ Click Add to add a second formatting condition.

⑨ Click OK to apply the conditional formatting.

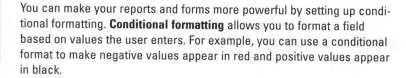

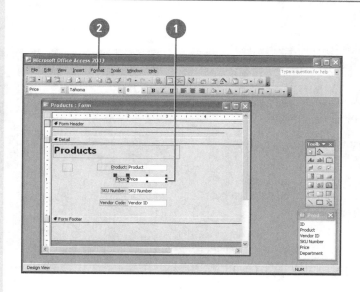

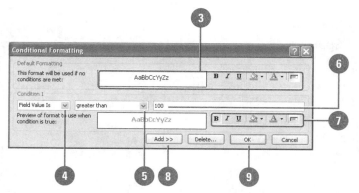

Did You Know?

You can use expressions in a conditional format. For more complicated conditional formats, select the input field, click the Format menu, and then click Conditional Formatting. Click the Condition 1 list arrow, select Expression Is, type the conditional formatting expression in the box to the right, and then click OK.

Aligning and Grouping Controls

AC03S-3-2, AC03S-3-3

Often when you work with multiple controls and objects, they look best when aligned with each other. For example, you can align three controls with the left-most control in the selection so that the left sides of all three controls align along an invisible line. You can also change the horizontal and vertical spacing between controls and objects. Access also lets you resize controls and objects relative to each other and group them together.

Align Objects and Controls to Each Other

1. Display the form or report in Design view, or, for a field border, in Form or Report view.

2. Select the controls and objects you want to align.

3. Click the Format menu, point to Align, and then click the alignment option you want.

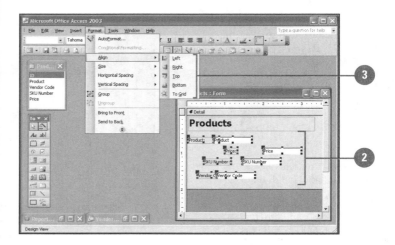

Change Horizontal or Vertical Spacing

1. Display the form or report in Design view, or, for a field border, in Form or Report view.

2. Select the controls and objects whose spacing you want to change.

3. Click the Format menu, point to Horizontal Spacing or Vertical Spacing, and then click the spacing option you want.

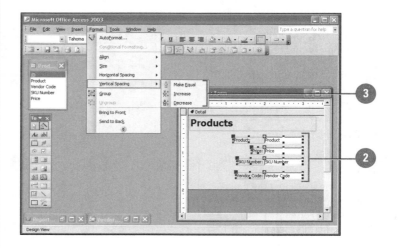

Change the Size of Controls and Objects

1. Display the form or report in Design view, or, for a field border, in Form or Report view.

2. Select the controls and objects you want to resize.

3. Click the Format menu, point to Size, and then click the sizing option that you want—To Fit, To Grid, To Tallest, To Shortest, To Widest, or To Narrowest.

Group or Ungroup Controls and Objects

1. Display the form or report in Design view, or, for a field border, in Form or Report view.

2. Select the controls and objects you want to group or the object you want to ungroup.

3. Click the Format menu, and then click Group or Ungroup.

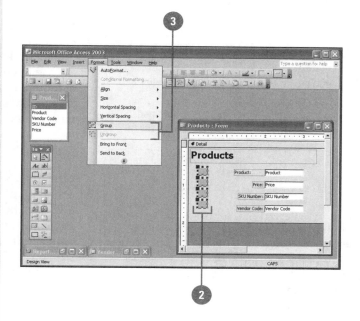

Did You Know?

You can turn off the Snap To Grid to align controls and lines the way you want. In Design view, the controls and other objects you create align themselves along an invisible grid as you move them. To gain greater control over the exact placement of lines and controls, you can turn off the Snap To Grid option. Click the Format menu, and then clear the Snap To Grid check box. Select this command to turn it on.

9

Sharing Information Among Documents

The ability to insert an object created in one program into a document created in another program allows you to create documents that meet a variety of needs. Access can convert data or text from one format to another using a technology known as **object linking and embedding (OLE)**. OLE allows you to move text or data between programs in much the same way as you move them within a program. The table below includes terms that you'll find useful in understanding how you can share objects among documents.

Embedding and Linking	
Term	**Definition**
Source program	The program that created the original object
Source file	The file that contains the original object
Destination program	The program that created the document into which you are inserting the object
Destination file	The file into which you are inserting the object

To better understand how these objects and terms work together, consider this example: If you place an Excel chart in an Access database, Excel is the source program and Access is the destination program. The chart is the source file; the database is the destination file.

There are three ways to share information in Windows programs: pasting, embedding, and linking.

Pasting

You can cut or copy an object from one document and then paste it into another using the Cut, Copy, and Paste buttons on the source and destination program toolbars.

Embedding

When you embed an object, you place a copy of the object in the destination file. When you activate the embedded object, the tools from the source program become available in the destination file. For example, if you insert an Excel chart into an Access database, the Excel menus and toolbars become available, replacing the Access menus and toolbars, so you can edit the chart if necessary. With embedding, any changes you make to the chart in the database do not affect the original file.

Linking

When you link an object, you insert a representation of the object itself into the destination file. The tools of the source program are available, and when you use them to edit the object you've inserted, you are actually editing the source file. Moreover, any changes you make to the source file are reflected in the destination file.

Copying and Pasting Objects

When you copy or paste an object, Access stores the object in the Office Clipboard. You can paste the object into the destination file using the Clipboard task pane, Paste button, or Paste Special command, which gives you more control over how the object will appear in the destination file. When you use the Paste button, you are sometimes actually embedding. Because embedding can greatly increase file size, you might want to use Paste Special. You can select a format that requires minimal disk space and paste the object as a simple picture or text.

Paste an Object

1. Select the object in the source program.

2. Click the Copy button on the source program's toolbar.

3. Switch to Access and display the area where you want to paste the copied object.

4. Click the Paste button on the toolbar and position the object.

Pasted object

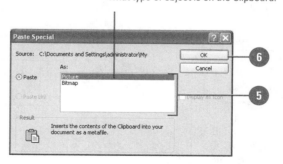

Paste Information in a Specified Format

1. Select the object in the source program.

2. Click the Copy button on the source program's toolbar.

3. Switch to Access and display the area where you want to paste the copied object.

4. Click the Edit menu, and then click Paste Special.

5. Click the object type you want.

6. Click OK.

The object types that appear depend on what type of object is on the Clipboard.

Inserting a New Object

You can create objects from scratch without leaving the Access program. After you drag to create a new unbound object frame control, the Insert Object dialog box appears, and you can select the program in which you want to create the graphic. The programs that appear correspond to the software installed on your computer. For example, if you want to create a picture in Microsoft Paint, a graphics accessory that accompanies the Microsoft Windows operating system, you can choose the Bitmap Image option.

Insert a New Object

1. In Design view, click the Unbound Object Frame button on the Toolbox.

2. With the Unbound Object pointer, drag a rectangle where you want the picture to appear. Make the rectangle approximately the same size as the picture you will insert.

3. Click the Create New option.

4. Double-click the program in which you want to create an object.

5. Create the new object using the tools that appear in the program you selected.

6. Click outside the window in which you created the unbound object.

   The program with which you created the object closes, and the new object is inserted in the form or report.

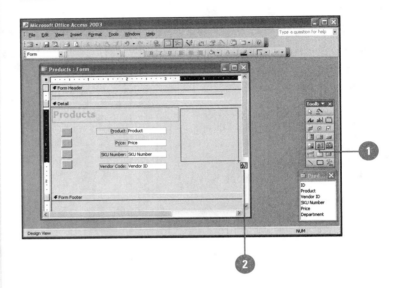

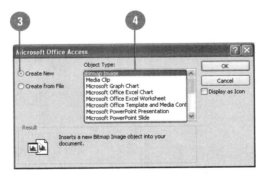

> ### Did You Know?
>
> **You can edit the original graphic.**
> Double-click the graphic object you created to redisplay the program in which you created the object, and then modify the graphic as necessary. When you close the program, the modified graphic will be inserted in the form or report.

Inserting an Object from a File

There are several ways to embed or link an object from a file. If you want to embed a new object that you create from scratch, you can use the Insert Object command. If you want to insert an existing file, you can also use Insert Object and you can specify whether or not you want to link the object. If your object is already open in the program that created it, you can copy it, and in some cases, paste it into a form or report, automatically embedding it. Finally, you can use the Paste Special command to paste link a copied object—pasting and linking it at the same time.

Insert an Object from a File

1. Click the Insert menu and then click Object.

2. Click the Create From File option, click the Browse button, select the file you want to insert, and then click O.K.

3. To embed the object, make sure the Link check box is not checked. To link it, click the Link check box to select it.

4. Click OK.

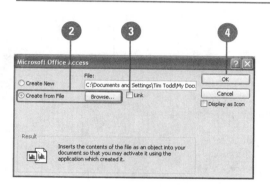

Paste Link an Object

1. In the source program, select the object you want to paste link.

2. Click the Cut or Copy button on the toolbar in the source program.

3. Switch to your database form or report.

4. Click the Edit menu, click Paste Special, and then click the Paste Link option.

5. Click the format you want, and then click OK.

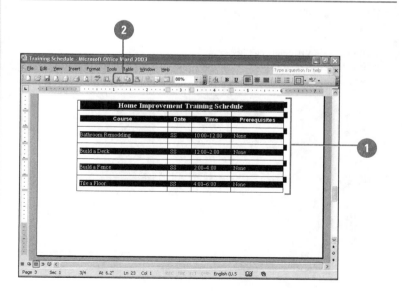

9

Inserting a Picture

You can insert interesting visuals, such as pictures, into your forms and reports or even fields. For example, in an employee table a field could contain employee photos. Or a field might contain a Word document that is a recent performance review. When you run a report that includes this field, the report will display the contents of the field. In Datasheet view, you can double-click the field to display the field's contents.

Insert a Graphic File

1. Display the form or report in Design view.

2. Click the Image button on the Toolbox.

3. Drag a rectangle where you want the picture to appear. Make the rectangle approximately the same size as the picture you will insert.

4. Click the Look In list arrow, and then locate the drive and folder containing the picture you want to insert.

   For example, if you want to insert a picture from the clip art collection provided with Office, open the Clip Art folder in the Office folder.

5. Click the file you want to insert, and then click OK.

6. If necessary, drag the sizing handles to resize the graphic as needed.

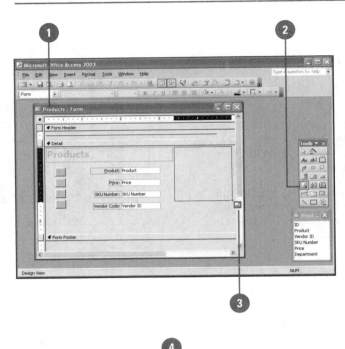

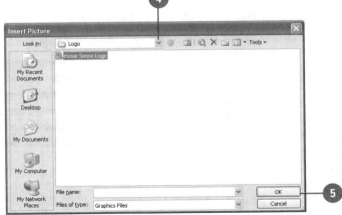

Insert a Clip Art Object

1 Click the Start button, point to All Programs, point to Microsoft Office, point to Microsoft Office Tools, and then click Microsoft Clip Organizer.

2 Use the Collection pane to locate the clip art you want to use.

3 Point to the clip art, and then click the image list arrow.

4 Click Copy on the submenu.

5 Click the Close button.

6 Display the form or report in Design view in which you want to paste.

7 Click the Paste button on the toolbar.

8 Use the sizing handles to resize the clip art object.

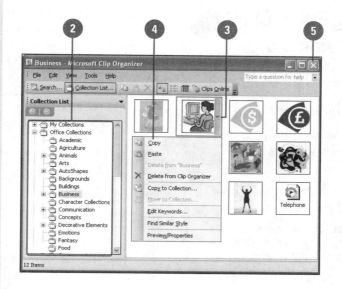

Did You Know?

You can crop parts of a graphic that you want to hide. Press and hold Shift, and then drag a sizing handle over the area you want to crop. To create more space around the graphic, drag the handle away (while holding down Shift) from the center of the graphic.

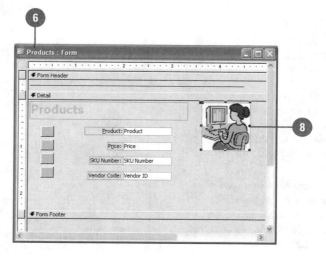

Inserting Excel Charts and Worksheets

There are several types of Excel objects that you can insert into your form or report. Two of the most common are worksheets and charts. You can insert a new Excel worksheet and then add data to it, or you can insert an existing Excel worksheet. You can also insert a chart from an Excel workbook.

Insert an Excel Chart

1. In Excel, click the chart you want to insert in the Access report or form.

2. In Excel, click the Copy button on the Standard toolbar.

3. Switch to Access, and, in Design view, display the form or report on which you want the chart.

4. Click the Paste button.

5. Click outside the chart to deselect it.

Did You Know?

You can drag and drop to Excel. You can drag objects from Excel right into Design view. Make sure that neither window is maximized and that both the object you want to drag and its destination are visible.

You can edit an inserted Excel worksheet. If you want to modify the worksheet, double-click it, and then use the Excel tools to edit. When you're done, click the Close button, and then click Yes to save changes.

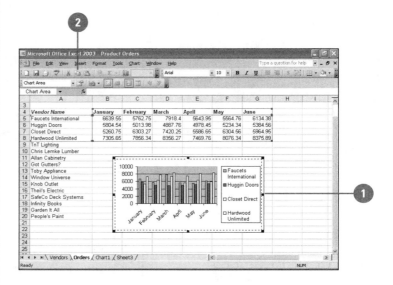

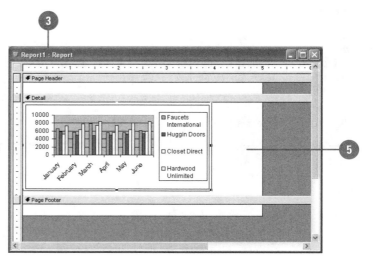

Insert an Excel Worksheet

1. Display the form or report into which you want to insert the Excel worksheet.

2. Click the Insert menu, and then click Object.

3. Click the Create From File option.

4. Click Browse, locate and select the worksheet, and then click OK.

5. Click OK.

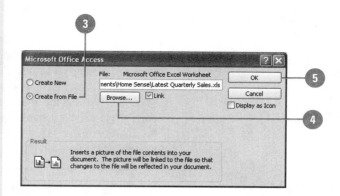

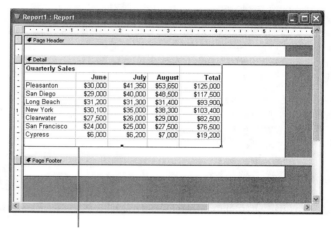

Excel worksheet in a report

Inserting a Graph Chart

You can create a chart from data in a table or query using the Chart Wizard. The wizard steps you through the process to select the data and chart type. The Graph chart uses two views to display the information that makes up a graph: the datasheet, which is a spreadsheet-like grid of rows and columns that contains your data, and the chart, which is the graphical representation of the data. A datasheet contains cells to hold your data. A cell is the intersection of a row and column. Graph Chart comes with a gallery that lets you change the chart type and then format the chart to get the result that you want. You can also save your customized settings as a format to use when you create other charts.

Create a Graph Chart

① In Design view, click the Insert menu, and then click Chart.

② Drag the pointer to create a rectangle the size of the chart you want to create.

③ When the Chart Wizard appears, click the Both option, and then click the table or query you want to use to make the chart. Click Next to continue.

④ Click a field, and then click the Add button for each field you want to chart. Click Next to continue.

⑤ Click the chart type you want, and then click Next.

⑥ Make any layout modifications that are desired, and then click Next.

⑦ If you want the chart to change from record to record, select the fields that link the document and the chart, and then click Next.

⑧ Enter a chart name, click the No option if you do not want to display the legend, and then click Finish.

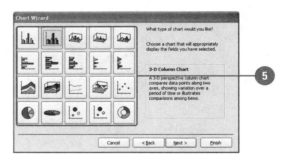

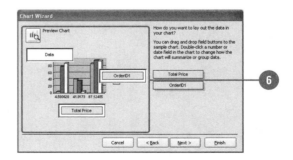

Change a Chart Type

1. In Design view, double-click the chart on your form or report.

2. Click the Chart Type button list arrow.

3. Click the button for the chart type you want.

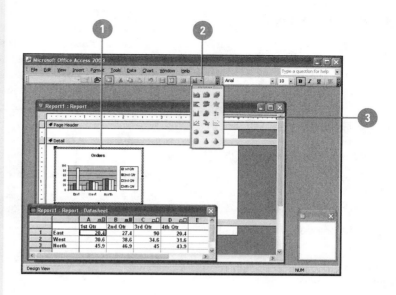

Save Chart Settings as a Custom Chart Type

1. In Design view, double-click the chart to select it.

2. Click the Chart menu, and then click Chart Type.

3. Click the Custom Types tab.

4. Click the User-defined option.

5. Click Add.

6. Type a name and description for the chart, and then click OK.

7. Click OK.

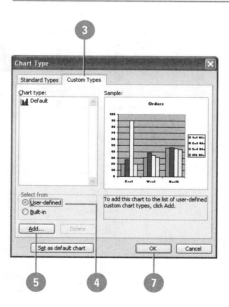

9

Formatting Chart Objects

Chart objects are the individual elements that make up a chart, such as an axis, the legend, or a data series. The **plot area** is the bordered area where the data are plotted. The **chart area** is the area between the plot area and the Microsoft Graph object selection box. To suit your needs, you can format chart objects and individual elements that make up a chart, such as an axis, legend, or data series.

Select a Chart Object

1. In Design view, double-click the chart on your form or report.

2. Click the Chart Objects list arrow on the Standard toolbar.

3. Click the chart object you want to select.

   When a chart object is selected, selection handles appear.

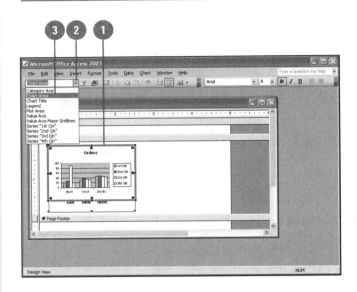

Format a Chart Object

1. In Design view, double-click the chart on your form or report.

2. Double-click the chart object you want to format, such as an axis, legend, or data series.

3. Click the tab corresponding to the options you want to change. Tabs differ depending on the chart object.

4. Select the options to apply.

5. Click OK.

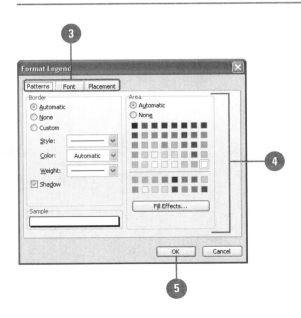

Customize a Chart

1. In Design view, double-click the chart on your form or report.

2. If necessary, select the chart object.

3. Click the Chart menu, and then click Chart Options.

4. Click the tab (Titles, Axes, Gridlines, Legend, Data Labels, or Data Table) corresponding to the chart object you want to customize.

5. Make your changes.

6. Click OK.

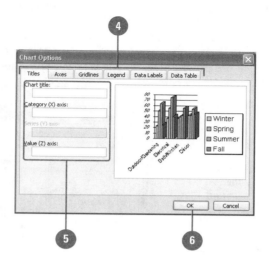

Change the View of a 3-D Chart

1. In Design view, double-click the chart on your form or report.

2. Select the 3-D chart you want to change.

3. Click the Chart menu, and then click 3-D View.

4. Click the left or right rotation button.

5. Click the up or down elevation button.

6. Click OK.

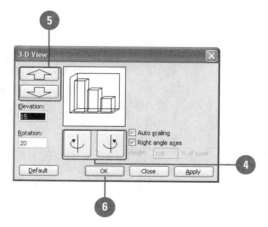

Moving and Resizing an Object

After you insert a graphic object, you can resize or move it with its selection **handles**, the little squares that appear on the edges of the object when you click the object to select it. If you need to select more than one object, you can drag a selection rectangle around the objects, or press and hold down the Shift key, and then click each object to select it.

Move an Object

1. In Design view, select an object you want to move.

2. Position the mouse pointer over the object, and then when the mouse pointer changes to a hand, drag it to move the outline of the object to a new location.

   Do not click a handle or else you will resize the object.

Resize an Object

1. In Design view, select the object you want to resize.

2. Position the mouse pointer over one of the handles.

3. When the pointer changes to a two-headed arrow, drag the handle until the object is the size you want.

Did You Know?

You can resize objects proportionately. To resize objects proportionately, drag one of the object's corner sizing handles until the object is the size you want.

Working on the Web

Introduction

The Internet and the World Wide Web have become an integral part of computing today. By providing quick and easy communication and data sharing to users around the world, the Internet has made it possible for data to have a global, rather than simply local, application. Microsoft Office Access 2003 provides support for the World Wide Web in four ways:

- ◆ By allowing database tables, queries, forms, and reports to contain links to objects on the Web

- ◆ With tools to navigate the Web from within the database

- ◆ Meeting with a remote audience over the Internet in "real time"

- ◆ With the ability to save tables, queries, forms, and reports as Web pages or to create Web pages based on data contained in the database

Each of these features makes it easier for you to include Web features in your database and makes your data available to the outside world.

What You'll Do

Integrate Access and the Internet

Create a Hyperlink Field

Insert a Hyperlink to a File or Web Page

Link to an Object in a Database

Link to a New Document

Navigate Hyperlinks

Work with the Web Toolbar

Export Database Objects to HTML

Export Database Objects to ASP Files

Hold an Online Meeting

Create a Data Access Page Using a Wizard

Work with a Data Access Page in Design View

Add a Theme to a Page

Group a Data Access Page

View a Data Access Page

Analyze Pivot Data from the Web

Integrating Access and the Internet

One of the chief uses of computers today lies in accessing the **Internet**, a structure of millions of interconnected computers that allows users to communicate and to share data with one another. In its early years, the Internet was limited to a small community of university and government organizations. This was due, in part, to the sometimes difficult commands needed to navigate the Internet.

However, the introduction of the World Wide Web in the early 1990s led to an explosion in Internet use by businesses and the general public. The **World Wide Web** (or simply the Web) made Internet navigation easy by replacing arcade commands with a simple point-and-click interface within an application called a **Web browser**. The Web made data accessible to a wider audience than ever before. Companies could create Web sites containing product information, stock reports, and information about the company's structure and goals. Later innovations allowed businesses to accept and process orders online and to enter those orders into databases containing inventory and customer information.

Because of the importance of these developments, Microsoft has worked to integrate Access more tightly with the Internet and the Web. You can now navigate the Web from inside Access. Access databases can contain links to Internet resources, and you can save tables, forms, and reports as Web documents. These features make it possible for you to manage Access data locally and across the globe.

Creating Hypertext Links

The Web is a giant structure of documents connected together through hypertext links.

Hypertext links, or **hyperlinks**, are elements on a Web page that you can activate, usually with a click of your mouse, to retrieve another Web document, which is called the **target** of the link. For example, a document about the national park system might contain a hypertext link whose target is a page devoted to Yosemite National Park. The great advantage of hypertext is that you don't have to know where or how the target is stored. You need only to click the hyperlink to retrieve the target. A target is identified by its **Uniform Resource Locator (URL)**, an address that uniquely identifies the location of the target on the Internet.

Access incorporates hypertext in two ways. First, through **hypertext fields**, fields in tables that contain hyperlinks, you can view and click a link and retrieve the link's target. Second, Access allows you to insert hyperlinks as elements within forms and reports. A footnote on a form, for example, could be a link to a Word document.

The targets of these links need not be pages on the Web. You can also direct the links to target other files on a hard disk drive, to an object within the current database, or to a different database altogether.

Navigating the Web

Once you activate a hyperlink, Access displays a toolbar, called the **Web toolbar**, which contains buttons that help you navigate the hyperlinks. As you progress through a series of links, the toolbar displays buttons that allow you to go forward and backward through the link sequence. The toolbar also includes a button to access a list of favorite Web pages or a start page, the Web page you initially see when you access the Web from your Web browser.

Creating Web Pages

Web pages are created in a special language called **HTML (Hypertext Markup Language)**, a cross-platform language which any operating system, including Microsoft Windows, Macintosh, and UNIX, can use to access a Web page. The cross-platform nature of HTML is one reason for the popularity of the Web.

Static Web Pages

Access allows you to export reports, forms, and tables to HTML format. Once you export these database objects, you can publish them as Web pages for others to view. These Web pages are **static Web pages** because their content is unchanged until you export the database object again. You have some control over the appearance of the Web page through the use of **HTML templates**, files that consist of HTML commands describing the page's layout. The templates can be used to insert company logos, graphics, and other elements. However, Access does not supply the templates for you, and you must have some working knowledge of HTML to create your own.

Active Server Pages

If you want your Web page to change whenever the source data changes, you need to create a **dynamic Web page**. Access provides two ways of exporting your reports, forms, and tables to this dynamic Web page format. The more established method is with **Active Server Pages**, or more simply, **ASP**. Unlike files in HTML format, an ASP file causes the Web browser to automatically retrieve the most current data from the database. The data is then formatted according to the layout of the ASP file. An ASP file can also be used to save new data in the database, as would be the case with an online order form.

To create an ASP file, you need the name of the current database, a user name and password to connect to the database, and the URL of the Web server that will store the ASP file.

In addition, the Web server must be running Microsoft Active Server 3.0 or later, have the ActiveX Server component installed, along with the Microsoft Access Desktop Driver, and have access privileges to the database. Because of these issues, creating an ASP file has to be done in cooperation with the administrator of the Web site.

Data Access Pages

Data access pages are Web pages bound directly to the data in the database. Data access pages can be used like Access forms, except that these pages are stored as external files, rather than within the database or database project. Although the pages can be used within Access, they are primarily designed to be viewed by a Web browser. Data access pages are written in **dynamic HTML or DHTML**, an extension of HTML that allows dynamic objects as part of the Web page.

Unlike ASP files, you can create a data access page within Access using a wizard or in Design view employing many of the same tools you use to create Access forms. However, a data access page requires that Internet Explorer 5.0 or later be installed.

10

Creating a Hyperlink Field

The Hyperlink data type allows you to create a Hyperlink field, a field that can store hyperlinks. The hyperlink can be a path to a file on your hard disk drive or network, or it can be a link to a page on the Web. When you click a Hyperlink field, Access jumps to the target specified by the link. For example, if you have a Clients table, and most of your clients have their own Web pages, you might want to create a Hyperlink field that contains links to each client Web page.

Create a Hyperlink Field in a Table

1. Display the table in Design view.

2. Create a new field in which you want to store a hyperlink.

3. Click the Data Type list arrow, and then click Hyperlink.

4. Click the Save button on the Table Design toolbar to save the changes to the table.

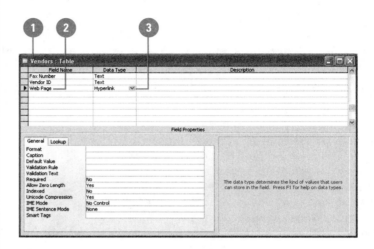

See Also

See "Viewing Field Properties" on page 69 and "Changing Field Properties" on page 70 for more information on working with data types.

Inserting a Hyperlink to a File or Web Page

Use the Insert Hyperlink button to create a hyperlink within a Hyperlink field or as hypertext within a form or report. A hyperlink consists of the text that the user sees that describes the link, the URL of the link's target, and a ScreenTip that appears whenever the pointer passes over the link. If you have created a Hyperlink field for client Web pages, you can use this method to add a URL for each client's Web page.

Insert a Hyperlink to a File or Web Page

1. Within a Hyperlink field or while editing a form or report in Design view, click the Insert Hyperlink button on the Design toolbar.

2. Click Existing File Or Web Page on the Link To bar.

3. Enter the hyperlink text.

4. Specify the linked document by either:

   ◆ Entering the file name or URL of the linked document

   ◆ Choosing the linked document from the Recent Files, Browsed Pages, or Inserted Links list

5. Click ScreenTip to create a ScreenTip that will be displayed whenever the mouse pointer moves over the hyperlink.

6. Click OK.

Did You Know?

You can use ScreenTips. ScreenTips appear in the Web browser window if you're using Internet Explorer 4.0 or later.

You can link to an e-mail address. To link to an e-mail address, click E-Mail Address in the Link To bar, and then enter the e-mail address and subject.

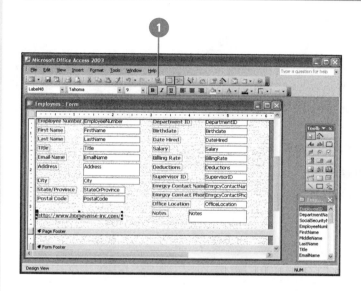

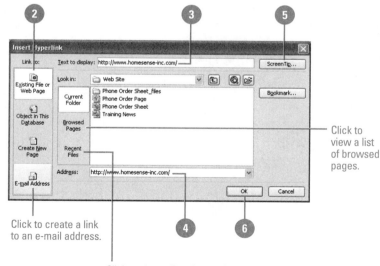

Click to view a list of browsed pages.

Click to create a link to an e-mail address.

Click to view a list of recently opened files.

Linking to an Object in a Database

You can create hyperlinks that target forms, tables, and reports within the current database. You can also link to objects in other databases by specifying the database's file name and selecting the form, table, or report you want to target. You will have immediate access to those objects by clicking the hyperlink you insert.

Link to a Database Object in the Database

① Within a Hyperlink field or while editing a form or report in Design view, click the Insert Hyperlink button on the Design toolbar.

② Click Object In This Database on the Link To bar.

③ Enter the hyperlink text.

④ Select the database object.

⑤ Click OK.

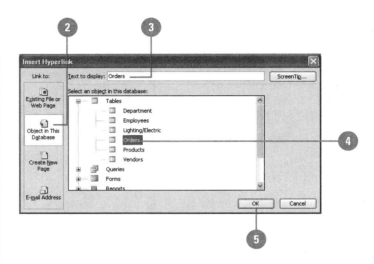

Link to an Object in Another Database

1. Within a Hyperlink field or while editing a form or report in Design view, click the Insert Hyperlink button on the Design toolbar.

2. Click Existing File Or Web Page on the Link To bar.

3. Enter the hyperlink text.

4. Enter the database file name or click Browse to locate and select a database file name.

5. Click Bookmark.

6. Select the database object.

7. Click OK.

8. Click OK.

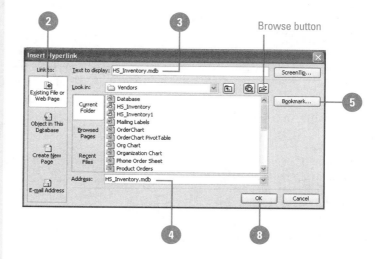

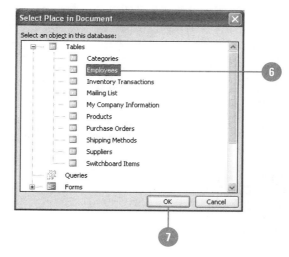

10

Linking to a New Document

You can create new documents at the same time you link to them. The documents can be Web pages, Office documents like Excel spreadsheets and PowerPoint presentations, or any other document type that is associated with an application on your computer. Once you create the new document, you have the choice of editing it immediately within the appropriate application, or editing it later.

Insert a Hyperlink to a New Document

1. Within a Hyperlink field or while editing a form or report in Design view, click the Insert Hyperlink button on the Design toolbar.

2. Click Create New Page on the Link To bar.

3. Enter the hyperlink text.

4. Enter the name of the new document and the location in which you want it created.

5. Click one of the When To Edit option to indicate whether you want to edit the document now or later.

6. Click OK.

   If you chose to edit the document immediately, the application for the document type opens.

7. Start editing your new document.

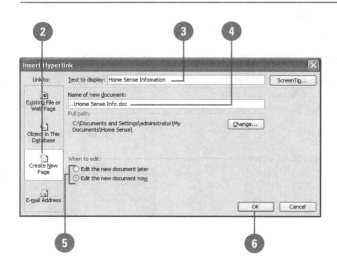

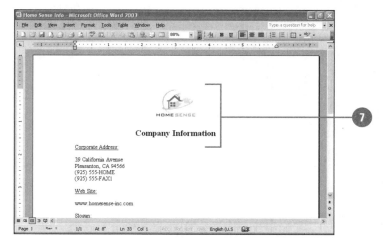

Did You Know?

You can choose a document type.
Document types are determined by the file name extension. For example, Word documents are identified by the .doc extension.

Navigating Hyperlinks

When you have added a hyperlink to a form, report, or table, you can activate the link by clicking it with the mouse. As the pointer moves over the hyperlink, the pointer changes to a hand, which indicates the presence of the link. If you have supplied a ScreenTip when you created the link, the tip appears, giving additional information about the link. The Web toolbar also appears, allowing you to move forward and backward through a series of links, and jump to a specific page on the Web or to a file on your hard disk drive.

Navigate a Hyperlink

1. Open a table, form, or report containing a hyperlink.

2. Move the pointer over the hyperlink so that the pointer shape changes to a hand.

3. Click the hyperlink to display the linked document.

Did You Know?

You can remove or edit a hyperlink. To remove or edit a Hyperlink field, right-click the link, point to Hyperlink, and then click Remove Hyperlink or Edit Hyperlink. To remove or edit a hypertext link from a form or report, right-click the link in Design view, and then click Remove or Edit.

Web toolbar

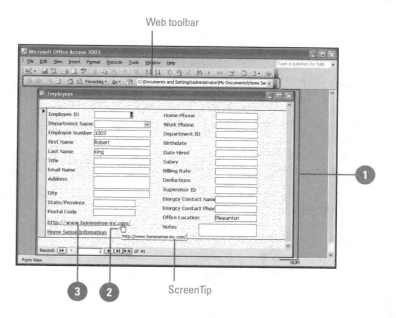

ScreenTip

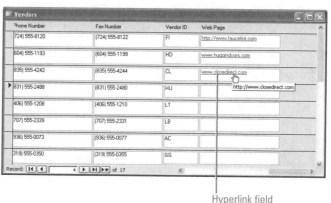

Hyperlink field

10

Working with the Web Toolbar

The Web toolbar provides an easy way to navigate Web pages in any Office program. You can use the Web toolbar to go to your start page (also known as a home page), access a Web search page, or open a specific Web page. You can jump directly to a document on your computer or network, or to a Web page on your intranet or the Internet. In the Address box on the Web toolbar, type the address of the document (including its path; for example,

C:\My Documents\Memo\To Do List.doc) or Web page (a URL; for example, *http://www.perspection.com*) that you want to view and press Enter. While you're browsing, you can hide all the other toolbars to gain the greatest space available on your screen and improve readability.

When you have jumped to a document that you would like to return to in the future, you can add the document to a list of favorites. The Favorites button provides shortcuts to files you explore frequently so you won't need to retype long file locations. These shortcuts can open documents on your computer, network, intranet, and the Internet.

Web Toolbar	
Button	**Description**
	Click to move back in a series of hyperlinks.
	Click to move forward in a series of hyperlinks.
	Click to stop the current jump.
	Click to refresh the current page.
	Click to go to the start page.
	Click to display a search page to search the Web.
Favorites ▾	Click to display a list of favorite Web pages and documents.
Go ▾	Click to go forward or backward, to the start page, or to define your start and search pages.
	Click to show only the Web toolbar.

Exporting Database Objects to HTML

In Access, the Export command allows you to save a table, query, form, or report as a Web page. If the page is saved in HTML format, it represents a snapshot of the data at the time you created the file. If your data changes, you must export it again if you want the Web page to be current.

Export to an HTML File

1. Open a table, query, form, or report.

2. Click the File menu, and then click Export.

3. Click the Save In list arrow, and then select a location for the file.

4. Enter a file name for the Web page.

5. Click the Save As Type list arrow, and then click HTML Documents.

6. Click Export All.

7. Select a HTML Template check box.

8. Enter the name of the HTML template you'll use for this Web page (if one exists).

9. Click OK.

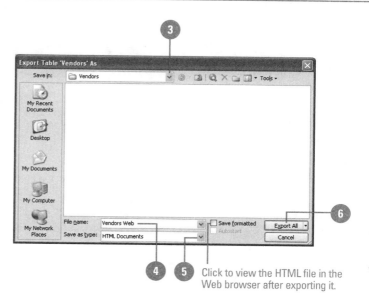

Click to view the HTML file in the Web browser after exporting it.

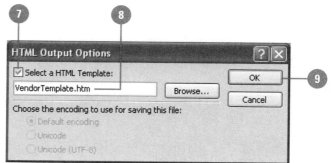

Did You Know?

You can use Export format. Tables, queries, and forms appear as HTML tables, but a report appears in HTML format with the same layout it had in Access.

You can use HTML templates. Templates are usually stored in the *Program Files\Microsoft Office\Templates\Access* folder. See online Help for more information on creating your own templates.

10

Exporting Database Objects to ASP Files

When you export a database object as an Active Server Page (ASP) file, you are giving Web users access to the information in your database. Unlike a static HTML file, an ASP file connects to the database and retrieves the most current information for the user to view.

Export a Database Object to an ASP File

① In the Database window, click the database object you want to export, click the File menu, and then click Export.

② Click the Save As Type list arrow, and then select Microsoft Active Server Pages.

③ Click the Save In list arrow, and then select the location where you want to save the file.

④ Click Export or Export All.

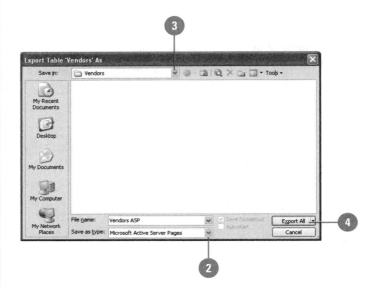

See Also

See "Exporting Data to Other Programs" on page 242 for more information on exporting data from Access.

⑤ Enter the name of the HTML template (if one exists).

⑥ Enter the name of the database file that contains the data you want the Web server to access.

⑦ Enter the user name you want the Web server to use to connect to the database.

⑧ Enter the password you want the Web server to use to log on to the database.

⑨ Enter the Web server URL.

⑩ Click OK.

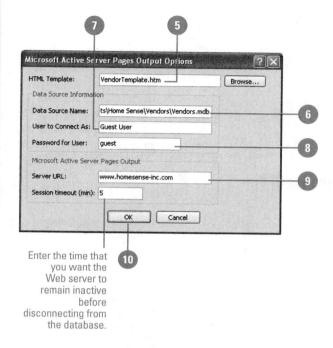

Microsoft Active Server Pages Output Options

HTML Template: VendorTemplate.htm   [Browse...]

Data Source Information

Data Source Name: ts\Home Sense\Vendors\Vendors.mdb

User to Connect As: Guest User

Password for User: guest

Microsoft Active Server Pages Output

Server URL: www.homesense-inc.com

Session timeout (min): 5

[OK]   [Cancel]

Enter the time that you want the Web server to remain inactive before disconnecting from the database.

Holding an Online Meeting

Microsoft NetMeeting is a program that comes with Access 2003. It allows you to host, participate, and collaborate in an online meeting over the Internet or an intranet. You can share and exchange information as if everyone were in the same room. As a host for an online meeting, you can start the meeting and control the database. You can allow participants to make changes to the database. Each person in the online meeting can then take turns editing and controlling the database. As a participant and collaborator, you can share applications and documents, send text messages in Chat, transfer files, and work on the Whiteboard.

Start an Impromptu Online Meeting

① Open the database you want to share.

② Click the Tools menu, point to Online Collaboration, and then click Meet Now.

③ If this is the first time you've worked in an online meeting, the Microsoft NetMeeting dialog box appears. Fill out the information in the My Information and Directory boxes, and then click OK.

④ Select the participants for the meeting.

⑤ Click Call to start NetMeeting running in the background.

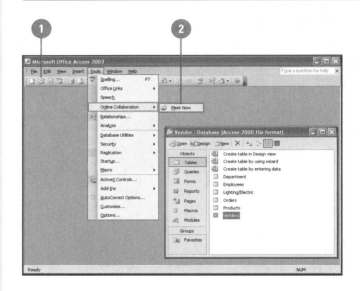

Enter the names of the people you want to invite to the meeting.

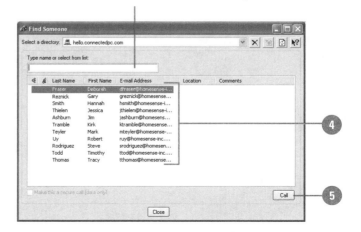

Collaborate in an Online Meeting

① As the host, click the Allow Others To Edit button on the Online Meeting toolbar.

② When collaboration is turned on, click anywhere in the database to gain control. If you are a participant, double-click anywhere in the database to gain control.

③ Click the Allow Others To Edit button again to turn off the collaboration, or press Esc if you don't have control of the database.

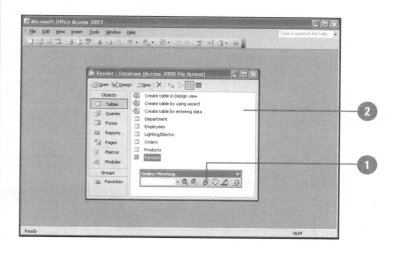

Participate in an Online Meeting

◆ Use the buttons on the Online Meeting toolbar to participate in an online meeting.

Did You Know?

You can start NetMeeting using the Start menu. Click Start on the taskbar, point to Programs, and then click NetMeeting.

You can receive an online meeting call. You must have NetMeeting running on your computer to receive an online meeting call.

You can join an online meeting. If you receive an online meeting call, click Accept in the Join Meeting dialog box. If you receive an Outlook reminder for the meeting, click Start This NetMeeting (host) or Join This NetMeeting (participant). To receive an Outlook reminder to join a meeting, you need to have accepted the meeting from an e-mail message.

Online Meeting Toolbar

Button	Description
	Allows the host to invite additional participants to the online meeting.
	Allows the host to remove a participant from the online meeting.
	Allows participants to edit and control the database during the online meeting.
	Allows participants to send messages in a Chat session during the online meeting.
	Allows participants to draw or type on the Whiteboard during the online meeting.
	Allows either the host to end the online meeting for the group or a participant to disconnect.

10

Creating a Data Access Page Using a Wizard

ACO3S-1-12, ACO3S-4-2

Data access pages allow you to create dynamic Web pages without the need of a Web server, unlike an Active Server Page (ASP) file. You can format data access pages, using many of the same tools you use when creating Access forms. Access organizes the data access pages in a separate object group in the Database window. Unlike other data objects, however, a data access page is stored in a file separate from the database file. One of the easiest ways to create a data access page is by using the Page Wizard. The wizard asks you to select the tables and fields you want to use, and how you want to group the fields on the Web page.

Create a Data Access Page Using a Wizard

1 In the Database window, click Pages on the Objects bar.

2 Double-click the Create Data Access Page By Using Wizard icon.

3 Select the table and fields that you want to appear in the data access page. Click Next to continue.

4 If you want, select any fields you want to act as group levels in the Web page. Click Next to continue.

Did You Know?

You can create a data access page with the New button. To create a data access page, click the New button on the Database Window toolbar, click Design View, and then choose the table or query you want placed in the data access page.

You can work in HTML. If you know HTML, click the View menu, and then click HTML Source to display the page's underlying HTML code.

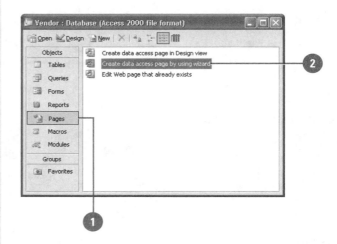

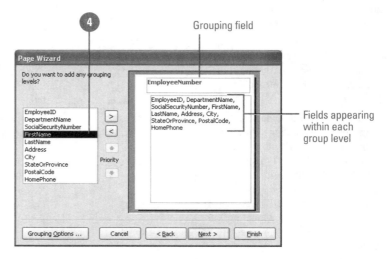

Grouping field

Fields appearing within each group level

5 Select the fields to sort the records in the page. Click Next to continue.

6 Enter a title for the data access page.

7 Indicate whether you want to open the page in Access or modify its design in Design view.

8 Click Finish.

Did You Know?

You can name a data access page. Access uses the title you enter as the page's file name, adding the .html file name extension.

You can export to a data access page. You can also create a data access page by using the Export command on the File menu, and then select Microsoft Access Data Access Page as the file type.

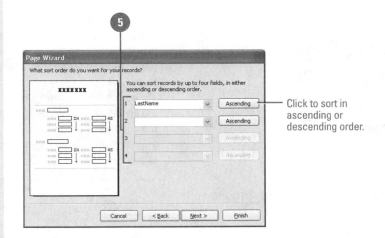

Click to sort in ascending or descending order.

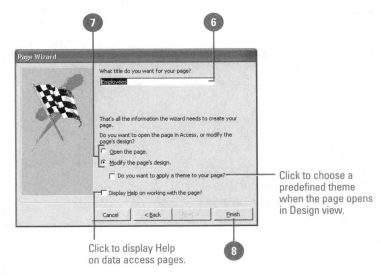

Click to choose a predefined theme when the page opens in Design view.

Click to display Help on data access pages.

10

Working with a Data Access Page in Design View

If you want to create a data access page without the Page Wizard, you can create it in Design view. Design view allows you to choose the tables, fields, and other objects that you want to appear on the Web page. You can format the appearance of the page using the same techniques you apply when you create Access forms. You can use tools on the Toolbox to insert hyperlinks and Office data, such as PivotTables, Excel Charts, and Excel Spreadsheets. A **PivotTable** is an interactive table linked to a database that summarizes the data in a table or query in tabular format. Similarly, a **PivotChart** is an interactive chart that is linked to a database.

Create or Modify a Data Access Page in Design View

1. In the Database window, click Pages on the Objects bar.

2. Double-click the Create Data Access Page In Design View icon, or click the page you want to modify, and then click the Design button.

3. If necessary, click the Field List button to display the list of tables and queries in the database.

4. Double-click the Tables or Queries folder, and then locate the table or query on which you want to base your page.

5. Drag a table or query icon from the field list to the Unbound section of the data access page.

6. Click a layout option, and then click OK.

7. Use the tools on the Toolbox to insert hyperlinks and other Office data, such as PivotTables, Charts, and Spreadsheets.

8. Click the Close button, click Yes, if prompted to save your work, and then enter a file name for the resulting Web page.

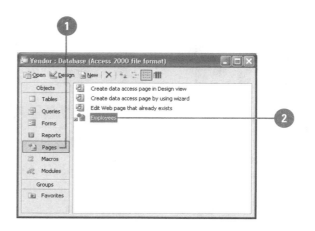

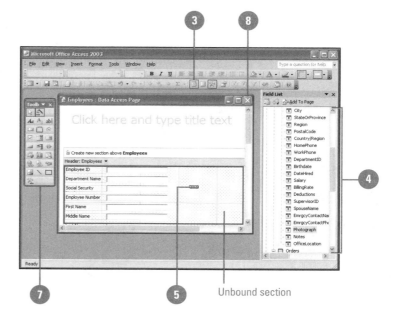

Unbound section

Adding a Theme to a Page

Access has a large collection of Web page themes that provide you with a variety of page designs. With the predefined themes you can format the background, fonts, and colors used in the Web page, or you can choose to format only one of these at a time. If you prefer a particular theme for your pages, you can set it as the default and all future pages will use that theme automatically.

Add a Theme to a Page

1. Display the data access page in Design view.

2. Click the Format menu, and then click Theme.

3. Select the theme you want to apply to your Web page.

4. Click to select the theme options you want.

   ◆ Use the theme's vivid colors.

   ◆ Apply the theme's active graphics.

   ◆ Use the theme's background image.

5. Click OK.

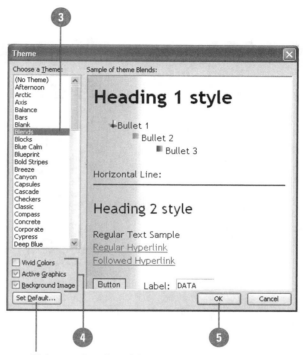

Click to set the selected theme as the default for future pages.

Did You Know?

You can choose a theme for your page with the Page Wizard. In the Page Wizard, choose to modify the page, and then click to select the Apply A Theme check box. When the page opens in Design view, you can choose the theme you want.

Grouping a Data Access Page

A **grouped data access page** is a hierarchical, interactive Web page in which records are grouped based on the values of a grouping field. When browsed, the page displays values of the grouping field, five records at a time. Each record will have a plus sign (+) button before it. Clicking this button will expand the page to show the complete record for that particular field value.

Group a Data Access Page

1. Display the data access page in Design view, and then select a field that will act as the grouping value.

2. Click the Promote button.

   Access creates a Group section that contains the group field and a plus sign that allows users to expand and collapse the record.

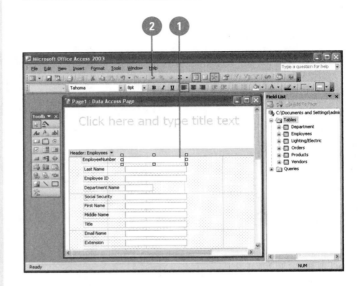

Remove a Group

1. Display the grouped data access page in Design view, and then select a grouping field.

2. Click the Demote button.

   Access removes the Group section, placing the grouping field in the Detail section.

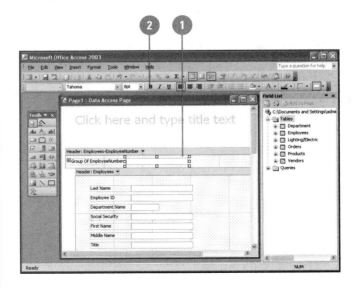

Specify Group Options

1. Display the grouped data access page in Design view.

2. Click the Group Level Properties list arrow.

3. Click Group Level Properties.

4. Change or modify any or all of the grouping properties.

5. Click the Close button.

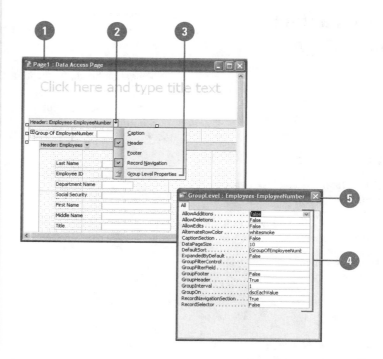

Did You Know?

You can create a group with the Page Wizard. Create a group and group your data access page with the Page Wizard. In the second step of the wizard, add a grouping level. You can also specify the grouping options that control how groups are selected.

Common Group Properties

Group Property	Group Property Function
Caption Section	Adds a caption to the Group section.
Group Header	Adds a header to the Group section.
Group Footer	Adds a footer to the Group section.
Record Navigation Section	Displays a record navigation box.
Expanded By Default	Expands the detail section when the browser opens the page.
Data Page Size	Determines the number of records shown at one time.
Group On	Determines the size of each group.
Group Interval	Determines the interval of each group
Default Sort	Sorts fields by group.
Group Filter Control	Specifies a combo or list box to filter the records in the group.
Group Filter Field	Specifies which field to filter the records in the group.

10

Viewing a Data Access Page

Once you create a data access page, you can open it from within the database or from your Web browser. If you choose to view the page in your browser, the browser will connect to the database and retrieve the information needed to display the page. The data access page contains a navigation box to help you retrieve the database records. The navigation box works in the browser the same way it works within Access. This tool allows you to move forward and backward through the database records, filter the data, sort it, or search for specific values.

View a Data Access Page

1. In the Database window, click Pages on the Objects bar.

2. Double-click the data access page you want to view.

   The page appears in a separate window.

Did You Know?

You can select data to copy. When you select data to copy, you can select an entire row or a single cell, but not multiple cells within a single row.

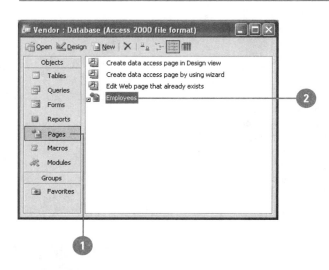

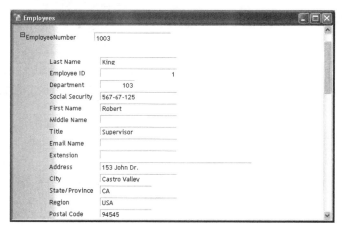

Preview a Data Access Page in a Web Browser

1. In the Database window, open a data access page from the list of pages.

2. Click the File menu, and then click Web Page Preview.

   Access starts your Web browser, loading the data access page.

3. Use the navigation box to review and modify the data.

Did You Know?

You can choose a Web browser for your data access page. You must use Internet Explorer 5.0 or later to view a data access page.

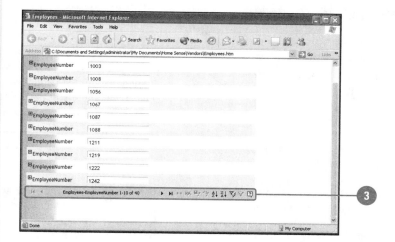

10

Analyze Pivot Data from the Web

AC03S-4-2

When you want to summarize information in a lengthy list using complex criteria, use the PivotTable to simplify your task. Without the PivotTable, you would have to manually count or create a formula to calculate which records met certain criteria, and then create a table to display that information. Once you determine what fields and criteria you want to use to summarize the data and how you want the resulting table to look, the PivotTable and PivotChart Wizard does the rest. Access comes with a control on the Toolbox to insert a Pivot Table in a data access page.

Insert a PivotTable in a Data Access Page

1. In the Database window, click Pages on the Objects bar.

2. Click the page you want to insert a PivotTable, and then click the Design button.

3. If necessary, click the Field List button to display the list of tables and queries in the database.

4. Click the Office PivotTable button on the Toolbox.

5. Drag a rectangle box to create a blank PivotTable.

6. Drag fields from the Field List to areas on the PivotTable.

7. When you're done, click the Close button, click Yes if prompted to save your work.

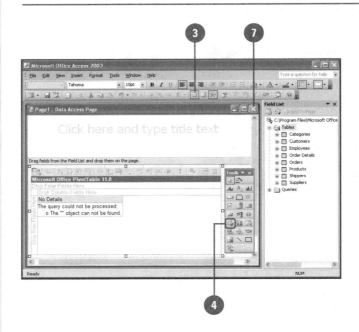

PivotTable

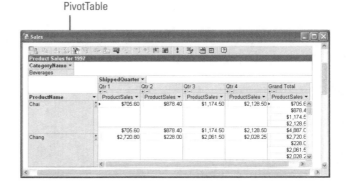

Did You Know?

You can insert a spreadsheet in a data access page. In a data Access page in Design view, click the Office Spreadsheet button on the Toolbox, and then drag a rectangle box to insert a blank Excel spreadsheet. You can enter or copy and paste data just like you were in the Excel program.

Importing and Exporting Information

Introduction

Microsoft Office Access 2003 allows you to incorporate information from a variety of sources into a database and exchange information from a database into other sources. You can use the Access import and export features to easily move data between your database and other databases and programs.

When you get data from other sources, you have the choice to import the data into a new table or link an existing table of the data to the database. When you import data, Access converts and copies the data into the database file. When you link to the data in another program, the data stays separate from the Access database. You can import data or link to data from several sources, including Microsoft Access, other databases (such as Paradox), HTML (a standard Web format), Microsoft Office Excel, Microsoft Exchange, and Microsoft Office Outlook.

If you work with XML (Extensible Markup Language), Access 2003 allows you to import and export XML data as well as transform the data to and from other formats using XML related files. XML is a new standard that enables you to move information across the Internet and programs where the data is stored independently of the format so you can use the data more seamlessly in other forms.

Microsoft Office 2003's data sharing techniques allow you to use other Office tools to work with your data. For example, you can merge your Access data with Microsoft Office Word to create form letters, or you can use Microsoft Office Excel's analysis tools on your Access data.

What You'll Do

Import and Link Data

Import or Link Data from an Access Database

Import or Link Data from an Excel Spreadsheet

Import or Link Data from a Mail Program

Get Data from Other Programs

Import and Export XML Data

Export Data to Other Programs

Merge Data with Word

Analyze Data in Excel

Importing and Linking Data

If you have data in other forms, yet need the information in Access, you can import the data into a new table or link the data to the database. When you import data, Access converts and copies the data into the database file. When you link to the data in another program, the data stays separate from the database, yet you can view and edit the data in both the original program and in the Access database.

If you need to use the data in different programs and sources, linking data is the most efficient way to keep the data up-to-date. However, if you plan to use your data only in Access, importing data is the most effective way. Access works faster and more efficiently when you import the data.

In addition to Access databases and projects, you can import or link data using the most common data formats from other programs, such as Microsoft Excel spreadsheets, Lotus 1-2-3 spreadsheets, Paradox for Windows databases, Microsoft SharePoint Services, Microsoft Exchange, text files, HTML, XML (Extensible Markup Language), and SQL tables with ODBC (Open Database Connectivity).

When you import data, you cannot append data to an existing table unless you import a spreadsheet or text files. When you link data, you can read and update the external data without altering the external data format in the original data source. Access uses different icons to represent linked tables and nonlinked tables.

If you no longer need a linked table, you can delete the linked table from the Access window. When you delete a linked table, you are deleting only the information that Access uses to open the table. You can re-link to the table again at any time.

Data Sources

Data Sources	Format Supported
Microsoft Access database	2.0, 7.0/95, 8.0/97, 9.0/2000, and 10.0/Access 2002, Access 2003
Microsoft Access project	9.0/2000, 10.0/Access 2002, and Access 2003
Microsoft Excel Spreadsheets	3.0, 4.0, 5.0, 7.0/95, 8.0/97, 9.0/2000, 10.0/Excel 2002, and Excel 2003
Paradox for Windows	3.x, 4.x, 5.0; and 8.0
Lotus 1-2-3 (Linking is read-only)	.wks, .wk1, .wk3, and .wk4
Microsoft Windows SharePoint Services	2.0
Microsoft Exchange	All versions
Delimited text file	All Character sets
Fixed-width text file	All Character sets
HTML	1.0 (if a list), 2.0, 3.x (if table or list)
XML	All versions
SQL tables from Microsoft Visual FoxPro	2.x, 3.0, 5.0, and 6.x (import only)
SQL tables from ODBC databases	See Microsoft Knowledge Base for an up-to-date list

You can import or link data in Access using the Import or Link Table commands on the Get External Data submenu on the File menu. When you choose one of these commands, the Import or Link dialog box opens, displaying a dialog box similar to the Open dialog box. You can use the Files Of Type list arrow to select the type of data you want to import or link.

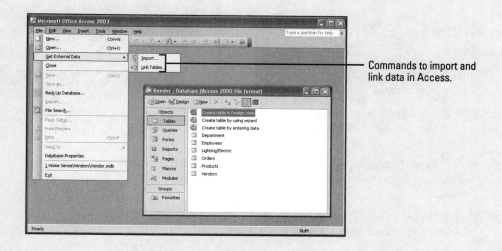

Commands to import and link data in Access.

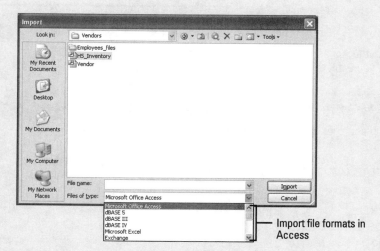

Import file formats in Access

Importing or Linking Data from an Access Database

If you have data in another Access database, you can import the information using the Import command. During the importing process, you select the tables you want to import. If you import a table that is already linked, Access links the table to its data source. In other words, Access copies the link to the table. If you link to a file on a network, make sure to use the full path name, such as \\server\share\path\file name (for example \\Server1\Projects\Data\Sales.mdb), instead of a mapped drive to avoid linking problems.

Import Data from an Access Database

1. Open the database in which you want to import data.

2. Click the File menu, point to Get External Data, and then click Import.

3. Click the Files Of Type list arrow, and then click Microsoft Office Access.

4. Locate and select the database from which you want data.

5. Click Import.

6. Click Options.

7. Click the tab with the Access database object you want to import.

8. Click the objects you want.

   To deselect an object, click it again.

9. Select the import options you want.

10. Click OK.

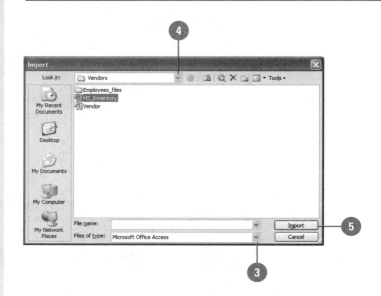

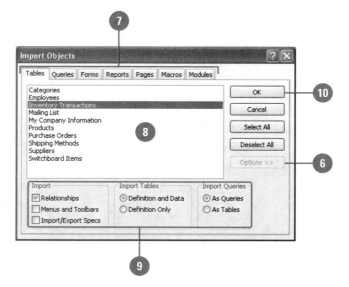

Did You Know?

You can delete the link to a linked table. In the Database window, click Tables, click the linked table you want to delete, and then press Delete.

Link Data from an Access Database

1. Open the database in which you want to link data.

2. Click the File menu, point to Get External Data, and then click Link Tables.

3. Click the Files Of Type list arrow, and then click Microsoft Office Access.

4. Locate and select the database from which you want data.

5. Click Link.

6. Click each table to which you want to link.

   To deselect a table, click it again.

7. Click OK.

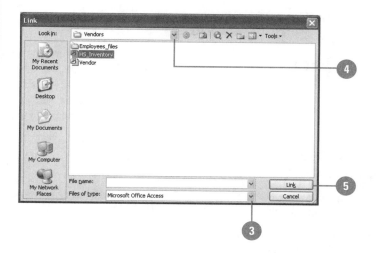

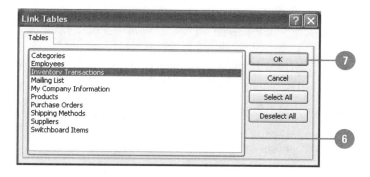

Convert a Linked Table to a Nonlinked Table

1. In the Database window, select the linked table you want to convert.

2. Click the Copy button on the Database toolbar.

3. Click the Paste button on the Database toolbar.

4. Type a name for the new table.

5. Click the Structured Only or Structure And Data option.

6. Click OK.

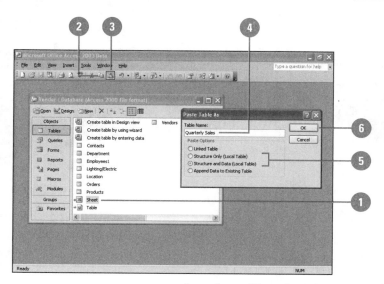

11

Importing or Linking Data from an Excel Spreadsheet

If you have data in an Excel spreadsheet, you can use the information in an Access database. You can import or link all the data from a spreadsheet or specific data from a named range. When you import or link data, Access normally creates a new table for the information. For Excel spreadsheet data, you can also append data to an existing table as long as the table field's and spreadsheet column headings match. After you import or link data, you should check to make sure Access assigned the appropriate data type to the imported fields.

Import or Link Data from an Excel Spreadsheet

1. Open the database in which you want to import or link data.

2. Click the File menu, point to Get External Data, and then click Import or Link Tables.

3. Click the Files Of Type list arrow, and then click Microsoft Excel.

4. Locate and select the spreadsheet from which you want data.

5. Click Import or Link.

6. Follow the wizard instructions; some of the requested information includes:

   ◆ A worksheet or named range

   ◆ First row column heading

   ◆ A new or existing table

   ◆ Field information

   ◆ Primary key

   ◆ Table name

7. When you're done, click Finish.

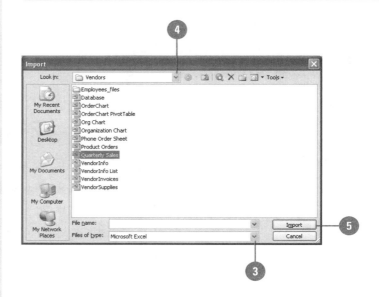

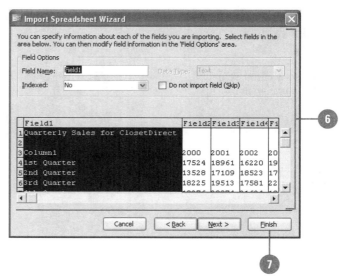

Importing or Linking Data from a Mail Program

If you have data in a mail program, such as Microsoft Exchange or Microsoft Outlook, you can use the Import From Exchange/Outlook Wizard or the Link To Exchange/Outlook Wizard to import or link your Contacts folder. You can use the information from your Contacts folder to create form letters and mailing labels by merging the data using the Microsoft Word Mail Merge Wizard. You need to have Microsoft Outlook, Outlook Express, or Microsoft Exchange installed on your computer to use these wizards to import or link data.

Import or Link Data from Microsoft Exchange or Outlook

1. Open the database in which you want to import or link data.

2. Click the File menu, point to Get External Data, and then click Import or Link Tables.

3. Click the Files Of Type list arrow, and then click Outlook or Exchange.

   The Import or Link Exchange/Outlook Wizard dialog box opens.

4. Click the Contacts folder icon (use the plus and minus signs to display folders), and then click Next.

5. Follow the remaining wizard instructions; some of the requested information includes:

   ◆ A worksheet or named range

   ◆ First row column heading

   ◆ A new or existing table

   ◆ Field information

   ◆ Primary key

   ◆ Table name

6. When you're done, click Finish.

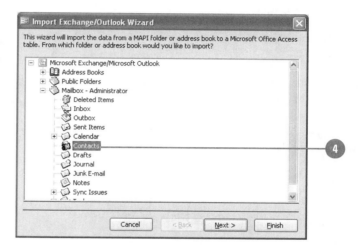

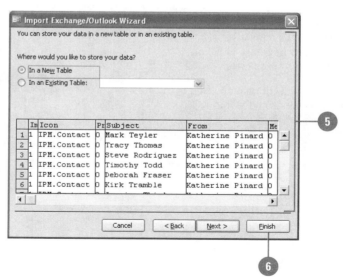

Getting Data from Other Programs

AC03S-2-3

When you import data, you insert a copy of one file into another—in this case, Access. When you import data into Access, Access creates a new table to store the data, using labels from the first row of a worksheet or table for the new table. If you need to keep the data in a separate file for use in other programs, you can also link your data to a table in Access, which allows you to keep both updated. You can import or link data from a variety of sources, such as dBase, Microsoft Excel, Microsoft Exchange, Microsoft Outlook, HTML, Lotus 1-2-3, Paradox, SharePoint Team Services, and text files. You can use Access commands to edit the imported data.

Import Data from Another Source

1. Open the database into which you want to import data.

2. Click the File menu, point to Get External Data, and then click Import.

3. Click the Files Of Type list arrow, and then click the type of file you are importing.

4. Locate and select the file you want to import.

5. Click Import.

6. If necessary, follow the instructions in the Import wizard to set up the data as an Access table.

7. Edit the imported information using Access commands and features, if necessary.

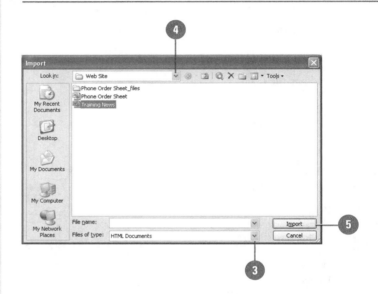

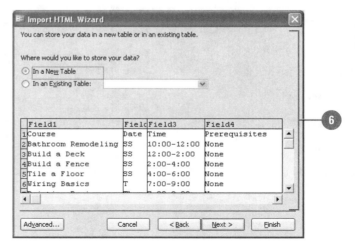

Link Data from Another Source

1. Open the database into which you want to link data.

2. Click the File menu, point to Get External Data, and then click Link Tables.

3. Click the Files Of Type list arrow, and then click the type of file you are importing.

4. Locate and select the file in which you want to link.

5. Click Link.

6. If necessary, follow the instructions in the link wizard to set up the data as an Access table.

7. From within the source program or Access, edit the linked information using the program's commands.

Did You Know?

You can identify linked tables. Right-click the table in the Object list in the Database window, and then click Properties on the shortcut menu. The property sheet shows that a table is linked to another data source and what that data source is.

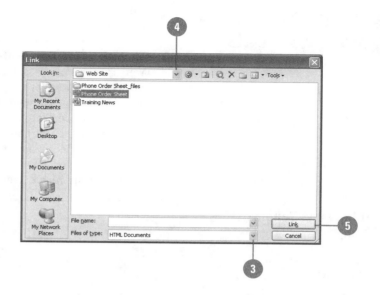

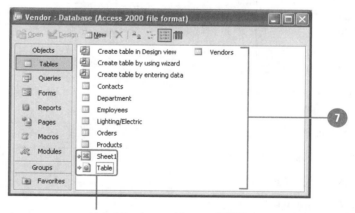

Linked Excel spreadsheet and HTML document

11

Importing and Exporting XML Data

XML (**Extensible Markup Language**) is a universal language that enables you to move information across the Internet and programs where the data is stored independently of the format so you can use the data more seamlessly in other forms. XML is fully supported in Office 2003 through Word, Excel, and Access. Access allows you to import and export XML data as well as transform the data to and from other formats using XML related files, such as Extensible Stylesheet Language (XSL), which provides a flexible and consistent way to present your data. When you import and export XML data, you can use an XML Schema (XSD)—a set of rules that defines the elements and content used in an XML file—to ensure the data conforms to a defined structure. XML schemas and XSL transformations are created by developers who understand XML.

Import Data and Schema from XML

1. Open the database in which you want to import.

2. Click the File menu, point to Get External Data, and then click Import.

3. Click the Files Of Type list arrow, and then click XML.

4. Select and locate the XML data or schema file.

5. Click Import.

6. Click Options.

7. Click an import option.

   ◆ Structure Only

   ◆ Structure And Data

   ◆ Append Data To Existing Table(s)

8. To select a transform, click Transform, click a transform, and then click OK.

9. Click OK, and then, if necessary, click OK again.

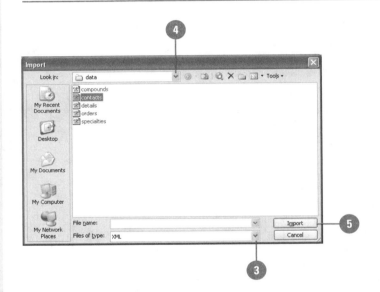

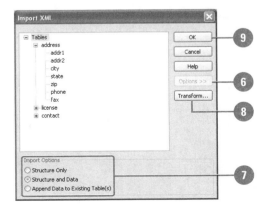

Export XML Data

1. Open the database containing the object you want to export, and then select the database object.

2. Click the File menu, and then click Export.

3. If necessary, click the Save In list arrow, and then select the drive and folder where you want to save the file.

4. Click the Save As Type list arrow, and then click XML.

5. If necessary, type a new name for the file.

6. Click Export.

7. Select the export check boxes you want.

   ◆ Data (XML)

   ◆ Schema Of The Data (XSD)

   ◆ Presentation Of Your Data (XSL)

8. Click More Options.

9. Click the tabs (Data, Schema, and Presentation) with the export type you want, and then select the related options you want.

10. Click OK.

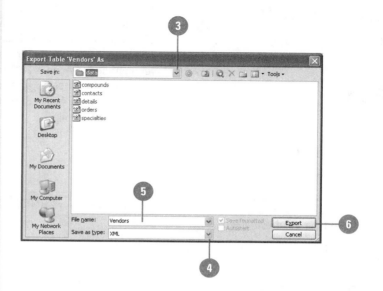

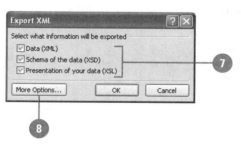

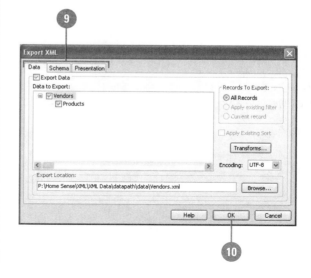

11

Exporting Data to Other Programs

AC03S-4-4

Export an Object to Another Program

① Open the database containing the object you want to export, and then select the database object.

② Click the File menu, and then click Export.

③ If necessary, click the Save In list arrow, and then select the drive and folder where you want to save the file.

④ Click the Save As Type list arrow, and then click the type of file you want to save the object as.

⑤ If necessary, type a new name for the file.

⑥ Click Export.

See Also

See "Exporting Database Objects to HTML" on page 217 and see "Exporting Database Objects to ASP Files" on page 218 for information on exporting data to the Web.

When you **export** Access data, you save a database object in a new format so that it can be opened in a different program. For example, you might export a table to an Excel worksheet. Or you might want to save your database as an earlier version of Access so someone who hasn't yet upgraded to Access 2003 can edit, format, and print it. You can also attach any database object to an e-mail message as an Excel (.xls), Rich Text Format (.rtf), Active Server Page (ASP), or Hypertext Markup Language (.html) file.

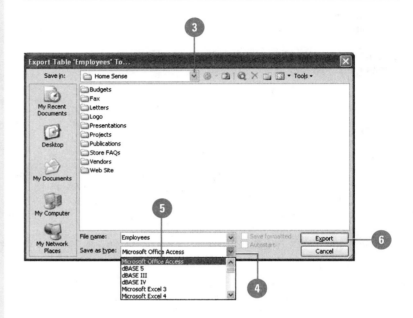

Attach a Database Object to an E-Mail Message

1. In the Database window, click the object you want to attach to an e-mail message.

2. Click the File menu, point to Send To, and then click Mail Recipient (As Attachment).

3. Click the file format you want.

4. Click OK.

5. Log on to your e-mail system if necessary, and then type your message.

   Access attaches the object to the message in the format you selected.

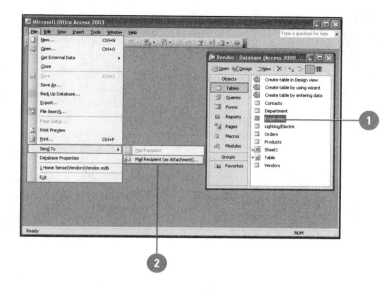

Did You Know?

You can attach part of an object to an e-mail message. Double-click the object in the Database window, select the portion you want to send, and then continue with step 2 of "Attach a Database Object to an E-Mail Message."

You can copy and paste Access data. If you want to place only part of an Access object in a file in another program, copy the information you want to insert, and then paste the information in the file where you want it to appear.

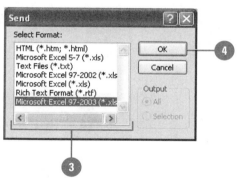

Database object in an Excel spreadsheet

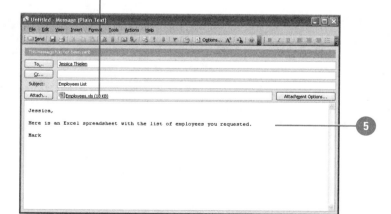

Merging Data with Word

AC03S-4-4

Access is a great program for storing and categorizing large amounts of information. You can combine, or **merge**, database records with Word documents to create tables or produce form letters and envelopes based on names, addresses, and other Access records. For example, you might create a form letter in Word and personalize it with an Access database of names and addresses. Word uses the Mail Merge task pane to step you through the process. Mail merge is the process of combining names and addresses stored in a data file with a main document (usually a form letter) to produce customized documents.

Insert Access Data into a Word Document

1. In the Database window, click the table or query that you want to insert in a Word document.

2. Click the OfficeLinks list arrow on the Database toolbar.

3. Click Merge It With Microsoft Office Word.

4. Click the linking option you want to use.

5. Click OK.

   If you selected the option for linking to an existing Word document, open the document.

6. In Word, follow the step-by-step instructions in the Mail Merge task pane to create a letter or mailing list using the data from Access.

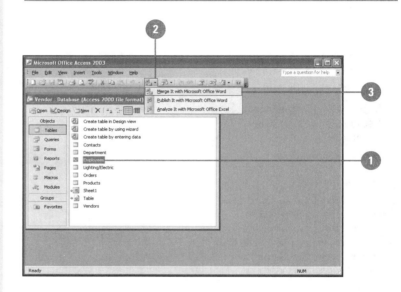

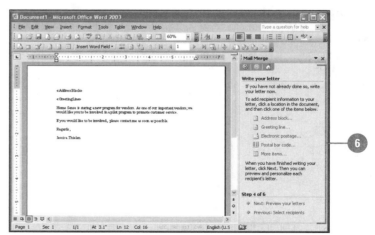

Create a Word Document from an Access Database

① In the Database window, click the table, query, report, or form that you want to save as a Word document.

② Click the OfficeLinks list arrow on the Database toolbar.

③ Click Publish It With Microsoft Office Word to save the data as a Rich Text Format file.

Word opens and displays the document.

④ Edit the document using Word commands and features.

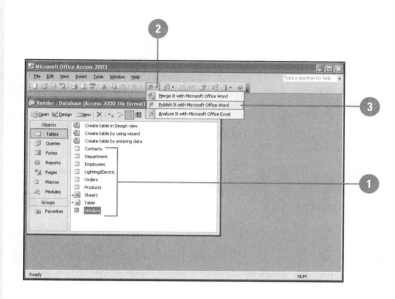

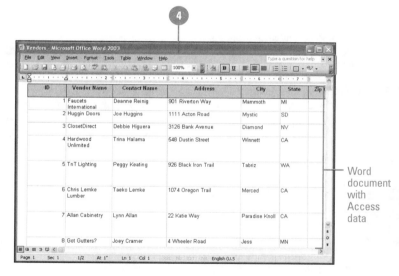

Word document with Access data

Analyzing Data in Excel

AC03S-4-4

Before you can analyze Access data in a workbook, you must convert it to an Excel file. You can either use the Analyze It With MS Excel command in Access to export data as an Excel table file or use the PivotTable And PivotChart Report wizard in Excel to use the Access data as a **PivotTable**, a table you can use to perform calculations with or rearrange large amounts of data. Once you determine what fields and criteria you want to use to summarize the data and how you want the resulting table to look, the wizard does the rest. You can also copy and paste or drag Access database objects (tables, queries, and so on) from the Database window to an Excel worksheet.

Export an Access Table into an Excel Workbook

1. In the Access Database window, click the table you want to analyze.

2. Click the OfficeLinks button on the Database toolbar.

3. Click Analyze It With Microsoft Office Excel to save the table as an Excel file, start Excel, and then open the workbook.

4. Use Excel commands to edit and analyze the data.

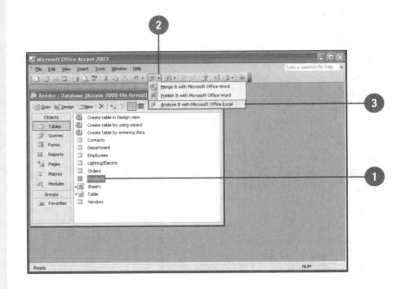

Create an Excel PivotTable from an Access Database

1. In Excel, click the Data menu, and then click PivotTable And PivotChart Report.

2. Click the External Data Source option button.

3. Click Next to continue.

4. Click Get Data, if necessary click Yes to install Microsoft Query, and then follow the wizard instructions to select the Access data.

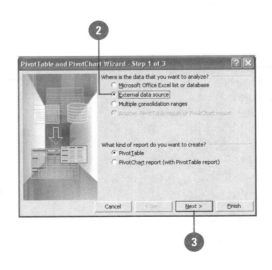

Managing a Database

Introduction

Once you're familiar with the basics of creating and using a database, you're ready to work with some of the more advanced features of Microsoft Office Access 2003 that can help you better manage your database. If you're working in a multi-user environment, where several people need access to the database, you need to explore ways of maintaining database security. Access provides several tools that help you control who can connect to your database and what a user can do once he or she is connected.

In addition to security issues, Access provides tools that help your database operate more efficiently. This includes the ability to compact your database file and to repair it if it is damaged. You can also use Access to analyze the design of your database and tables in order to improve performance and reliability.

Finally, if you're interested in making your database easier to use, Access provides a Switchboard Manager that can put a user-friendly face on your database. With a switchboard, new users can access database reports and forms with a single click of a button, and you can control what parts of the database you want users to be able to access.

What You'll Do

Secure a Database

Create and Join a Workgroup

Create User and Group Accounts

Activate User Logons

Set User and Group Permissions

Set Object Ownership

Set a Database Password

Encode a Database

Lock Database Records

Replicate and Back Up a Database

Compact and Repair a Database

Split, Document and Analyze a Database

Convert Access Databases

Use Add-Ins

Create a Database Switchboard

Manage a Switchboard

Create a Splash Screen

Setting Access Startup Options

Securing a Database

As long as you are the only one working with a database, security issues are not usually a big concern. However, in a multi-user environment, you will probably need to consider how to secure the information your database contains. There are many threats to your data's integrity. It needs to be protected from users accidentally deleting important records or reports. Some parts of your database, such as a table containing employee salaries and social security numbers, will need to be restricted to a select group of users. You may even need to devise ways to protect your database from being hacked by someone using special programs designed to view your most sensitive data. Access security features help you ensure that your data will be secure under almost all circumstances.

Creating and Using Workgroups

A **workgroup** is a group of users in a multi-user environment who share data. A company's workgroup might consist of all of its employees, and to a certain extent, its customers and shareholders. Access stores workgroup information in a special file called the **workgroup information file**, also known as the **system database**. Access created a default workgroup information file during its initial setup. The information is typically stored in the System.mdw file located in the *C:\Windows\System* folder. You have been using this workgroup file since the first day you started Access, even if you weren't aware of it.

If you need to support several different workgroups, such as when there are several different multi-user environments (employees, customers, and shareholders, for example) Office 2003 supplies a utility called the **Workgroup Administrator**, which allows you to create new workgroup information files. Even if you don't intend to support several workgroups, it is recommended that you replace the default workgroup information file with one of your own, because it is possible for unauthorized users to copy the default workgroup file and use it to gain access to your data.

If you do support several workgroups, you have to use the Workgroup Administrator to join the appropriate group before you start Access. As long as you're using only the default workgroup, you automatically joined the workgroup when you ran the Access Setup program and have remained joined to it since.

Working with User and Group Accounts

Access allows you to organize the users in a workgroup into **groups**. Each group might enjoy different privileges. Users in some groups might have the ability to add, edit and delete data; other user groups might be limited to viewing data. You can create workgroups and populate them with users. You can also specify the privileges for these groups or for individual users within a group. You can apply privileges to specific tables, queries, and reports or to whole databases. The list of users, groups and privileges also becomes part of the workgroup information file.

Using the Admins Group

Access, by default, creates the Admins group (short for Administrative), which is the group of users that have complete control over all database objects and the database itself. When you initially start Access, you are a member of the Admins group with the user name "Admin." As long as you are the sole user of your database, you are probably not even aware that you have such an account and are a member of such a group. Access keeps this feature hidden from you. However, if others will have access to your database, you may want to take steps to keep them from being given the same default privileges that you were given.

Activating Account Logons

To protect your data from other users acting as the Admin user, you have to specify a password for the Admin account. When you specify a password, you activate Access's logon procedure, requiring users to enter a user name and password before being able to start Access. You can then insert passwords for each individual account, requiring users to enter their own user name and password to start Access. User names and passwords are also stored in the workgroup information file.

You cannot assign a single user name and password to an entire group; each user must have a unique name and password. A user can create or change his or her own password; however, only the Admin user can clear a password if a user forgets it.

Assigning Ownership

Another Access security feature allows the **ownership** of the various tables, reports, forms, and databases. By default, the owner of an object is the account that created the object

(usually the Admin account). An account that owns a database object always has full privileges to edit or delete that object. An account that owns a database can always open the database. You can use the Admin account to assign ownership of these objects to various users and groups, even if they did not create the object themselves. In this way, you can prohibit certain users from accessing sensitive databases by assigning ownership to accounts not included in their workgroup information file.

Using Database Passwords

Access prompts for the user password once, when the user starts Access. After that, Access does not query the user again, unless you assign a **database password** to a specific database. In this case, all users must enter a password before gaining access to that database. Adding a database password is an easy way to keep unauthorized users out of sensitive material; however, once the user gains access to the database, you will still need to use the other security features to control the user's privileges and behavior in that database.

Employing Encoding

A final area where the security of your data could be compromised is unauthorized data retrieval with applications other than Access. By using specialized utility programs, or even word processors, a user can bypass Access's security features to view your sensitive material. If this is a concern, you can encrypt your data. When you encode a database file, Access makes it indecipherable to unauthorized viewing, especially during electronic transmission or when it's stored on a disk or tape. The encoding does not affect Access, however, except that it can slow performance by 10 to 15 percent.

12

Creating a Workgroup Information File

When you install Access, the Setup program automatically creates a workgroup information file for you. The workgroup is identified by the Workgroup ID (WID), a text string that the Setup program automatically creates based on your name and organization. Since this information can be determined by unauthorized users, you may want to create a new version of the workgroup information file, and with it a new WID, not so easily determined. Only someone who knows the WID will be able to create a copy of your workgroup information file and thus potentially gain access to Access's administrative accounts.

Create a Workgroup Information File

1. Open a database.

2. Click the Tools menu, point to Security, and then click Workgroup Administrator.

3. Click Create.

4. Type your name or the name of the Access database administrator.

5. Type the name of your organization.

6. Type any combination of up to 20 numbers and letters for the workgroup ID (keep this information in your records).

7. Click OK.

8. Type a new name and location for the new workgroup information file.

9. Click OK.

10. Click OK twice to confirm.

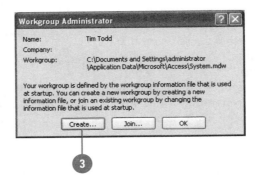

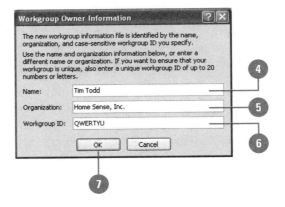

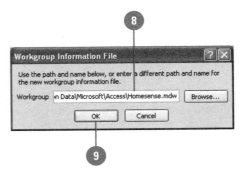

Joining a Workgroup

If you have several workgroup information files, you may have to choose which workgroup to join before starting Microsoft Access. You can do so with the same Workgroup Administrator program used to create new workgroup information files. Once you join a workgroup, Access uses that workgroup as the default group each time it starts—until you join a different group.

Join a Workgroup

① Open a database.

② Click the Tools menu, point to Security, and then click Workgroup Administrator.

③ Click Join.

④ Enter the location and filename of the workgroup information file for the workgroup you want to join.

⑤ Click OK.

⑥ Click OK to confirm the change.

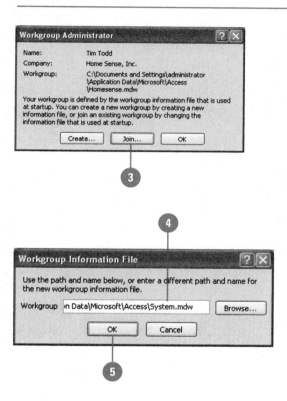

Did You Know?

You can use the Security Wizard. Create and join a workgroup using the Security Wizard within Access. To start the wizard, click Security on the Tools menu, and then click User-Level Security Wizard.

You can locate the Workgroup Administrator. If you cannot find the Workgroup Administrator, return to your Access Setup program and choose this option from the set of installation options.

12

Creating User and Group Accounts

If many users work on the same database or a database contains confidential information, you might want to restrict access to specific information for certain users. You can do this by setting up individual accounts for each user. If users share a common characteristic or job description (such as those in charge of entering personnel data), you may want to place them in a common group. Members of the same group would share the same rights and privileges within Access. Before you set up accounts, you are, by default, the Admin user in the Admin group. This gives you complete control over all databases.

Create a User Account

1. Click the Tools menu, point to Security, and then click User And Group Accounts.

2. Click the Users tab.

3. Click New.

4. Type a name for the new user.

5. Type a personal identifier.

6. Click OK.

7. Click OK.

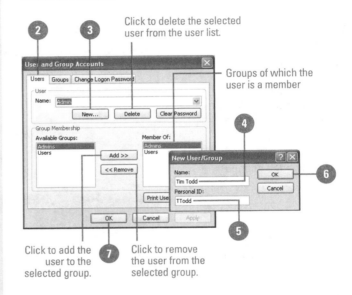

Click to delete the selected user from the user list.

Groups of which the user is a member

Click to add the user to the selected group.

Click to remove the user from the selected group.

Create a Group Account

1. Click the Tools menu, point to Security, and then click User And Group Accounts.

2. Click the Groups tab.

3. Click New.

4. Type a name for the new group.

5. Type a personal identifier.

6. Click OK.

7. Click OK.

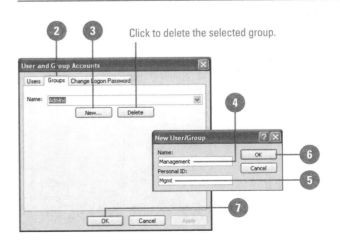

Click to delete the selected group.

Activating User Logons

Until you activate the logon procedure for a workgroup, Access automatically logs on all users in the Admin account, giving them complete control over all databases. You can force users to log on to Access by creating a nonblank password in the Admin account.

Activate the Logon Procedure

1. Start Access as the Admin user (the initial setting for Access).

2. Click the Tools menu, point to Security, and then click User And Group Accounts.

3. Click the Change Logon Password tab.

4. Verify that the current user is Admin.

5. Type a password.

   You do not need to type a password in the Old Password box, because until this moment, no password should have been defined for the Admin account.

6. Verify the password by retyping it in the Verify box.

7. Click OK.

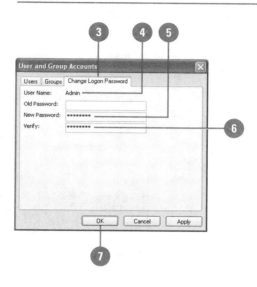

When you try to open a database, Access will prompt you for your name and password.

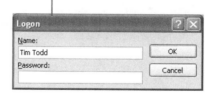

Did You Know?

You can add other user passwords. To create passwords for other users, log on as those users and create a password in the same way you created a password for the Admin account.

You can remove a password. If a user forgets his or her password, log on as Admin, and then click Clear Password, on the Users tab in the User And Group Accounts dialog box.

You can disable user logons. To disable user logons, remove the password for the Admin account.

Setting User and Group Permissions

Once you have defined users and groups, you will want to define permissions for them. **Permissions** indicate the ability of each user or group to modify databases or database objects. Permissions also control a user's ability to create new objects. For example, you might want to limit the ability to view the Salaries table to a small group of users, and limit the ability to edit that table to an even smaller group.

Change Account Permissions

1. Start Access, type **Admin** as the user name, press Tab, and then enter the password for the Admin account.

2. Click the Tools menu, point to Security, and then click User And Group Permissions.

3. Click the Permissions tab.

4. Click the Users option or the Groups option, depending on whether you want to modify the rights of individual users or entire groups.

5. Click the name of the person or group for whom you want to change permissions.

6. Click the Object Type list arrow, and then select an object type.

7. Click the name of an existing object or click <New Object>.

8. Select the applicable check boxes to add or remove permissions for the selected object.

9. Click Apply.

10. Click OK.

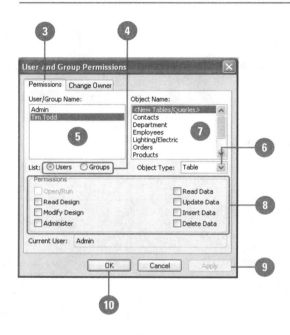

Select Permissions

◆ When you add or remove permissions for a selected object, refer to the Database Permissions table to the right.

Did You Know?

You can set personal identifiers for user accounts. Personal IDs contain between 4 and 20 letters (capitalization matters) or numbers or both. Along with the account name, a personal ID uniquely tags a user or group in a workgroup. Make sure you keep a copy of both the personal ID and account name in a secure location in case you need to retrieve an account that has been accidentally deleted or moved.

You can simplify user permissions. Instead of assigning permissions to each user, assign permissions to groups, and then add users to the appropriate groups.

You can print a list of permissions. Use the Documenter to print a report describing the permissions for each object in the database.

Database Permissions

Permission	Permits a User to	Applies
Open/run	Open a database, form, or report, or run a macro	Databases, forms, and macros
Open Exclusive	Open a database with exclusive access	Databases
Read Design	View objects in Design view	Tables, queries, forms, macros, and modules
Modify Design	View and change the design of objects, or delete them	Tables, queries, forms, macros, and modules
Administer	Have full access to objects and data, including the ability to assign permissions	Tables, queries, forms, macros, and modules
Read Data	View data	Tables and queries
Update Data	View and modify data	Tables and queries
Insert Data	View and insert data	Tables and queries
Delete Data	View and delete data	Tables and queries

12

Setting Object Ownership

By default, the Admin account owns all objects in a database (and the database itself). You can change the ownership of any object and assign the object to a specific user or group. The owner of an object has administrative-like powers. That individual can assign permissions for the object and thereby control who else can gain access to that object. However, the Admin account will also have full privileges to every object, regardless of ownership.

Set Ownership

1. Start Access, type **Admin** as the user name, press Tab, and then enter the password for the Admin account.

2. Click the Tools menu, point to Security, and then click User And Group Permissions.

3. Click the Change Owner tab.

4. Click the Object Type list arrow, and then select the type of object you want to own.

5. Click the specific object in the Object list.

6. Click whether you want to assign the object to a group or a specific user.

7. Click the New Owner list arrow, and then select the user or group you want.

8. Click Change Owner.

9. Click OK.

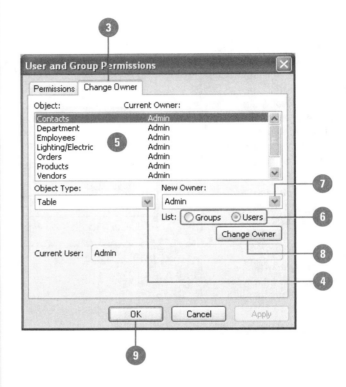

Setting a Database Password

If you want to provide extra security for a database, you can protect it by forcing users to enter a password before they can gain access to the database. This password is different from the account password used to log on to Access and applies to all users, even those with an Admin account. Don't lose or forget the password you assign to a database because it cannot be recovered. If you forget your password, you won't be able to open the database.

Set a Database Password

1. Make sure all users close the database, and then create a backup copy of the database.

2. Start Access, and then log on to an account with administrative permissions.

3. Click the File menu, and then click Open.

4. Select the database you want to use.

5. Click the Open list arrow, and then click Open Exclusive to open the database exclusive of all other users.

6. Click the Tools menu, point to Security, and then click Set Database Password.

7. Type a password.

8. Retype the password.

9. Click OK.

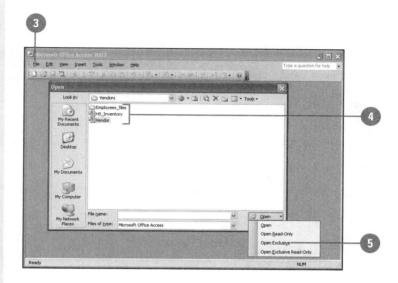

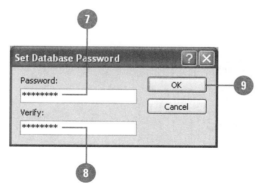

Did You Know?

You can remove a database password. Open the database in exclusive mode under an administrative account, click the Tools menu, click Security, and then click Unset Database Password. Enter the current password, and then click OK.

Encoding a Database

An unauthorized user could access your data by bypassing Access entirely. Special utility programs exist that allow users to retrieve data without going through Access. You can guard yourself from this problem by encoding your database. **Encoding** makes the database file indecipherable to these types of programs. Be aware, however, that encoding does not prohibit someone from using Access to open and read an encoded database file.

Encode a Database

1. Make sure all users close the database.

2. Click the Tools menu, point to Security, and then click Encode/Decode Database.

3. Locate and select the database file you want to encode.

4. Specify a name and location for the encoded version of your database file.

5. Click Save.

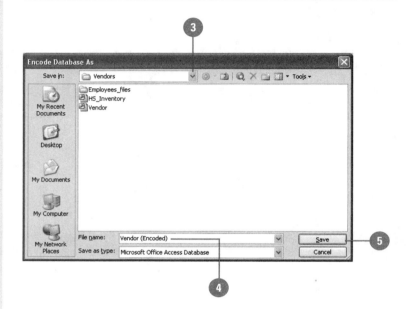

Did You Know?

You lose performance speed when you encode a database. An encoded database will perform 10 to 15 percent slower.

You can decode a database. Open the encoded database, click the Tools menu, point to Security, click Encode/Decode Database, and then either replace the encoded file or create a new, decoded version.

Locking Database Records

In a multi-user environment, several users could attempt to edit the same record simultaneously. Access prevents conflicts of this sort using **record locking**, ensuring that only one user at a time can edit data. You can also prevent conflicts by opening the database in **exclusive mode**, preventing all other users from accessing the database while you're using it. This technique is useful for administrators who need sole access to the system while making changes to the database itself.

Set Record Locking

1. Click the Tools menu, and then click Options.

2. Click the Advanced tab.

3. Indicate whether the default strategy for opening the database is shared (allowing simultaneous access by other users) or exclusive (keeping out other users).

4. Click the Default Record Locking strategy option you want to use.

5. Verify that the Open Databases Using Record-Level Locking check box is selected.

6. Click OK.

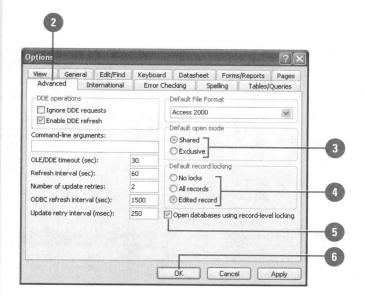

Record Locking Strategies

Locking Type	Description
No Locks	Access does not lock the record you're editing. When you save changes, Access gives you the option to overwrite another user's changes, copy your version to the clipboard, or discard your changes.
All Records	Access locks all records in the table for the entire time you have it open, so no one else can edit or lock the records.
Edited Record	Access locks the record you're currently editing and displays a locked record indicator to other users who may try to edit the record.

12

Replicating a Database

In some multi-user environments, users are scattered over a wide area, making it impossible for them to use the same database file. One method of providing access for these users is by **replicating** the database. The original database becomes the **Design Master**, and the other database files are **replicas**. You can add records to any of the database files, but you can only make structural changes (such as adding tables) to the Design Master. Periodically, you should synchronize each replica with the Design Master. This ensures that each file has the most current data and database design. If a conflict arises between the values entered in the databases, you can choose which values are correct.

Create a Replica

1 If necessary, remove the database password from the database.

2 Open the database in exclusive mode. In the Open dialog box, click the Open button list arrow, and then click Open Exclusive.

3 Click the Tools menu, point to Replication, and then click Create Replica.

4 Click Yes to close the database.

5 If necessary, click Yes to make a backup copy of the database.

6 Enter the name for the replica.

7 Specify the location where you want to save the replica.

8 Click OK.

9 Click OK to confirm the creation of the Design Master and the replica.

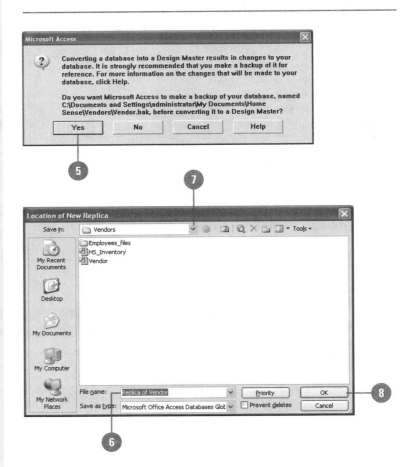

Update a Replica

1. Open the replica you want to update.

2. Click the Tools menu, point to Replication, and then click Synchronize Now.

3. Click the Directly With Replica option.

4. Enter the name and location of the Design Master, if necessary.

5. Click OK.

6. Click Yes to close and re-open the replica.

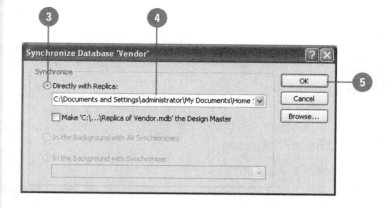

Backing Up a Database

 AC03S-4-5

Back up an Access Database

1. Save and close all objects in a database.

2. Click the File menu, and then click Back Up Database.

3. Click the Save-In list arrow to select a location for the back up copy.

4. Specify a different backup name.

5. Click Save.

It is vital that you make back up copies of your database on a regular basis so you don't lose valuable data if your computer encounters problems. Access makes it easy to create a back up copy of a database with the Back Up Database command, which works like the Save As command. When you make a back up copy of your database, save the file to a removable disk or network drive to make sure the file is safe if your computer encounters problems. If you need the back up copy of the database, you can use the Open button to restore and view your data.

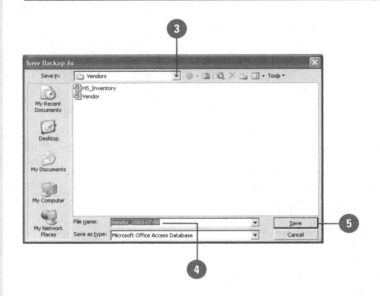

Compacting and Repairing a Database

AC03S-4-6

What do you do when your database starts acting erratically, or when even the simplest tasks cause Access to crash? Problems of this type can occur when a database gets corrupted or when the database file becomes too large. A database can become corrupted when, for example, Access suffers a system crash. Access can repair many of the problems associated with a corrupted database. The size of the database file may also be the trouble. When you delete objects such as forms and reports, Access does not reclaim the space they occupied. To use this space, you have to **compact** the database, allowing Access to rearrange the data, filling in the space left behind by the deleted objects.

Compact and Repair a Database

1. Make sure all users close the database.

2. Open the database with administrative privileges.

3. Click the Tools menu, and then point to Database Utilities.

4. Click Compact And Repair Database.

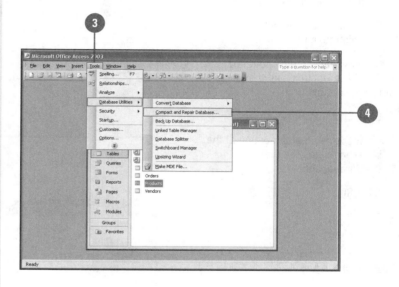

Splitting a Database

You can reduce the size of a database file by splitting the database. When Access **splits** a database, it places the tables in one file, called the **back-end database**, and the other database objects, like forms and reports, in the current database file. This technique stores all of the data in one location, while allowing each user to create his or her own forms and reports in his or her own database files.

Split a Database

1. Make sure all users close the database, and then close the switchboard, if necessary.

2. Open the database with administrative privileges.

3. Click the Tools menu, point to Database Utilities, and then click Database Splitter.

4. Click Split Database.

5. Enter the name and location of the back-end database that contains the database tables.

6. Click Split.

7. Click OK.

> ### Did You Know?
>
> **You can make a backup copy of your database.** It is a good idea to back up your database before compacting or splitting it. If an error occurs during either process and data is lost, you can retrieve data from your backup.

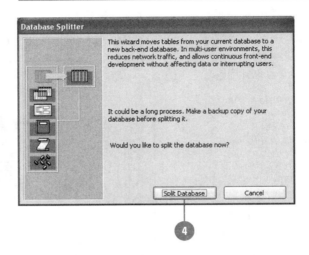

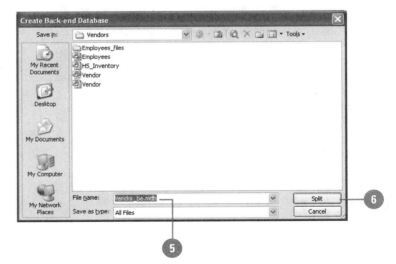

Documenting a Database

Complex databases can include many tables, forms, permissions, and user accounts. Access helps you keep tabs on all the elements in a database with the **Documenter** utility. You can use Documenter to print all the information about a database in a summary report.

Document a Database

1 Click the Tools menu, point to Analyze, and then click Documenter.

2 Click the All Object Types tab.

3 Select the check boxes for the objects you want to document.

4 Click Options.

5 Click the definitions you want to print for the selected object(s).

6 Click OK.

7 Click OK.

8 Check how many pages will print, and then click the Print button or the Print Preview button.

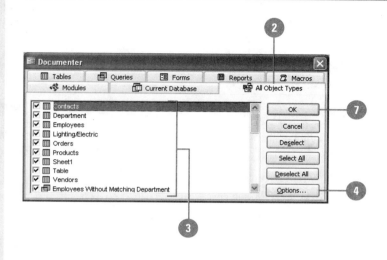

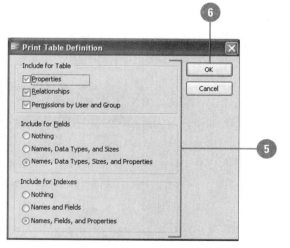

> ### Did You Know?
>
> **You can save the Documenter output.**
> To save the summary report created by the Documenter, click the File menu, and then click Export. Access will then export the report to a Word file, Excel worksheet, or another format.

Analyzing a Database

From time to time, you should analyze your database to ensure that it works as efficiently as possible. Begin by running the **Performance Analyzer**, which provides ways to organize your database optimally and helps you make any necessary adjustments. Whenever you determine that several fields in a table store duplicate information, run the **Table Analyzer** to help you split the data into related tables (a process called **normalization**), but leave the original table intact.

Optimize Database Performance

1. Open the database you want to analyze.

2. Click the Tools menu, point to Analyze, and then click Performance.

3. Click the All Object Types tab.

4. Select the check boxes for the objects whose performance you want to analyze.

5. Click OK.

   If the Performance Analyzer has suggestions for improving the selected object(s), it displays them in its analysis results.

6. Click each item, and then review its analysis notes.

7. Press and hold Ctrl, and then click the suggested optimizations you want Access to perform.

8. Click Optimize.

9. Click Close.

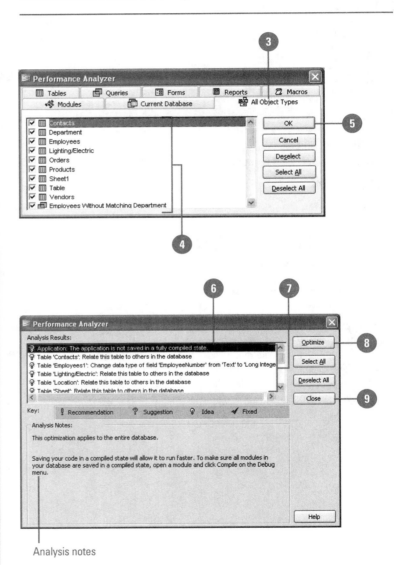

Analysis notes

Analyze the Design of Your Tables

1. With your database open, click the Tools menu, point to Analyze, and then click Table.

2. If an explanation screen for the Table Analyzer Wizard opens, read it, click Next to continue, and then read the second explanation screen. Click Next to continue.

3. Click the table you want to analyze. Click Next to continue.

4. Click the option for letting the wizard decide which fields to place in which tables. Click Next to continue.

5. Continue following the wizard instructions for naming the new tables, specifying the primary key for the new tables, and so on.

6. Click Finish, or click Cancel if the wizard recommends not to split the table.

Did You Know?

You can apply performance Analyzer results. The Performance Analyzer returns recommendations, suggestions, and ideas. You should have Access perform the recommended optimizations. Suggested optimizations have potential tradeoffs, and you should review the possible outcomes in the Analysis Notes box before having Access perform them. You can perform idea optimizations manually by following the instructions in the Analysis Notes box.

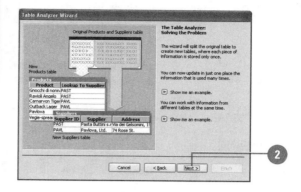

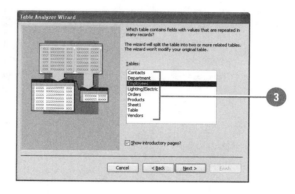

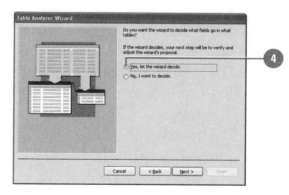

12

Converting Access Databases

In a multi-user environment, you may need to support users that run different versions of Access, or you may need to upgrade older databases to Access 2003. When you open a database from a previous Access version, Access 2003 prompts you to either upgrade the database file or open it without upgrading. You can also convert a database to the previous Access format.

Set Default Access File Format

1. Click the Tools menu, and then click Options.

2. Click the Advanced tab.

3. Click the Default File Format list arrow, and then click a format.

4. Click OK.

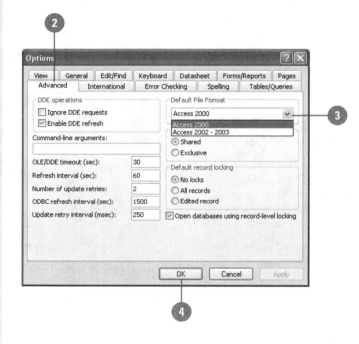

Convert a Database to Another Version of Access

1. Click the Tools menu, point to Database Utilities, and then point to Convert Database.

2. Click the command with the version in which you want to convert the database.

3. Enter the name for the converted database.

4. If necessary, click the Save In list arrow, and then select the drive and folder where you want to save the database.

5. Click Save.

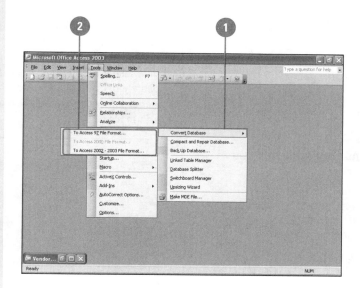

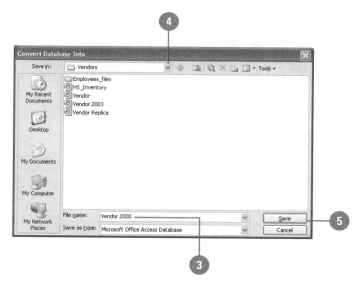

12

Using Add-Ins

Add-ins are additional programs, designed to run seamlessly within Access. Some add-ins are installed when you run the Access Setup program, while others can be purchased from third-party vendors. One of these add-ins is the Switchboard add-in, used to create and manage database switchboards. Another add-in, the Linked Table Manager, helps users work with linked tables in their database. To work with add-ins, Access provides the **Add-In Manager**, a utility to install and remove your add-in files.

Install and Uninstall Add-Ins

1. Open a database.

2. Click the Tools menu, point to Add-Ins, and then click Add-In Manager.

3. Click Add New, and then locate and open the add-in you want to install.

4. Double-click the available add-in you want install.

5. Click any installed add-in you want to remove, and then click Uninstall.

6. Click Close.

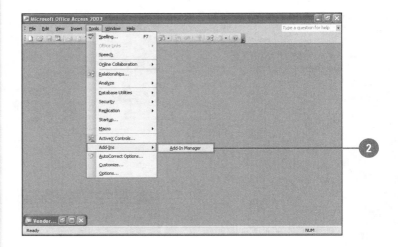

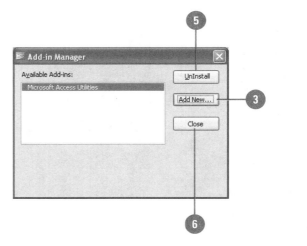

Creating a Database Switchboard

Switchboards are forms that provide easy access to many of your database's features. With a properly designed switchboard, your database users can display forms, print reports, and run macros with a single click of an action button. You can even hide all the other features of Access, making your switchboard the only thing the users see when interacting with your database. To help you create a switchboard, Access provides the Switchboard Manager add-in. The Switchboard Manager makes it easier to create new switchboards or edit the content of existing switchboards.

Create a Switchboard

1. Click the Tools menu, point to Database Utilities, and then click Switchboard Manager.

2. Click Yes when you are asked to create a switchboard.

3. Click Edit to edit the content of the switchboard's main page.

4. Type a name for the main page.

5. Click New to add an action button to the page.

6. Enter text for the button.

7. Click the Command list arrow, and then select a command.

8. Click the Report list arrow, and then select a form, report, macro, switchboard or function name.

9. Click OK.

10. Repeat steps 5 through 9 to add additional action buttons to the switchboard.

11. Click Close.

12. Click Close.

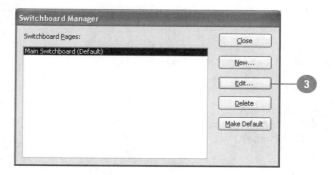

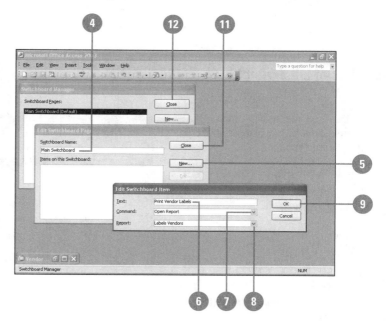

Managing a Switchboard

After you create a switchboard, you can edit it using the same Switchboard Manager command you used to create it in the first place. In your revisions, you may want to add extra pages to the switchboard or delete action buttons you've previously created. You can also edit action buttons so that they perform new tasks. The switchboard can thereby grow and change as your database changes.

Add a Switchboard Page

1. Click the Tools menu, point to Database Utilities, and then click Switchboard Manager.

2. Click New.

3. Type a name for the new page.

4. Click OK.

5. Select the new page from the Switchboard Pages list, and then click Edit to edit the page's content.

6. Click Close to close the Switchboard Manager.

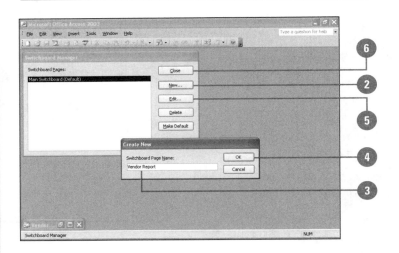

Define the Default Switchboard Page

1. Click the Tools menu, point to Database Utilities, and then click Switchboard Manager.

2. Select the page that you want to act as the default.

3. Click Make Default.

4. Click Close.

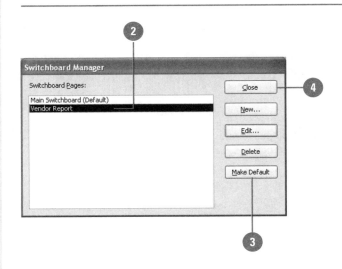

> **Did You Know?**
>
> *You can edit the switchboard design.* To edit your switchboard's design, open the switchboard form in Design view.

Creating a Splash Screen

In Access, you can create a splash screen—the initial screen that appears when you start a program—by creating a form or data access page and adding the pictures and text that you want to display on database startup. You can might also want to add a Close button to the form or data access page to let the user close it. You specify the name of the form or data access page in the Startup dialog box, so that Access opens it automatically each time the database is opened. Changes to the Startup dialog box take effect the next time you start the Access database.

Display a Form or Data Access Page at Startup

1. If necessary, create a splash screen in a form.

2. Click the Tools menu, and then click Startup.

3. Click the Display Form/Page list arrow, and then click the form or page you want to use at startup.

4. Click OK.

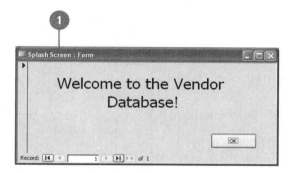

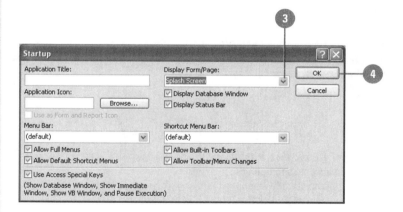

Did You Know?

You can ignore startup options. To bypass startup options in the Startup dialog box, hold down the Bypass key (the Shift key) while you open the database. If you encounter security messages, continue to hold down the Bypass key until you have closed the security messages.

See Also

See "Setting Access Startup Options" on page 274 for more information on startup options.

12

Setting Access Startup Options

You can use startup options to specify how an Access database opens. For example, you can specify what form or data access page to display, whether users can customize toolbars, and whether shortcut menus are available. You can also use a special macro named AutoExec to carry out one or more actions. When you open a database, Access looks for a macro named AutoExec. If Access finds the AutoExec macro, it automatically runs it.

Change Startup Options

1. Click the Tools menu, and then click Startup.

2. Type a title for the application database.

3. Select the form/page options you want.

4. Select the menu bar and shortcut options you want.

5. Click OK.

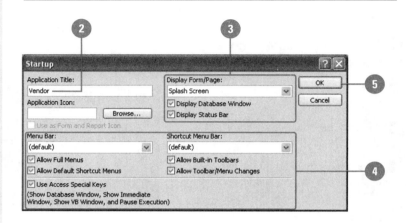

See Also

See "Creating a Macro" on page 284 for information on creating a macro named AutoExec for startup purposes.

Did You Know?

You can open a switchboard automatically. To cause Access to open the switchboard automatically whenever the database is opened, click the Tools menu, click Startup, click the Display Form/Page list arrow, and then click Switchboard.

Customizing Access

Introduction

There are several ways you can customize Microsoft Office Access 2003 to meet your needs and the needs of those who will use the databases you create. You can:

◆ Edit Access's menus and toolbars, adding new commands and subtracting unused ones

◆ Create new menus and toolbars

◆ Design a complete custom application with menu bars and toolbars tailored to a specific database

Access also allows you to create macros, stored collections of actions that perform a specific task. Macros allow you to create new commands designed to work with a particular database. You can attach macros to menus, toolbars, and form controls. You can write a macro so that it executes its actions only if a particular condition is met.

If you have a microphone installed on your computer, you can use the Office Language bar to dictate text directly into your database and also to control buttons, menus, and toolbar functions by using the Voice Command option. For those of you with an electronic stylus, an ink device, or a handwriting tablet, such as Tablet PC attached to your computer, you can can insert handwritten text into an Access database.

What You'll Do

Add and Remove Toolbar Buttons

Customize a Toolbar

Customize the Menu Bar

Edit Toolbar Buttons and Menu Entries

Learn About Macros

Create a Macro

Run and Test a Macro

Create Macro Groups

Create Conditional Macros

Assign a Macro to a Button

Assign a Macro to an Event

Create a Message Box

Control Access with your Voice

Execute Voice Commands

Dictate Text

Recognize Handwriting

Use Multiple Languages

Adding and Removing Toolbar Buttons

Each toolbar initially appears in a default configuration, but many toolbars actually contain many more commands than are displayed. When monitors are set to low resolution, sometimes not all toolbar buttons are visible. You can modify Access's toolbars so that they display only the buttons you want. For example, you can add buttons to a toolbar for commands you frequently use, or you can remove buttons from toolbars that have too many. You can use the Add Or Remove command on the Toolbar Options menu to quickly show or hide buttons on a toolbar. If a button doesn't appear on the button list for a toolbar, you can add it. If you no longer need a button on the button list, you can remove it.

Show or Hide a Toolbar Button

1. Click the Toolbar Options list arrow on the toolbar.

2. Point to Add Or Remove Buttons.

3. Click to select or clear the check box next to the button you want to show or hide.

4. Click outside the toolbar to deselect it.

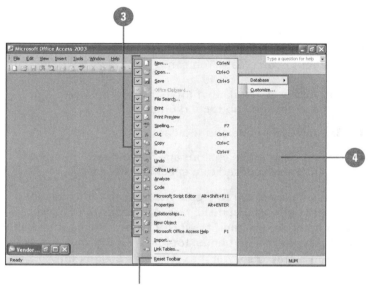

Click to reset the toolbar to its default state.

Add or Remove a Toolbar Button

① Click the Tools menu, and then click Customize.

② Click the Commands tab.

③ Click the category containing the toolbar button you want to add.

④ Drag a command from the Commands tab to the toolbar to add a button, or drag a button off a toolbar to a blank area to remove it.

⑤ Click Close.

Did You Know?

You can set options for toolbars and menus. To set some general options for toolbars and menus, click the Tools menu, click Customize, click the Options tab, select the options you want, and then click OK.

A solid vertical line appears to the right of where the new button will be inserted.

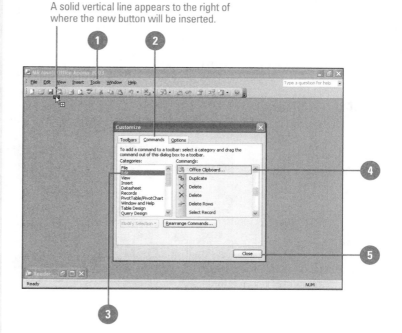

Customizing a Toolbar

You can create your own toolbars to increase your efficiency. You might, for example, create a toolbar that contains macros and other features that you use most often when you are performing a particular task, such as editing records in a table. You can change the properties of an existing Access toolbar or one that you create using the Customize dialog box, which allows you to control the toolbar's placement.

Create a New Toolbar

1. Click the Tools menu, and then click Customize.

2. Click the Toolbars tab.

3. Click New.

4. Type a name for the new toolbar.

5. Click OK.

6. Add buttons to the new toolbar by dragging commands found on the Commands tab.

7. Click Close.

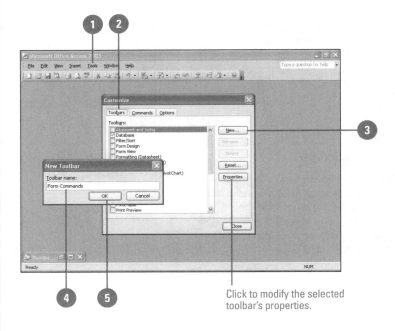

Click to modify the selected toolbar's properties.

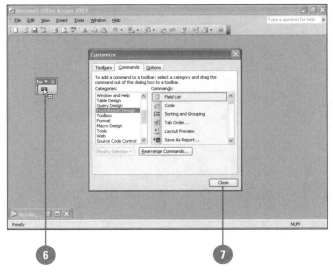

Change a Toolbar's Properties

1. Click the View menu, and then click Customize.

2. Click the Toolbars tab.

3. Select the toolbar from the list.

4. Click the Properties button.

5. Modify the toolbar properties.

6. Click Close.

Did You Know?

The Undo button does not undo when you are customizing a toolbar.
Remember not to click the Undo button while you are customizing a toolbar. Rather than reversing the last change, clicking the Undo button selects the button so you can copy or move it.

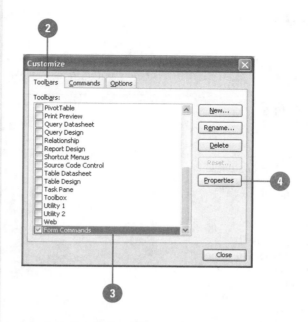

Customizing the Menu Bar

You can customize the existing Access menu bar by adding buttons, commands, and macros that you use frequently. Adding items to the menu bar is a great way to have easy access to features without adding more buttons or toolbars. The ability to drag features from different parts of the program window makes it easy to add items to the menu bar.

Add or Remove a Menu Command

1 Click the View menu, point to Toolbars, and then click Customize.

2 Click the Commands tab.

3 Select a category.

4 To add a button, drag the command to the appropriate place on the menu you want to modify. A solid horizontal line appears below the place where the new menu command will be placed.

5 To remove a button, drag the menu command you want to remove to an empty area in the database workspace.

6 Click Close.

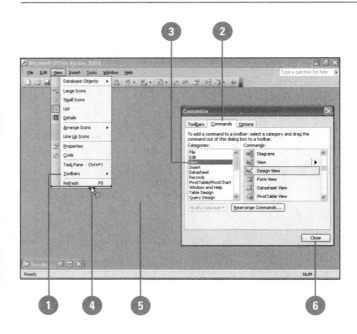

Did You Know?

You can assign an accelerator key to a menu. An accelerator key is the key you press to display a menu or run a menu command. For example, the accelerator key for the File menu is "F." To add an accelerator key to a menu item, type an ampersand (&) before the letter that will be the accelerator key. For example, enter the menu name "&New Menu" to create the menu entry New Menu with the accelerator key "N."

Create a New Menu

1. Click the View menu, point to Toolbars, click Customize, and then click the Commands tab.

2. Click New Menu in the Categories box.

3. Drag New Menu from the Commands list to an empty spot on the menu bar.

4. Click Close.

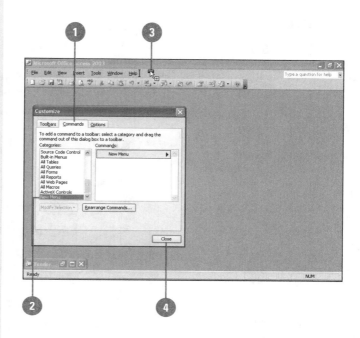

Name a New Menu

1. Click the View menu, point to Toolbars, click Customize.

2. Click New Menu on the menu bar.

3. Click Modify Selection.

4. Click the Name box, and then type a new name.

5. Press Enter.

6. Click Close.

Did You Know?

You can copy a command to toolbars and menus. Copy commands from other menus or toolbars to new menus and toolbars by pressing and holding Ctrl as you drag the new command.

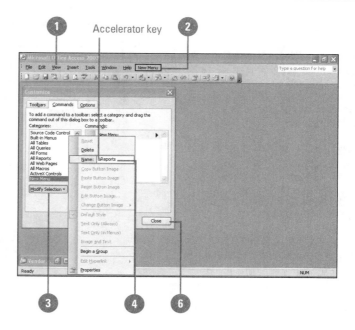

Accelerator key

Editing Toolbar Buttons and Menu Entries

Access includes tools that allow you to edit toolbar buttons and menu entries. You can specify whether the button or menu item will display text, an image, or both text and an image. If you choose to display an image, you can edit the image, copy it from another button or use one of Access's predefined images. You can use the Customize dialog box to makes these and other changes to your buttons and menus.

Edit a Button or Menu Entry

1. Click the View menu, point to Toolbars, and then click Customize.

2. Select the button on the toolbar or command on the menu you want to edit.

3. Click Modify Selection.

4. Choose the commands that will modify the selection in the way you prefer.

   ◆ Click Copy Button Image to copy the button image.

   ◆ Click Paste Button Image to paste the button image.

   ◆ Click Reset Button Image to reset the selected item to its default image.

   ◆ Click Edit Button Image to edit the button image.

   ◆ Click Change Button Image to select from a group of predefined images, as shown.

   ◆ Click Image And Text to paste a button image into the selected item.

   ◆ Click Begin A Group to begin a group of menu items, separated by horizontal lines.

5. Click Close.

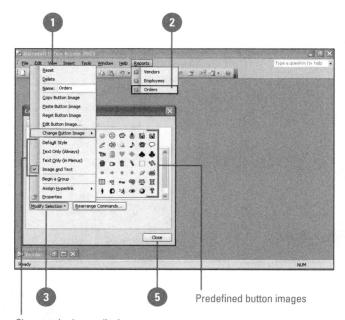

Choose whether to display text, an image, or both text and image.

Predefined button images

Learning About Macros

A **macro** is a stored collection of actions that perform a particular task, such as opening a specific form and report at the same time or printing a group of reports. You can create macros to automate a repetitive or complex task or to automate a series of tasks. Using a macro to automate repetitive tasks guarantees consistency and minimizes errors caused when you forget a step. Using a macro can also protect you from unnecessary complexity. You can perform multiple tasks with a single button or keystroke. For whatever reason you create them, macros can dramatically increase your productivity when working with your database.

Macros consist of actions or commands that are needed to complete the operation you want to automate. Sorting, querying, and printing are examples of **actions**. **Arguments** are additional pieces of information required to carry out an individual action. For example, an Open Table macro action would require arguments that identify the name of the table you want to open, the view in which to display the table, and the kinds of changes a user would be able to make in this table. Because there are no wizards to help you make a macro, you create a macro by entering actions and arguments directly in Design view. After creating a macro, make sure you save your work and give the macro a meaningful name.

Actions that make up the macro

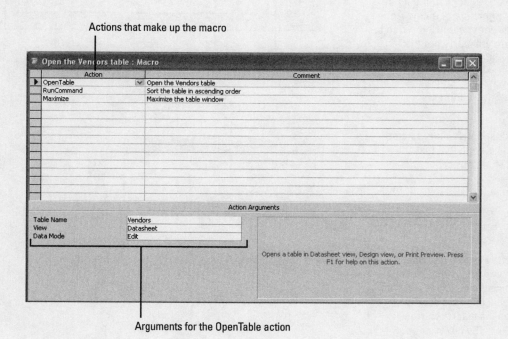

Arguments for the OpenTable action

Creating a Macro

Before you begin creating a macro, you should plan the actions required to complete the tasks you want to automate. Practice the steps needed to carry out the operation and write them down as you go. Finally, test your written instructions by performing each of the steps yourself.

Create and Save a Macro

1. In the Database window, click Macros on the Objects bar.

2. Click the New button.

3. Click the Action list arrow, click the action you want to use, and then press Tab.

4. Type a comment if you want to explain the action.

5. Click the table name in the first Action Arguments box, click the list arrow, and then select a value.

6. To add more actions to the macro, click the right side of a new Action row, and repeat steps 2 through 5. The macro will carry out the actions in the order in which you list them.

7. Click the Save button on the toolbar.

8. Enter a descriptive macro name that helps identify the tasks the macro carries out.

9. Click OK.

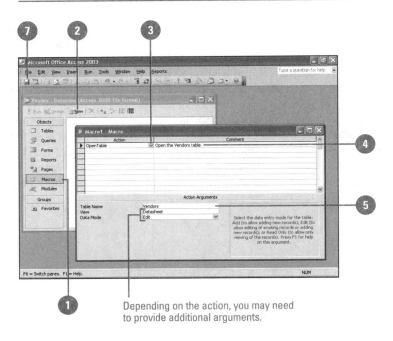

Depending on the action, you may need to provide additional arguments.

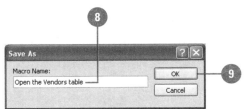

Did You Know?

You can create a macro that runs when an Access file opens. Create a macro containing the actions you want to run when you open the database, and then save the macro with the name AutoExec. The next time you open the database, the macro runs.

Edit an Existing Macro

1. In the Database window, click Macros on the Objects bar.

2. Click the macro you want to edit.

3. Click the Design button.

4. Change the actions and arguments you want.

   ◆ To insert a new action, click the Insert Rows button on the Macro Design toolbar.

   ◆ To remove an action, select the action row, and then click the Delete Rows button.

5. Click the Save button on the toolbar.

6. When you're done, click the Close button.

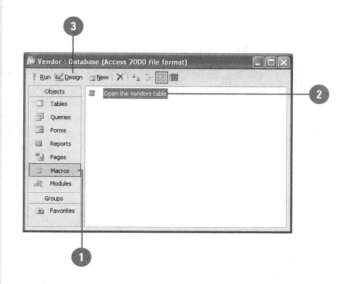

Did You Know?

You can create a new macro based on an existing one. Open the macro in Macro Design view, and then click the Save As command on the File menu. Give the macro a new name, and then modify the new macro as needed.

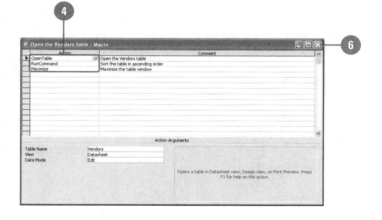

Running and Testing a Macro

To have a macro perform its actions, you must run it, or instruct it to execute its actions. There are two ways to run a macro. You can have the macro perform all the steps in a sequence at once, or you can test a macro by running it to perform one step at a time, allowing you to review the results of each step. By testing your macro, you might discover that it did not perform all its tasks in the way you expected. If so, you can make changes and retest the macro as you continue to make adjustments in Macro Design view. Keep in mind that a macro will perform only the actions that are appropriate in the currently active view, so be sure to display the correct view before you run the macro; you can have the first action in the macro display the view in which you want to run the macro.

Run a Macro in a Sequence

1. Display the macro you want to run in Macro Design view.

   If your macro does not automatically switch you to the correct view, switch to the view in which you want to run the macro.

2. Click the Run button on the Macro Design toolbar.

   If the macro encounters an action it cannot perform, a message box appears, indicating a problem.

3. If necessary, click OK to close the message box.

4. Click Halt to stop the macro.

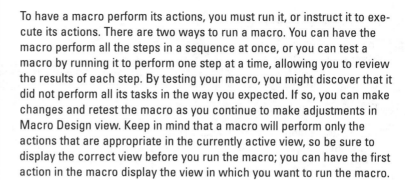

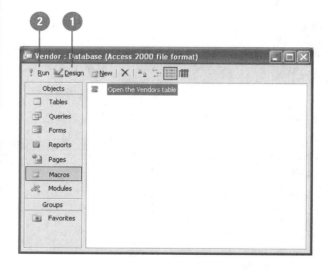

Did You Know?

You can run a macro from the Database window. In the Database window, click the Macros tab, and then double-click the name of the macro you want to run.

You can place a macro on a toolbar. If you want to place a macro on the toolbar, click the Tools menu, click Customize, click the Commands tab, choose the All Macros category, drag the macro you want to the toolbar, and then click OK.

Test a Macro Step-by-Step

1. Display the macro you want to run in Macro Design view.

2. Click the Single Step button on the Macro Design toolbar.

   If necessary, switch to the view in which you want to run the macro.

3. Click the Run button on the toolbar.

   If the Run button does not appear, click the Tools menu, click a macro, click Run Macro, click the Macro Name list arrow, and then double-click the macro you want to run, and then click OK.

4. Click Step to perform the first action in the macro.

5. Repeat step 4 until the macro finishes.

   If the macro encounters an action it cannot perform, you see a message box stating the action it could not carry out.

6. Click OK to close the message box.

7. Click Halt to stop the macro.

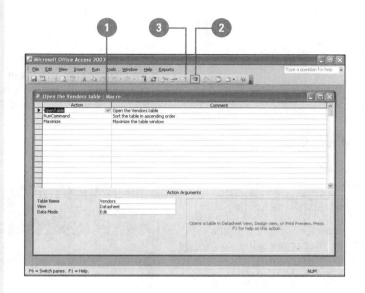

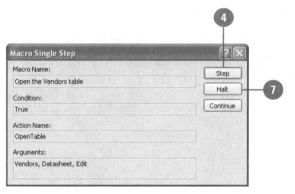

Did You Know?

You can stop the macro before it finishes. In the Macro Single Step dialog box, click Halt.

You can run all steps in a macro. If the Single Step button on the Macro Design toolbar is active, you can still run all the steps in the macro without stopping. In the Macro Single Step dialog box, click Continue.

Creating Macro Groups

If you have numerous macros, grouping related macros in macro groups can help you to manage them more easily. When Access runs a macro group, the first macro in the group starts with the first action, continuing until it reaches a new macro name or the last action in the window. To run a macro group, use the macro group name followed by the macro name. For example, you can refer to a macro group named *Report1* in the *Employees* macro as *Report1.Employees*.

Create a Macro Group

1 Open a macro in the Macro window.

2 Click the Macro Names button.

3 Type a name for the macro group next to the first action in the Macro Name column.

4 Click the Save button to save your changes.

5 Click the Close button.

Did You Know?

You can display the Macro Name column. Display the Macro Name column by clicking Macro Names on the View menu.

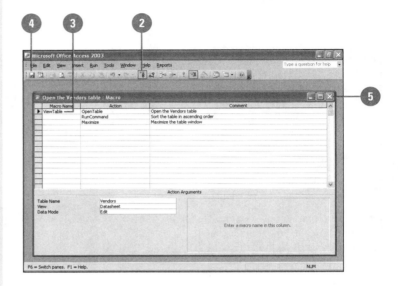

Creating Conditional Macros

Sometimes you may want a macro to run only if some prior condition is met. For example, you could create a macro that prints a report only if the number of records to print is greater than zero. You can do this by creating a **conditional expression**, an expression that Access evaluates as true or false. If the condition is true, Access carries out the actions in the macro or macro group.

Create a Macro Condition

1. Open a macro in the Macro window.

2. Click the Conditions button on the Macro Design toolbar.

3. Click the Build button on the Macro Design toolbar to open the Expression Builder.

4. Enter an expression that Access could evaluate as either true or false.

5. Click OK.

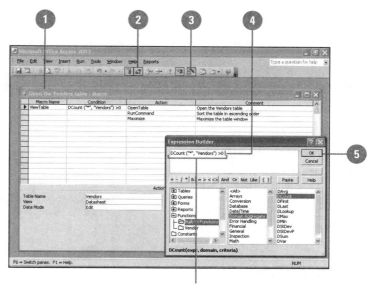

Check whether the number of records in the Customers table is greater than zero.

Assigning a Macro to a Button

Database designers often attach macros to form controls, particularly buttons, so that when a user clicks the button, the macro is activated. If you create a button, you can use the Command Button Wizard to specify the action that will occur when the button is clicked. If you want to assign a macro to a button, you choose the action of running the macro.

Assign a Macro to a Button

1. In Design view for a form, click the Command Button tool on the Toolbox.

2. Click the Control Wizards button on the Toolbox.

3. Drag the image onto the form, report, or page.

4. Click Miscellaneous.

5. Click Run Macro and then click Next.

6. Choose the macro you want to run, and then click Next.

Select the Control Wizards button to display the Command Button Wizard.

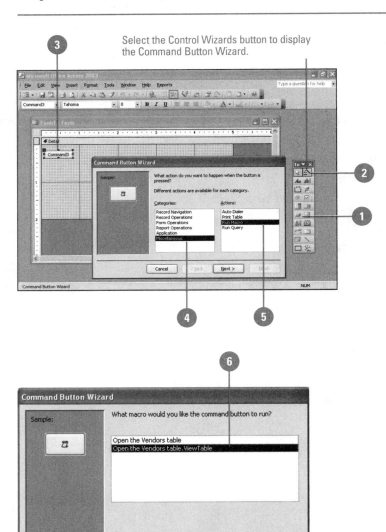

7 Specify the text or image that will appear on the button, and then click Next.

8 Enter a name for the command button control, and then click Finish.

9 Save the form or report, and then test the button to verify that your macro runs when the button is clicked.

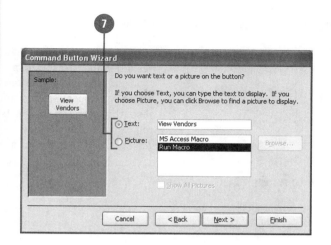

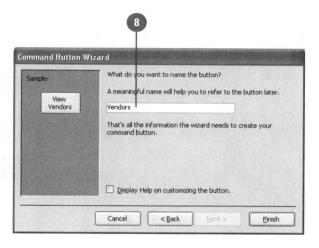

13

Assigning a Macro to an Event

An **event** is a specific action that occurs on or with a certain object. Clicking a button is an event, called the Click event. The Click event in this case occurs on the button object. Other events include the Dbl Click event (for double-clicking) and the On Enter event, which occurs, for example, when a user "enters" a field by clicking it. If you want to run a macro in response to an event, you have to work in the object's property sheet. The property sheet lists all of the events applicable to the object. You can choose the event and then specify the macro that will run when it occurs, or create a new macro in the Macro window.

Assign a Macro to an Event

1. In Design view, double-click the object in which the event will occur.

2. Click the Event tab.

3. Click the box for the event you want to use.

4. Click the list arrow, and then click the macro you want to use.

5. Click the Close button on the Properties window.

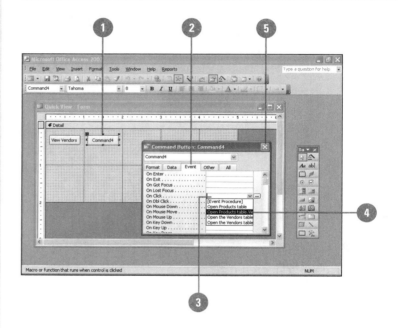

Create a New Macro for an Event

1. In Design view, double-click the object.

2. Click the Event tab.

3. Click the specific event to which you want to assign the macro.

4. Click the Build button.

5. Click Macro Builder.

6. Click OK.

7. Enter a name for the new macro, and then click OK.

8. Enter the actions for the new macro, and then close the Macro window.

9. Click the Close button on the Properties window.

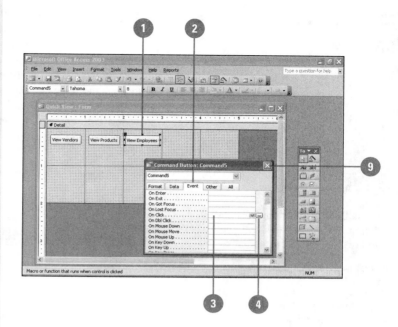

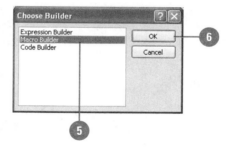

Creating a Message Box

When you create a macro, you may want to give database users information about how the macro works as it runs. You can create message boxes for your macros that, for example, ask the user if he or she wants to proceed. You do this with the MsgBox action. The MsgBox action allows you to specify the text of the message, whether or not a beep sounds when the box is displayed, the type of box that appears, and the box's title. Access supports five different types of message boxes. Each one has a different icon. The icons convey the importance of the message box, ranging from merely being informative to indicating a serious error.

Create a Message Box

1. In the Database window, display the macro in Design view to which you want to add a message box.

2. Click in an action box, and then type **MsgBox**.

3. Specify the text you want contained in the message box.

4. Indicate whether a beep will accompany the message.

5. Specify the box type.

   ◆ Critical

   ◆ Warning?

   ◆ Warning!

   ◆ Information

   ◆ None

6. Enter the box title.

7. When you're done, click the Close button.

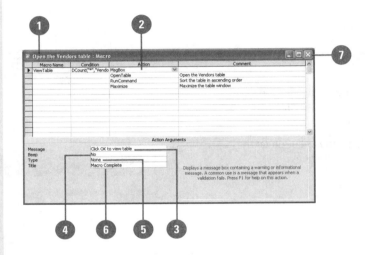

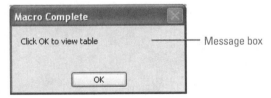

Message box

Controlling Access with your Voice

The Office Language bar allows you to dictate text directly into your database and also to control buttons, menus, and toolbar functions by using the Voice Command option. When you first install an Office program, the Language bar appears at the top of your screen. If you are using English as a default language, the toolbar is denoted by the letters EN. (Other languages have appropriate abbreviations as well.) Before you can use speech recognition, you need to install it first. You can choose the Speech command on the Tools menu, or you can use Add Or Remove Programs in the Control Panel to change the Office 2003 installation. Before you can use the Language bar for either dictation or voice commands, you need to connect a microphone to your computer, and you must train your computer to your voice using the Speech Recognition Wizard.

Work with the Language Bar

◆ **Open.** Right-click a blank area on the taskbar, point to Toolbars, and then click Language Bar.

◆ **Minimize.** Right-click the Language bar, and then click Minimize. The Language bar docks in the taskbar at the bottom right of the screen, near the system clock.

◆ **Restore.** Right-click the Language bar, and then click Restore The Language Bar.

◆ **Display or hide option buttons.** Click the Options button (the list arrow at the right end of the toolbar), and then click an option to display or hide.

◆ **Change speech properties.** Click the Speech Tools button, and then click Options.

◆ **Change Language Bar properties.** Click the Options button (the list arrow at the right end of the toolbar), and then click Settings.

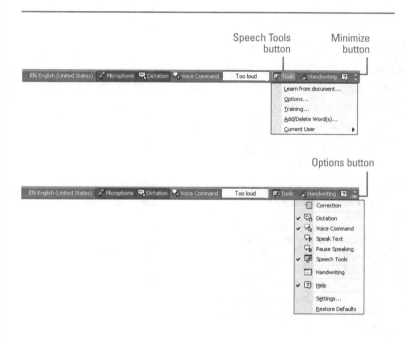

Executing Voice Commands

The two modes, Dictation and Voice Command, are mutually exclusive of one another. You do not want the word File typed, for example, when you are trying to open the File menu. Neither do you want the menu to open instead of the word File being typed when you are in the middle of a sentence. As such, you must manually click either mode on the Language bar to switch between them. The Voice Command mode allows you to talk your way through any sequence of menus or toolbar commands, simply by reading aloud the appropriate text instead of clicking it. For example, if you wanted to print mailing labels from a report, you would simply open the report and say File, Print, All, OK (without saying the commas between the words as written here). You need not worry about remembering every command sequence because as you say each word in the sequence, the corresponding menu or submenu appears onscreen for your reference.

Execute Voice Commands

① If necessary, display the Language bar.

② Click the Microphone button on the Language bar. The toolbar expands so that the Voice Command button becomes available on the toolbar.

③ Click the Voice Command button to shift into that mode.

④ Work with your Access database normally. When you are ready to issue a command, simply speak the sequence just as you would click through it if you were using the menus or toolbar normally (i.e. with the mouse or via keyboard shortcuts).

Say "File" to display the menu.

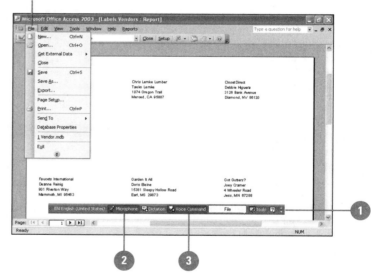

Did You Know?

You can have text read back to you.
Display the Speak Text button on the Language bar. Select the text you want read back to you, and then click Speak Text.

Dictating Text

Dictating text in an Access database using Office speech recognition functions may be easier for some users than typing, but don't think that it is an entirely hands free operation. For example, you must manually click the Voice Command button when you want to format anything that has been input, and then click again on Dictation to resume inputting text. Additionally, the Dictation function is not going to be 100% accurate, so you will need to clean up mistakes (such as inputting the word *Noir* when you say *or*) when they occur. Finally, although you can say punctuation marks, such as comma and period, to have them accurately reflected in the database, all periods are followed by double spaces (which may not be consistent with the formatting you want between sentences) and issues of capitalization remain as well.

Dictate Text

1. Display the Language bar, if necessary.

2. Click the Microphone button on the Language bar. The toolbar expands so that the Dictation button becomes available on the toolbar.

3. Click to position the insertion point inside the Access database where you want the dictated text to appear, and then begin speaking normally into your microphone. As you speak, the words will appear on the page.

4. When you have finished dictating your text, click the Microphone button again to make the speech recognition functions inactive.

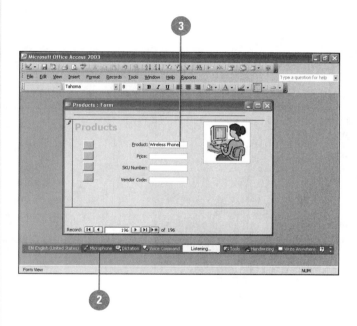

Recognizing Handwriting

Although entering information through the keyboard is fast and efficient, you may find that you need to enter information in handwritten form. Office provides handwriting recognition to help you convert handwriting into text. Before you can insert handwritten text into an Access database, you need to have a mouse, a third party electronic stylus, an ink device, or a handwriting tablet, such as Tablet PC, attached to your computer. Although you can use the mouse, for best results you should use a handwriting input device. When you insert handwritten text into a database that already contains typed text, the handwritten text is converted to typed text and then inserted in line with the existing text at the point of the cursor. The program recognizes the handwriting when there is enough text for it to do so, when you reach the end of the line, or if you pause for approximately two seconds. In addition, the converted text will take on the same typeface attributes as the existing text.

Insert Handwritten Text

1. Display the Language bar, if necessary.

2. Click the Handwriting button on the Language bar, and then click Write Anywhere.

3. Move the mouse over a blank area of your database, and then write your text.

    After recognition, the characters that you write appear as text in the Access database.

4. Use the additional handwriting tools to move the cursor, change handwriting modes, and correct text.

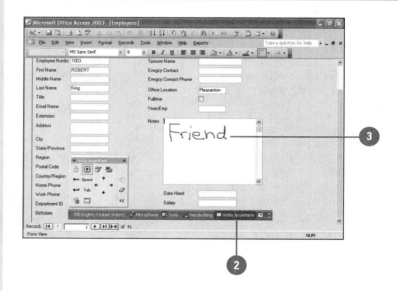

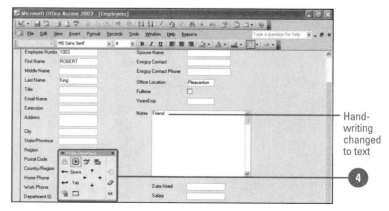

Handwriting changed to text

Insert Handwritten Text on a Writing Pad

1. Display the Language bar, if necessary.

2. Click the Handwriting button on the Language bar, and then click Writing Pad.

3. Move the cursor over the writing area of the Writing Pad dialog box. (The cursor turns into a pen.)

4. Write your text with the pen.

   After recognition, the characters that you write appear in the Access database.

5. Use the additional handwriting tools to move the cursor, change handwriting modes, and correct text.

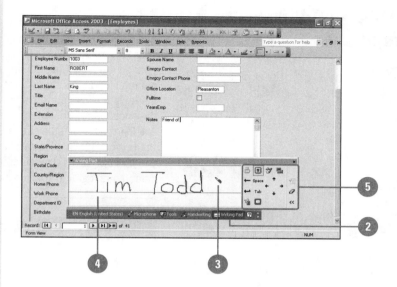

For Your Information

Using Additional Handwriting Tools

When you click the Handwriting button on the Language bar and then click the Writing Pad or Write Anywhere option, a dialog box opens on your screen with another toolbar. It has the same options that are available through the Handwriting button on the Language bar. In addition, the toolbar has the following buttons: Ink, Text, Backspace, Space, directional cursors, Enter, Tab, Recognize Now, and Write Anywhere. You use these buttons to control the input.

Using Multiple Languages

If you work with information that contains text in more than one language, you can use the Office 2003 multi-language features to edit in additional languages. You might need to modify your computer, including your keyboard layout, to do so. International Microsoft Office users can change the language that appears on their screens by changing the default language settings. Users around the world can enter, display, and edit text in all supported languages, including European languages, Japanese, Chinese, Korean, Hebrew, and Arabic, just to name a few. You'll probably be able to use Office programs in your native language. If the text in your Access database is written in more than one language, you can automatically detect languages or designate the language of selected text so the spelling checker uses the right dictionary.

Add a Language to Office Programs

1. Click Start on the taskbar, point to All Programs, point to Microsoft Office, point to Microsoft Office Tools, and then click Microsoft Office 2003 Language Settings.

2. Select the language you want to enable.

3. Click Add.

4. Click OK, and then click Yes to quit and restart Office.

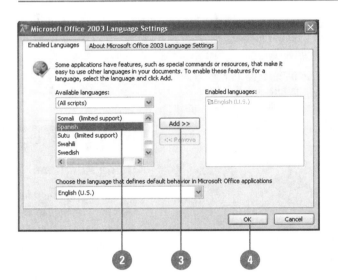

Did You Know?

You can check your keyboard layout.
After you enable editing for another language, such as Hebrew, Cyrillic, or Greek, you might need to install the correct keyboard layout so you can enter characters for that language. In the Control Panel, double-click the Regional And Language icon, click the Language tab, and then click Details to check your keyboard.

Enhancing a Database with Programming

14

Introduction

If you want to create customized Microsoft Office Access 2003 applications, you'll need to learn how to work with the Microsoft Office 2003 programming language, **Microsoft Visual Basic for Applications**, or **VBA**. VBA is more powerful and more flexible than Access macros, and you can use it in all major Office applications.

To create a VBA application, you have to learn VBA conventions and syntax. Access provides extensive online Help available to assist you in this task. Office 2003 makes VBA more user-friendly by providing the Visual Basic Editor, an application that includes several tools to help you write error-free VBA applications.

With VBA you can create applications that run when the user initially opens a database, or you can link applications to buttons, text boxes, or other controls. You can even use VBA to create your own custom functions, supplementing Access's library of built-in functions.

VBA may be a difficult language for the new user, but its benefits make the effort of learning it worthwhile.

What You'll Do

Enhance a Database with VBA

Create a Standard Module

Understand Parts of the Visual Basic Editor

Create a Sub Procedure

Write VBA Commands

Run a Sub Procedure

Copy Commands from the Object Browser

Create a Custom Function

Run a Custom Function

Create a Class Module for a Form or Report

Set Project Properties

Debug a Procedure

Identify VBA Debugging Tools

Optimize Performance with an MDE File

Enhancing a Database with VBA

Office 2003 applications like Access, Excel, and Word share a common programming language: VBA. With VBA, you can develop applications that combine tools from these Office 2003 products, as well as other programs that support VBA. Because of the language's power and flexibility, programmers often prefer to use VBA over Access macros to customize their Access applications.

Introducing the Structure of VBA

VBA is an **object-oriented** programming language because, when you develop a VBA application, you manipulate objects. An object can be anything within your database, such as a table, query, or a database. Even Access itself is considered an object. Objects can have properties that describe the object's characteristics. Text boxes, for example, have the Font property, which describes the font Access uses to display the text. A text box also has properties that indicate whether the text is bold or italic.

Objects also have methods, actions that can be done to the object. Deleting and inserting are examples of methods available with a record object. Closely related to methods are events. An **event** is a specific action that occurs on or with an object. Clicking a form button initiates the Click event for the button object. VBA also refers to an event associated with an object as an event property. The form button, for example, has the Click event property. You can use VBA to either respond to an event or to initiate an event.

Writing VBA Code

Unlike Access macros, which are created in the Macro Design window, the VBA programmer types the statements, or **code**, that make up the VBA program. Those statements follow a set of rules, called **syntax**, that govern how commands are formulated. For example, to change the property of a particular object, the command follows the general form:

    Object.Property = Expression

where **Object** is the name of a VBA object, **Property** is the name of a property that object has, and **Expression** is a value that will be assigned to the property. The following statement sets the Caption property of the Departments form:

    Forms!Departments.Caption="Department Form"

You can use Access's online Help to learn about specific object and property names. If you want to apply a method to an object, the syntax is:

    Object.Method arg1, arg2, ...

where **Object** is the name of a VBA object, **Method** is the name of method that can be applied to that object, and **arg1, arg2**, ... are optional **arguments** that provide additional information for the method operation. For example, to move to page 2 of a multipage form, you could use the GoToPage method as follows:

    Forms!Departments.GoToPage 2

Working with Procedures

You don't run VBA commands individually. Instead they are organized into groups of commands called **procedures**. A procedure either performs an action or calculates a value. Procedures that perform actions are called **Sub procedures**. You can run a Sub procedure directly, or Access can run it for you in response to an event, such as clicking a button or opening a form. A Sub procedure initiated by an event is also called an **event procedure**. Access provides event procedure templates to help you easily create procedures for common events. Event procedures are displayed in each object's event properties list.

A procedure that calculates a value is called a **function procedure**. By creating function procedures you can create your own function library, supplementing the Access collection of built-in functions. You can access these functions from within the Expression Builder, making it easy for them to be used over and over again.

Working with Modules

Procedures are collected and organized within **modules**. Modules generally belong to two types: class modules and standard modules. A **class module** is associated with a specific object. For example, each form or report can have its own class module, called a **form module** or **report module**. In more advanced VBA programs, the class module can be associated with an object created by the user. **Standard modules** are not associated with specific objects, and they can be run from anywhere within a database. This is usually not the case with class modules. Standard modules are listed in the Database window on the Modules Object list.

Building VBA Projects

A collection of modules is further organized into a **project**. Usually a project has the same name as a database. You can create projects that are not tied into any specific databases, saving them as Access add-ins that provide extra functionality to Access.

Using the Visual Basic Editor

You create VBA commands, procedures, and modules in Office's **Visual Basic Editor**. This is the same editor used by Excel, Word, and other Office applications. Thus, you can apply what you learn about creating programs in Access to these other applications.

The Project Explorer

One of the fundamental tools in the Visual Basic Editor is the Project Explorer. The **Project Explorer** presents a hierarchical view of all of the projects and modules currently open in Access, including standard and class modules.

The Modules Window

You write all of your VBA code in the **Modules** window. The Modules window acts as a basic text editor, but it includes several tools to help you write error-free codes. Access also provides hints as you write your code to help you avoid syntax errors.

The Object Browser

There are hundreds of objects available to you. Each object has a myriad of properties, methods, and events. Trying to keep track of all of them is daunting, but the Visual Basic Editor supplies the **Object Browser**, which helps you examine the complete collection of objects, properties, and methods available for a given object.

14

Creating a Standard Module

Create a New Standard Module

1. In the Database window, click Modules on the Objects bar.

2. Click the New button.

   Access starts the Visual Basic Editor, opening a new module window.

Did You Know?

You can open the Visual Basic Editor. You can open the Visual Basic Editor directly by pressing and holding Alt while you press F11. You can also toggle back and forth between Access and the Visual Basic Editor by pressing and holding Alt while you press F11.

All standard modules in a database are listed in the Modules section of the database window. You can open a module for editing or create a new module. When you edit a module or design a new one, Access automatically starts the Visual Basic Editor.

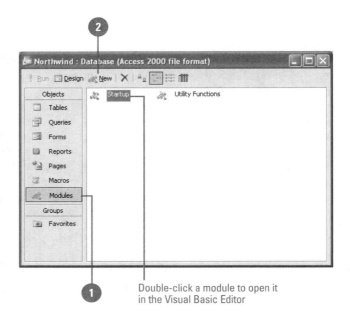

Double-click a module to open it in the Visual Basic Editor

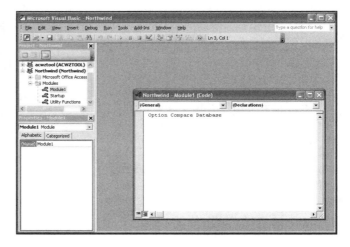

Understanding Parts of the Visual Basic Editor

The Project Explorer displays a hierarchical list of all open projects and modules.

The Modules window allows you to enter VBA commands.

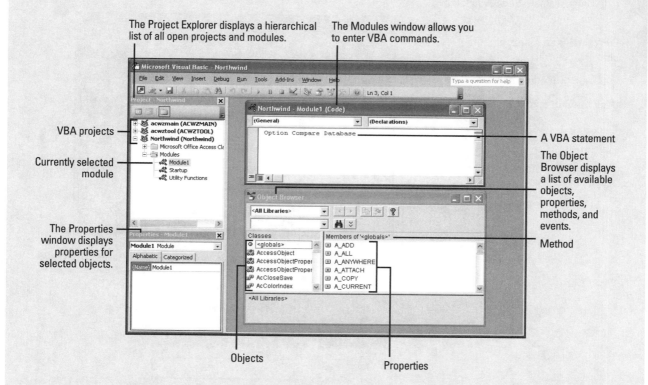

VBA projects

Currently selected module

The Properties window displays properties for selected objects.

A VBA statement

The Object Browser displays a list of available objects, properties, methods, and events.

Method

Objects

Properties

Creating a Sub Procedure

You can either type a Sub procedure directly into the Modules window, or the Visual Basic Editor can insert it for you. Sub procedures all begin with the line: Sub ProcedureName( ) where *ProcedureName* is the name of the Sub procedure. If the Sub procedure includes arguments, enter them between the opening and closing parentheses. Not every Sub procedure requires arguments. After entering the first line, which names the procedure, you can insert the procedure's VBA commands. Each Sub procedure ends with the line: End Sub

Create a Sub Procedure

1 In the Visual Basic Editor, click the Module window to select it.

2 Click the Insert menu, and then click Procedure.

3 Enter the procedure's name.

4 Click the Sub option, if necessary.

5 Click OK.

The Editor inserts the opening and closing lines of the new Sub procedure.

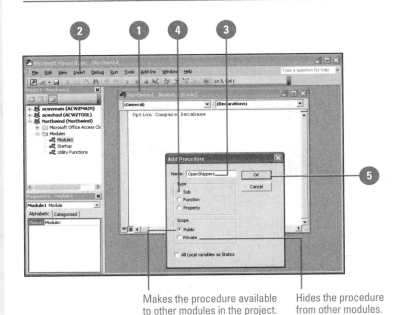

Makes the procedure available to other modules in the project.

Hides the procedure from other modules.

Indicates the Sub procedure is available to other modules.

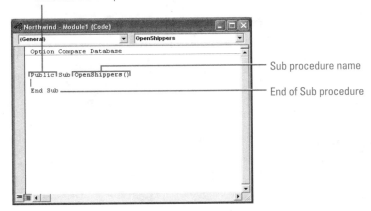

Sub procedure name

End of Sub procedure

Writing VBA Commands

You insert VBA commands by typing them into the appropriate place in the Module window. This, of course, requires some knowledge of VBA. Access provides online Help to assist you in writing VBA code. The Visual Basic Editor also helps you with hints that help you complete a command accurately. If you have entered a command incorrectly, the Editor notifies you of the error and may suggest ways of correcting the problem. One of the most useful VBA objects you'll encounter in writing VBA code is the *DoCmd* object, which represents Access commands. You can use DoCmd in your commands to perform basic operations, like opening tables, reports, and forms.

Write a VBA Command to Open a Table

① Click the Modules window to activate it.

② Click a blank line after the Sub *ProcedureName* command in the Modules window.

③ Type **DoCmd.** Make sure you include the period.

④ Double-click OpenTable in the list box that appears, and then press the Spacebar.

⑤ As indicated by the hints supplied by the Editor, type the name of a table from the current database. Make sure you enclose the name in quotation marks.

⑥ Type a comma.

⑦ Double-click acViewNormal to open the table in Normal view.

⑧ Type a comma.

⑨ Double-click acReadOnly to open the table in Read-only mode.

⑩ Press Enter to add a new blank line below the command.

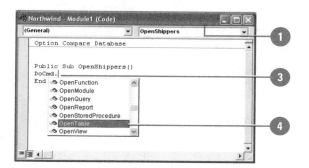

As you type the VBA command, the Editor displays the correct syntax. Optional arguments are enclosed in square brackets [ ].

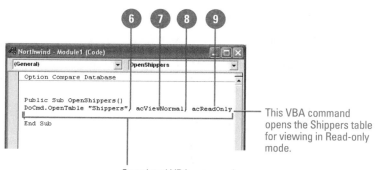

This VBA command opens the Shippers table for viewing in Read-only mode.

Completed VBA command

Running a Sub Procedure

After writing a Sub procedure, you may want to test it. You can run a Sub procedure from within the Visual Basic Editor, but you might have to return to Access to view the results. If the Sub procedure is a long one, you can also click buttons to pause it or to stop it altogether.

Run a Sub Procedure

1. Click the Save button on the Database toolbar to save changes to the VBA project.

2. Enter a name for your module if requested.

3. Click anywhere within the Sub procedure that you want to run.

4. Click the Run Sub/User Form button on the Database toolbar.

   If the Macros dialog box appears, select the macro you want to run, and then click Run.

5. Return to Access, if necessary, to view the results of your Sub procedure.

Did You Know?

You can rename a module. If you want to rename a module, select the module from the Project Explorer, and then enter a new name in the Name box, located in the Properties window.

You can run a procedure from the keyboard. You can also run a Sub procedure by pressing F5. If you need to halt the procedure, press the Ctrl and the Break keys simultaneously.

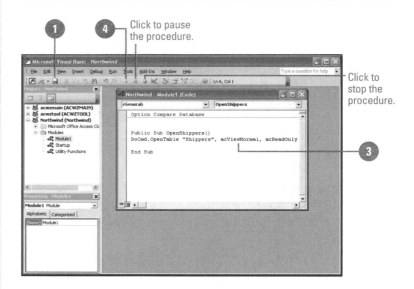

Click to pause the procedure.

Click to stop the procedure.

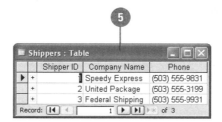

Copying Commands from the Object Browser

The Object Browser displays a hierarchical list of all of the objects, properties, methods, and events available to VBA procedures. The browser organizes these different objects into *libraries*. The list of libraries is not limited to those built into Access itself. It also includes libraries from other Access projects and add-ins. You can use the Object Browser as a reference tool, or you can copy and paste commands from the browser directly into your Sub procedures.

Insert an Object from the Object Browser

1. In the Visual Basic Editor, click the Object Browser button to display the Object Browser.

2. Click the Libraries list arrow, and then select the library that contains your object.

3. Select the object you want to insert.

4. Click the Copy button.

5. Return to the Sub procedure in the Modules window.

6. Click the location in the Sub procedure where you want to paste the object name.

7. Click the Paste button on the toolbar.

> ### Did You Know?
>
> **You can search for objects.** The Object Browser contains a search tool that helps you locate an object's name.

Enter a search string for an object, property, method, or event.

2 Click to search for an object, property, method, or event.

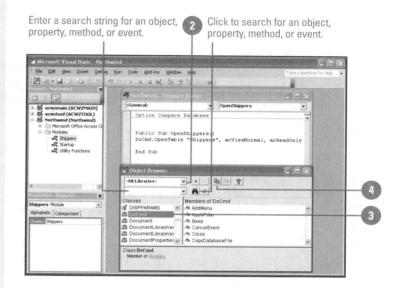

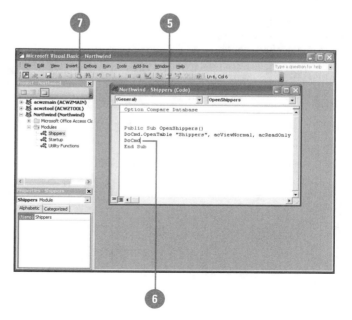

Creating a Custom Function

In addition to Sub procedures, you can also create function procedures that Access uses as custom functions. Each function procedure begins with the line: FunctionName( ) where *FunctionName* is the name of the function procedure. Within the parentheses, place any variables needed for the calculation of the function. You can learn more about variables from Access's online Help. After statement of the function's name and variables, add VBA commands to calculate the result of the function. The function concludes with the End Function line.

Create a Custom Function

1. In the Visual Basic Editor, open a Modules window, click the Insert menu, and then click Procedure.

2. Enter the function's name.

3. Click the Function option.

4. Click OK.

   The Editor inserts the opening and closing lines of your new custom function.

5. Enter variable names needed for the function.

6. Enter VBA commands required to calculate the function's value.

7. Insert a line assigning the calculated value to a variable with the same name as the function.

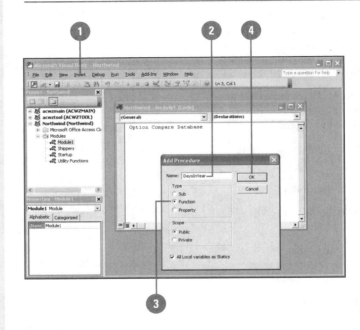

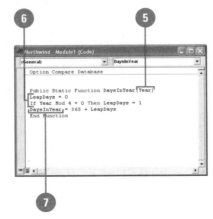

Running a Custom Function

Once you've completed a custom function, you can use it in any Access query, report, or form. The easiest way to access the function is through the Expression Builder. After you open the Expression Builder, you can access the custom function using the Functions folder.

Run a Custom Function

1. Open Expression Builder from any query, report, or form.

2. Double-click the Functions folder.

3. Double-click the name of the project containing your custom function (usually the name of the current database).

4. Click the module containing the custom function.

5. Double-click the name of the custom function.

6. Edit the function, replacing the variable names within the parentheses with the appropriate field names or constants.

7. Click OK.

8. Test your query, form, or report to verify the values returned by the custom function.

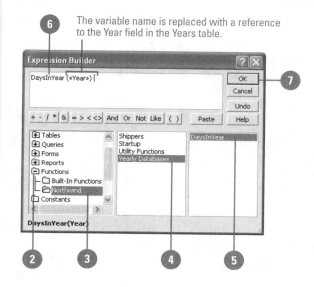

6 The variable name is replaced with a reference to the Year field in the Years table.

Did You Know?

You can save a module. Save changes to your module before using a customized function. Otherwise, the function will not appear in the Expression Builder.

Creating a Class Module for a Form or Report

Similar to the standard modules that you create, you can also create class modules with the Visual Basic Editor. You usually begin a class module in Design view for a form or report. In most cases, class modules are associated with events such as clicking a form button or opening the form. Unlike standard modules, class modules do not appear in the Modules Object list in the Database window. Instead, you can access them from within the Project Explorer.

Create a Class Module for a Form or Report

① Display a form or report in Design view.

② Click the control or object within the form or report in which you want to create a class module, and then click the Properties button on the toolbar.

③ Click the Event tab.

④ Click the event box that you want to associate with a VBA procedure.

⑤ Click the Build button.

⑥ Click Code Builder.

⑦ Click OK.

The Visual Basic Editor opens a Modules window and automatically creates an Event procedure for the control and event you selected.

⑧ Enter the VBA commands you want.

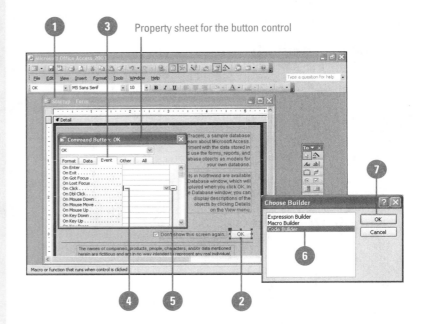

Property sheet for the button control

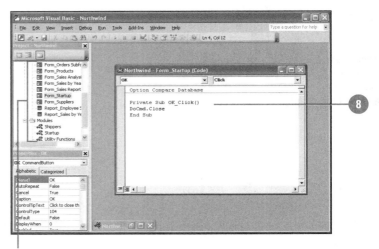

The Project Explorer lists all of the form and report modules, as well as other class modules.

Setting Project Properties

By default, Access assigns the same name to the project containing your VBA modules and procedures as your database's name. You can change the project's name to make it more descriptive. You can also password-protect your VBA project to keep other users from accessing and changing your procedures.

Set Project Properties

① Open the Visual Basic Editor by pressing and holding Alt while pressing F11.

② Select your project from the list of projects in Project Explorer.

③ Click the Tools menu, and then click *ProjectName* Properties, where *ProjectName* is the current name of your project.

④ Click the General tab.

⑤ Enter a new name for your project, if necessary.

⑥ Enter a description of your VBA project.

⑦ Click the Protection tab.

⑧ Click the Lock Project For Viewing check box if you want to keep others from viewing your project's source code.

⑨ Enter a password to unlock the project for viewing.

⑩ Confirm the unlocking password.

⑪ Click OK.

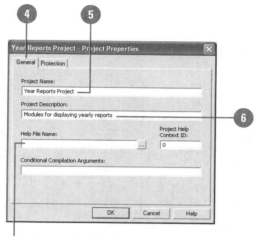

If you've created a Help file for your project, enter the name and location here.

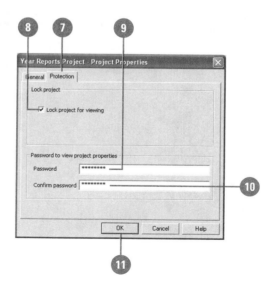

Did You Know?

You need to remember your project password. Save your password. If you lose it, you will not be able to open your code to edit it later.

Debugging a Procedure

The Visual Basic Editor provides several tools to help you write error-free code. However, sometimes a procedure does not act the way you expect it to. To deal with this problem, you can use the Editor's debugging tools to help you locate the source of the trouble. One the most common approaches to debug failed code is to "walk through" the procedure step by step, examining each thing the procedure does. In this way, you can try to locate the exact statement that is causing you trouble.

Stepping Through a Procedure

1. Click the View menu, point to Toolbars, and then click Debug.

2. Click the first line of the procedure you want to debug.

3. Click the Step Into button on the Debug toolbar to run the current statement and then to move to the next line in the procedure.

4. Continue clicking the Step Into button to move through the procedure one line at a time, examining the results of the procedure as you go.

5. Click the Stop button on the Debug toolbar to halt the procedure at a specific line.

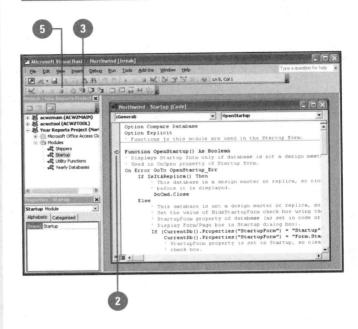

Identifying VBA Debugging Tools

Click to open the Immediate window.

Click to open the Locals window.

Click to Open the Watch window.

The Locals window shows the value and type of all variables used in your VBA procedure. You can use the Locals window to check the effect of your VBA procedure on all variables.

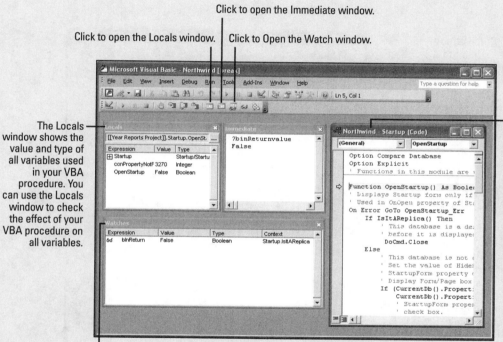

You can enter VBA commands into the Immediate window and then view the results of those commands immediately. The Immediate window saves you the time and effort of creating a VBA procedure and then running it.

You can view the changing values of selected variables in the Watch window. The Watch window helps you check the effect of your VBA procedure on these variable values.

Optimizing Performance with an MDE File

If you share your modules with others, you may want to convert the database file to MDE format. In creating an MDE file, Access removes the editable source code and then compacts the database. Your VBA programs will continue to run, but others cannot view or edit them. There are several advantages to converting a database to MDE format. In MDE format, a database is smaller, and its performance will improve as it optimizes memory usage. Note, however, that you should create an MDE file only after the original database has been thoroughly tested.

Make an MDE File

1. Close your database.

2. In the Access program window, click the Tools menu, point to Database Utilities, and then click Make MDE File.

3. Locate and select the database you want to convert to MDE format.

4. Click Make MDE.

5. Specify a location.

6. Enter a name for the MDE file.

7. Click Save.

Did You Know?

You can save the original database. Make a backup copy of the original database. You'll need it if you have to edit your VBA modules or add new ones.

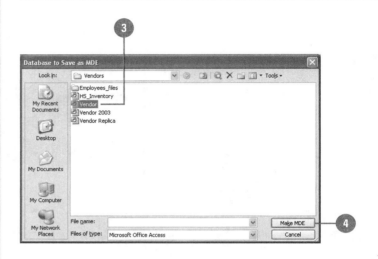

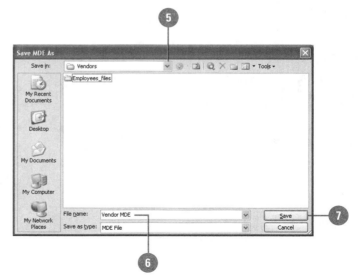

Working Together on Office Documents

15

Introduction

Microsoft SharePoint technology, known as SharePoint Team Services, is a collection of products and services which provide the ability for people to engage in communication, document and file sharing, calendar events, sending alerts, tasks planning, and collaborative discussions in a single community solution. SharePoint enables companies to develop an intelligent application which connects their employees, teams, and information so that users can be part of a Knowledge Community.

Before you can use SharePoint Team Services, SharePoint needs to be set up and configured on a Windows 2003 Server by your network administrator or Internet service provider.

In Access, you can use the Import and Export commands to exchange data from lists or views in Windows SharePoint Services. When you import or export data to Windows SharePoint Services, the Windows SharePoint Services Wizard steps you through the process to access the SharePoint server and convert the data list between the two programs.

What You'll Do

View SharePoint Team Services

Administer SharePoint Team Services

Store Documents in the Library

View Team Members

Set Up Alerts

Assign Project Tasks

Create an Event

Create Contacts

Hold Web Discussions

Import and Export Access Data with SharePoint

Install Windows 2003 and SharePoint Server 2003

Viewing SharePoint Team Services

Microsoft SharePoint displays the contents of its home Page so you can work efficiently with your site. The available pages are: The Home Page, Manage Content Page, Manage Users Page, Change Portal Site Navigation Page, Change Settings Page, and Site Settings Page. You can navigate within the site by clicking on each of the links within the home page. Certain Administrative Access rights are needed in order to view these pages.

Home Page view is the first page your users see when they access the URL for Microsoft SharePoint Server. If you are within a Windows 2003 Active Domain and have a Domain Account, you will not be prompted to type in your user credentials and password. If you do not have an account you will be asked to type in your credentials to have the page display your SharePoint Site. Please contact your Systems Administrator if you do not have access to the SharePoint Server.

Documents and Lists Page view allows you to manage content to your SharePoint Site. You can create Portal sites, a Document Library, Upload Graphic Images in an Image Library Site, Create Calender Events, Create an Address Book of Contents, setup Project Events, Create a Web Discussion site, and setup Surveys. Within your Document and Lists page you will be able to administer your content to provide users with content management capabilities.

Manage Users Page view allows you to add users to your SharePoint Site. If their e-mail address is located within their Domain Account on Windows 2003, SharePoint will e-mail the users you created, and then invite them to join in to the SharePoint Server. From the Manage Users page you can add, delete, and change the permissions of a user for your site.

Home Page

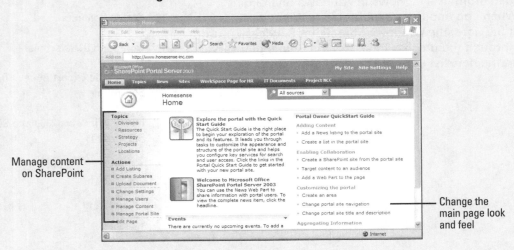

Manage content on SharePoint

Change the main page look and feel

Documents and Lists Page

Adds a new portal site

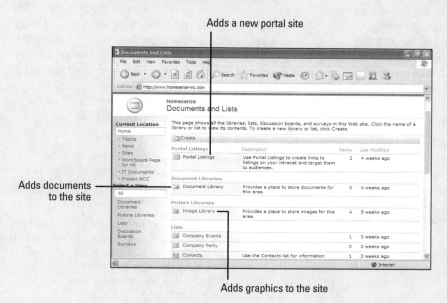

Adds documents to the site

Adds graphics to the site

Manage Users Page

Adds new users

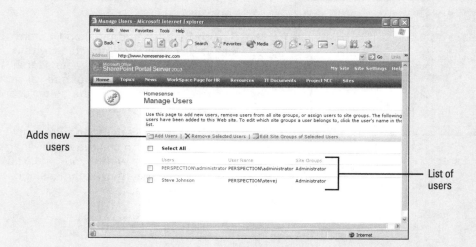

List of users

Administering SharePoint Team Services

Administering Microsoft SharePoint is easy within the site settings. The available pages are: The Home Page, Manage Content Page, Manage Users Page, Change Portal Site Navigation Page, Change Settings Page, and Site Settings Page. You can navigate within the site by clicking on each of the links within the home page. Certain Administrative Access rights are needed in order to view these pages.

Change Portal Site Navigation Page gives you a hierarchy structure to make changes to other portal sites within SharePoint. If you want to move your site to the top-level within SharePoint or modify your sub-level pages, you can do so with the SharePoint Portal Site Navigation Page.

Change Settings Page allows you to swiftly customize the look and feel of your portal site. You can change the title, description, and logo for the site. You can change the URL for creating sites based on the published templates for your site. You can also add a change management process by having the site approved by a manager before being published, and allowing you to change your contact information for your site.

Site Settings Page has four different categories: General Settings, Portal Site Content, Search Settings and Indexed Content, and User Profile, Audiences, and Personal Sites.

- ◆ **General Settings** offers additional security features, which allows you to manage the alerts settings, change your default SMTP e-mail server, change the location of your SharePoint Site, and modify the Regional Language Settings to your site.

- ◆ **Portal Site Content** allows you to manage the site structure, view your site lists and document libraries, import data into your SharePoint Server, and add link listings to your site.

- ◆ **Search Settings and Indexed Content** allows you to create Meta tags within your SharePoint Server, create search crawlers to investigate your site for new key words which will create better search results within your site.

- ◆ **User Profile, Audiences, and Personal Sites** allows you to change and manage your user profiles within your site. You can also manage your audiences and personal settings.

Quick Launch bar

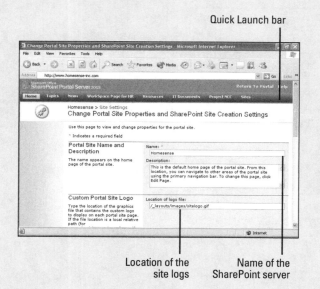

Location of the site logs

Name of the SharePoint server

Change Settings Page

Change publishing settings

Change home page settings

Change template settings

Change Search and Index results

Change site navigation

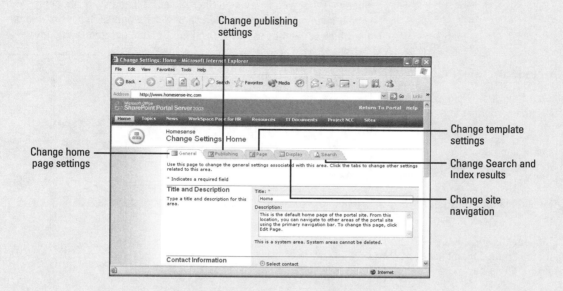

Site Settings Page

Administer the SharePoint site

Administer portal site content

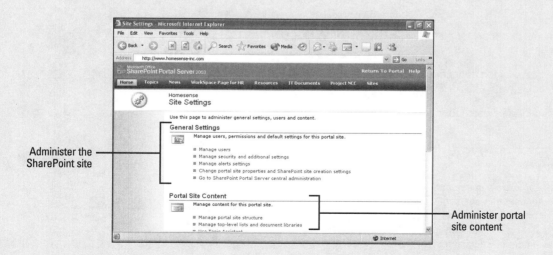

Storing Documents in the Library

A SharePoint **Document Library** is a central depository of files you can share with company employees, team members and permissible members with access. Within the Document Library you can create a list of common documents for a project, documented procedures, and company wide documents for departments such as human resources or finance. When you first install SharePoint 2003, the Web site comes with a built-in document library called **shared documents**. This is located on the Quick Launch bar as well as on the Documents And Lists page.

Upload a Document

1. Log into your SharePoint server with your domain account and password.

2. On the main Home page, click Create Manage Content under the Actions Sidebar.

3. On the Documents And Lists page, click Create.

4. Click Document Library, and then type the name of the document library for creating a new page.

5. Click Upload Document.

6. Type the location of the document, or click Browse to search for the document on your system.

7. Type the name of the owner and a brief description.

8. Select the status of the document, and then click Save.

9. Click the Save And Close button.

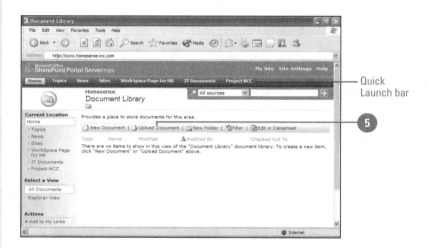

Quick Launch bar

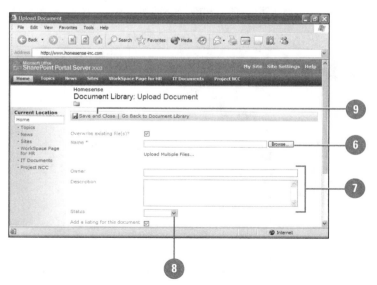

> ### Did You Know?
>
> **You can check documents in and out.** SharePoint's document management system ensures that only one person at a time can access a file. You can check out a document by clicking the Content menu in the document library, and then clicking Check Out.

Viewing Team Members

After you have setup a portal page, you need to specify a user access list to the site. Specifying a user access list controls who can access the site, as well as who has administrative privileges. With integration to Microsoft Active Directory, users can be managed with the same groups as your domain. The access will allow your users to perform a specific action in your site by assigning them to the appropriate groups.

Add New Members to the Site

1. Log into your SharePoint server with your domain account and password.

2. On the main Home page, click Give User Access To The Portal.

3. On the Manage Users page, click Add Users.

4. Type the name of their domain account.

5. Click the type of permissions you want to give this user:

   ◆ **Reader.** Gives the user read-only access to the portal site.

   ◆ **Contributor.** Gives the user write access to the document libraries and lists.

   ◆ **Web Designer.** Gives the user the ability to create lists and document libraries and customize the overall look and feel of the site.

   ◆ **Administrator.** Gives the user full access of the portal site.

   ◆ **Content Manager.** Gives the user the ability to manage lists, libraries, sites and moderate the discussions.

   ◆ **Member.** Gives the user the ability to personalize the portal site content and create lists.

6. Click Next, fill out any additional information, and then click Finish.

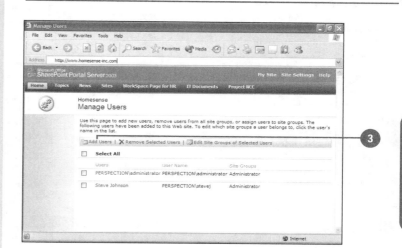

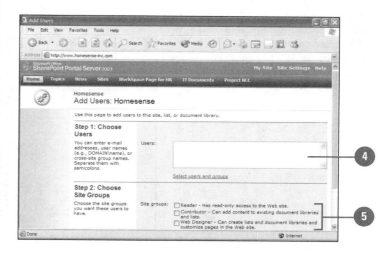

Setting Up Alerts

An Alert notifies you when there is new information which has been changed on the portal site. You can customize your areas of interests and define when you want to be notified after the site has been updated. You can define an alert to track new matches to a search query, changes to the site page, or a new site addition.

Create Your E-Mail Alert

1. Log into your SharePoint server with your domain account and password.

2. In a Portal Site, click Alert Me.

3. Define your delivery options, and then click Next.

4. Click Advanced Options if you want to set up filters.

5. Click OK.

Did You Know?

You can use the following filter categories to be alerted with: Search queries, document and listings, areas, new listings, sites added to the site directory, sharepoint lists and libraries, list items, portal site users, and backward compatible document library folders.

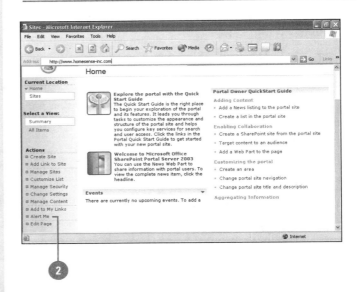

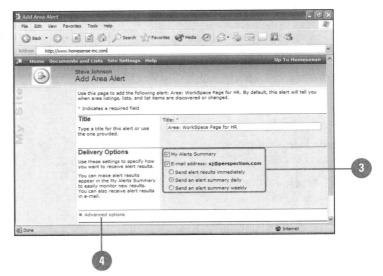

Assigning Project Tasks

Assigning a project task is another way you can use SharePoint to collaborate on the site. By creating a task, you can manage your team with status updates. You can also provide a central way to manage the effectiveness of a project. Since this is a Web based system, everyone can access this with a simple Web browser.

Add a Task Item to Your Site

1. Log into your SharePoint server with your domain account and password.

2. On the main home page, click Create Manage Content under the Actions Sidebar.

3. Click Create, and then click Tasks.

4. Type the name of the task, add in an optional description, click Yes, if you want to add the task to the menu bar, and then click Create.

5. Click New Item.

6. Type the title, set the priority, status, and completion percentage, assign your resource, add a description, and then set your due date.

7. Click the Save And Close button.

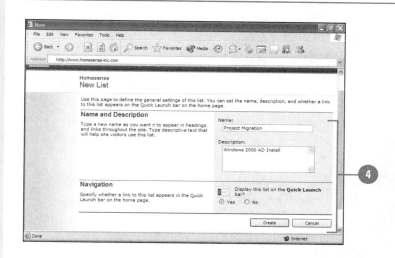

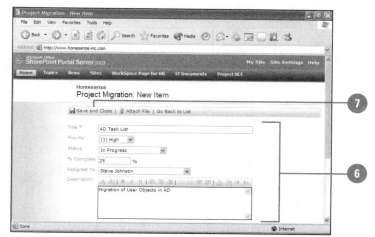

Did You Know?

You can use the Upload button to add an attachment. A general rule of thumb would be to keep your attachments under 1 MB, however, unless your administrator has set rights on your site, you are free to upload as much as you want.

15

Creating an Event

Creating an event allows you to send out notices on upcoming meetings, deadlines, and other important events. This is helpful if you need to send out information to a wide range of people or in a project you are working on. If you are looking to set up a meeting to a large group of people, you may want to set up an event which is seen by everyone who logs in.

Setup New Events

1. Log into your SharePoint server with your domain account and password.

2. On the main Home page, click Create Manage Content under the Actions Sidebar.

3. Click Create, and then click Events.

4. Type the name of the event, add in an optional description, click Yes , if you want to add the event to the menu bar, and then click Create.

5. Click New Item.

6. Type the event title, select a begin and end event time, a description, the location, and then select an recurrence option.

7. Click the Save And Close button.

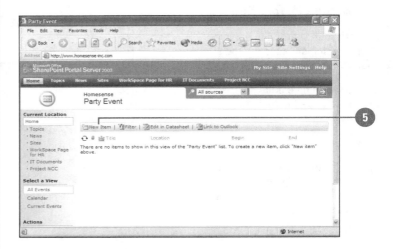

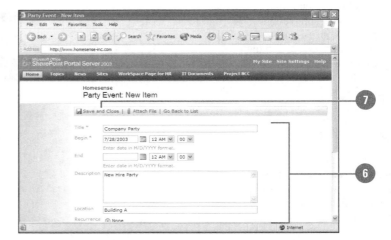

Did You Know?

You can use a new collaboration feature in Outlook 2003 called Meeting Workspace. Meeting Workspace allows you to gather information and organize everyone when you create a scheduled meeting event. To create a Meeting Workspace in Outlook 2003, prepare a calender event and set up your attendees for the event. Then click Meeting Workspace to link this to your SharePoint Server. You may need to type in the URL of your SharePoint server. Please get this from your System Administrator.

Link to Events in Outlook

1. On the Events page, click Link To Outlook.

2. If a security dialog box appears asking for your approval prior to adding a folder, click Yes.

   You will be prompted to type in the credentials of your user account.

3. Type in your Domain User credentials and password, and then click OK.

4. Click Other Calendars to view your SharePoint calendar.

Did You Know?

You will not be able to change the events in your SharePoint calendar folder within Outlook 2003. You will only have read access rights within Outlook 2003. To change the SharePoint calendar information, return to your SharePoint Site, and then modify the information under your Events Site.

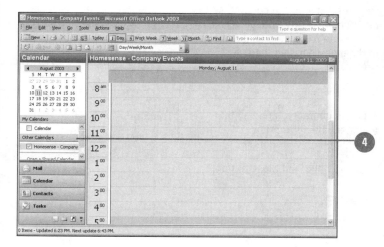

Creating Contacts

You can create a contact list when you want to have a central database of your team information. You will have the ability to manage information about sales contacts, vendors, and employees that your team has involvement with.

Create a Contact List

1. Log into your SharePoint server with your domain account and password.

2. On the main Home page, click Create Manage Content under the Actions Sidebar.

3. Click Create, and then click Contacts.

4. Type the name of the contact, add an optional description, click Yes, if you want to add the contacts list to the menu bar, and then click Create.

5. Click New Item.

6. Type the contact name, and then add in all the appropriate information on your contact.

7. Click the Save And Close button.

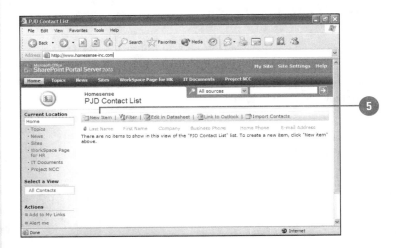

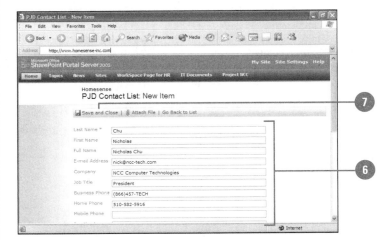

Link to Contacts in Outlook

1. On the Contacts page, click Link To Outlook.

2. If a security dialog box appears asking for your approval prior to adding a folder, click Yes.

   You will be prompted to type in the credentials of your user account.

3. Type your Domain User credentials and password, and then click OK.

4. Click Other Contacts to view your SharePoint contacts.

Did You Know?

You will not be able to change the contact information in your SharePoint contacts folder within Outlook 2003. You will only have read access rights within Outlook 2003. To change the SharePoint contacts information, return to your SharePoint Site, and then modify the information under your Contacts Site.

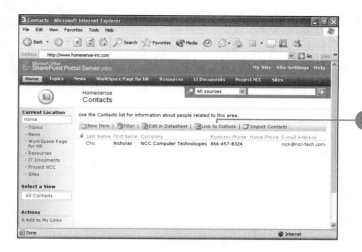

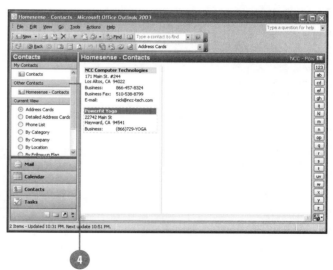

15

Holding Web Discussions

Web discussions are threaded discussions which allow users to collaborate together in a Web environment. Users can add and view discussion items, add in documents during the discussion and carry on conversations. Since the discussions are entered into a different area than the shared document, users can modify the document without effecting the collaborative discussion. Users can add changes to read-only documents and allow multiple users to create and edit discussion items simultaneously.

Hold a Web Discussion

1. Log into your SharePoint server with your domain account and password.

2. On the main Home page, click Create Manage Content under the Actions Sidebar.

3. Click Create, and then click Discussion Boards.

4. Type the name of the Discussion Board, add an optional description, click Yes, if you want to add this to the menu bar, and then click Create.

5. Click New Discussion.

6. Type the subject name, and then add in all the appropriate information on your discussion.

7. Click the Save And Close button.

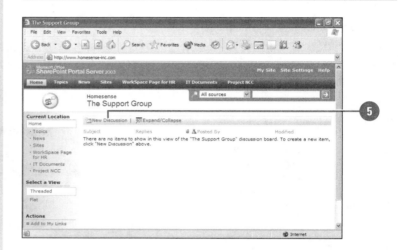

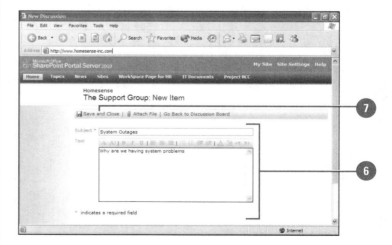

Importing and Exporting Access Data with SharePoint

You can use the Import, Link Tables, and Export commands in Access to exchange data from lists or views in Windows SharePoint Services. When you import or export data with SharePoint, the Windows SharePoint Services Wizard steps you through the process to convert the data between the two programs. Before you start the process be sure to have access information to connect to the SharePoint server.

Import or Link Data from SharePoint

1. Open the database in which you want to import data.

2. Click the File menu, point to Get External Data, and then click Import or Link Tables.

3. Click the File Of Type list arrow, and then click Windows SharePoint Services.

4. Enter the address of your SharePoint server.

5. Click Next, and then follow the remaining wizard instructions.

Export Data to SharePoint

1. Open the database containing the object you want to export, and then select the database object.

2. Click the File menu, and then click Export.

3. Click the Save In list arrow, and then select the drive and folder where you want to save the file.

4. Click the Save As Type list arrow, and then click Windows SharePoint Services.

5. Enter the address of your SharePoint server.

6. Click Finish, and then follow the remaining instructions.

Installing Windows 2003 and SharePoint Server 2003

In order for you to install the new version of SharePoint, you must Install Windows 2003 Server. Windows 2003 Server uses the new .NET Architecture Internet Information Server (IIS) 6.0, Microsoft SMTP (Simple Mail Transport Protocol) Service and Microsoft SQL Server 2000 Desktop Engine (MSDE 2000) or Microsoft SQL Server 2000 Enterprise or Standard Edition (64-bit), with Microsoft SQL Server 2000 SP3 or later.

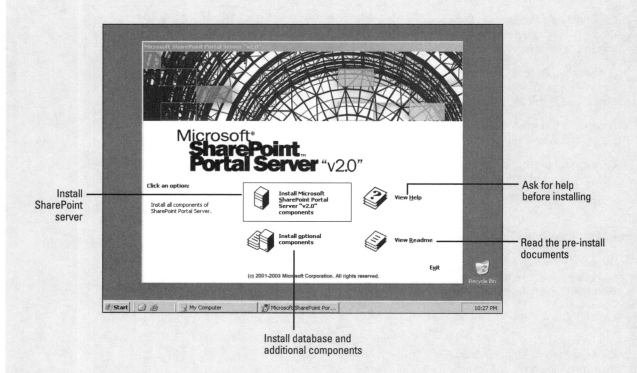

Install SharePoint server

Install database and additional components

Ask for help before installing

Read the pre-install documents

Microsoft Office Specialist

About the Microsoft Office Specialist Program

The Microsoft Office Specialist certification is the globally recognized standard for validating expertise with the Microsoft Office suite of business productivity programs. Earning an Microsoft Office Specialist certificate acknowledges you have the expertise to work with Microsoft Office programs. To earn the Microsoft Office Specialist certification, you must pass one or more certification exams for the Microsoft Office desktop applications of Microsoft Office Word, Microsoft Office Excel, Microsoft Office PowerPoint, Microsoft Office Outlook, or Microsoft Office Access. The Microsoft Office Specialist program typically offers certification exams at the "specialist" and "expert" skill levels. (The availability of Microsoft Office Specialist certification exams varies by program, program version, and language. Visit *www.microsoft.com/officespecialist* for exam availability and more information about the program.) The Microsoft Office Specialist program is the only Microsoft-approved program in the world for certifying proficiency with Microsoft Office programs.

What Does This Logo Mean?

It means this book has been approved by the Microsoft Office Specialist program to be certified courseware for learning Microsoft Office Access 2003 and preparing for the certification exam. This book will prepare you fully for the Microsoft Office Specialist exam at the specialist level for Microsoft Office Access 2003. Each certification level has a set of objectives, which are organized into broader skill sets. Throughout this book, content that pertains to a Microsoft Office Specialist objective is identified with the Microsoft Office Specialist logo and objective number below the title of the topic:

AC03S-1-1
AC03S-2-2

Access 2003 Specialist Objectives

Objective	Skill	Page
AC03S-1	**Structuring Databases**	
AC03S-1-1	Create Access databases	40-41, 46-47
AC03S-1-2	Create and modify tables	50-51, 56
AC03S-1-3	Define and create field types	56, 68, 70, 84-85
AC03S-1-4	Modify field properties	70, 76-77
AC03S-1-5	Create and modify one-to-many relationships	60-61
AC03S-1-6	Enforce referential integrity	62
AC03S-1-7	Create and modify queries	119-121, 129-131, 136-137
AC03S-1-8	Create forms	142-145
AC03S-1-9	Add and modify form controls and properties	148-151, 184-185
AC03S-1-10	Create reports	160-161, 164-165
AC03S-1-11	Add and modify report controls properties	172-173
AC03S-1-12	Create a data access page	222-223
AC03S-2	**Entering Data**	
AC03S-2-1	Enter, edit and delete records	88, 96-97
AC03S-2-2	Find and move among records	89, 90
AC03S-2-3	Import data to Access	55, 238-239
AC03S-3	**Organizing Data**	
AC03S-3-1	Create and modify calculated fields and aggregate functions	128
AC03S-3-2	Modify form layout	184-185, 192-193
AC03S-3-3	Modify report layout and page setup	164-165, 180, 192-193
AC03S-3-4	Format datasheets	106
AC03S-3-5	Sort records	108-109
AC03S-3-6	Filter records	112-113
AC03S-4	**Managing Databases**	
AC03S-4-1	Identify and modify object dependencies	63-64
AC03S-4-2	View objects and object data in other views	181, 222-224, 230
AC03S-4-3	Print database objects and data	182
AC03S-4-4	Export data from Access	244-246, 242-243
AC03S-4-5	Back up a database	262
AC03S-4-6	Compact and repair databases	263

Preparing for a Microsoft Office Specialist Exam

Every Microsoft Office Specialist certification exam is developed from a list of objectives, which are based on studies of how Microsoft Office programs are actually used in the workplace. The list of objectives determine the scope of each exam, so they provide you with the information you need to prepare for Microsoft Office Specialist certification. Microsoft Office Specialist Approved Courseware, including the Show Me series, is reviewed and approved on the basis of its coverage of the objectives. To prepare for the certification exam, you should review and perform each task identified with a Microsoft Office Specialist objective to confirm that you can meet the requirements for the exam.

Taking a Microsoft Office Specialist Exam

The Microsoft Office Specialist certification exams are not written exams. Instead, the exams are performance-based examinations that allow you to interact with a "live" Office program as you complete a series of objective-based tasks. All the standard menus, toolbars, and keyboard shortcuts are available during the exam. Microsoft Office Specialist exams for Office 2003 programs consist of 25 to 35 questions, each of which requires you to complete one or more tasks using the Office program for which you are seeking certification. A typical exam takes from 45 to 60 minutes. Passing percentages range from 70 to 80 percent correct.

The Exam Experience

After you fill out a series of information screens, the testing software starts the exam and the Office program. The test questions appear in the exam dialog box in the lower right corner of the screen.

◆ The timer starts when the first question appears and displays the remaining exam time at the top of the exam dialog box. If the timer and the counter are distracting, you can click the timer to remove the display.

◆ The counter at the top of the exam dialog box tracks how many questions you have completed and how many remain.

◆ If you think you have made a mistake, you can click the Reset button to restart the question. The Reset button does not restart the entire exam or extend the exam time limit.

◆ When you complete a question, click the Next button to move to the next question. It is not possible to move back to a previous question on the exam.

◆ If the exam dialog box gets in your way, you can click the Minimize button in the upper right corner of the exam dialog box to hide it, or you can drag the title bar to another part of the screen to move it.

Tips for Taking an Exam

◆ Carefully read and follow all instructions provided in each question.

◆ Make sure all steps in a task are completed before proceeding to the next exam question.

◆ Enter requested information as it appears in the instructions without formatting unless you are explicitly requested otherwise.

◆ Close all dialog boxes before proceeding to the next exam question unless you are specifically instructed otherwise.

◆ Do not leave tables, boxes, or cells "active" unless instructed otherwise.

◆ Do not cut and paste information from the exam interface into the program.

◆ When you print a document from an Office program during the exam, nothing actually gets printed.

◆ Errant keystrokes or mouse clicks do not count against your score as long as you achieve the correct end result. You are scored based on the end result, not the method you use to achieve it. However, if a specific method is explicitly requested, you need to use it to get credit for the results.

◆ The overall exam is timed, so taking too long on individual questions may leave you without enough time to complete the entire exam.

◆ If you experience computer problems during the exam, notify a testing center administrator immediately to restart your exam where you were interrupted.

Exam Results

At the end of the exam, a score report appears indicating whether you passed or failed the exam. An official certificate is mailed to successful candidates in approximately two to three weeks.

Getting More Information

To learn more about the Microsoft Office Specialist program, read a list of frequently asked questions, and locate the nearest testing center, visit:

www.microsoft.com/officespecialist

New! Features

Microsoft Office Access 2003

Microsoft Office Access 2003 is the database management program that gives you an improved user experience and an expanded ability to import, export, and work with XML data files. Working in Access 2003 is easier because common errors are identified and flagged for you with options to correct them.

◆ **Macro Security (p. 44)** Protect against potentially unsafe Visual Basic for Applications (VBA) code by setting the macro security level. You can set the security level so that you are prompted every time that you open a database containing VBA code, or you can automatically block databases that are from unknown sources. When you set the macro security level, you can run macros based on whether they are digitally signed by a developer on your list of trusted sources.

◆ **Block Potentially Unsafe Functions (p. 44)** Block potentially unsafe functions from being used in expressions using the Microsoft Jet Expression Service enhanced sandbox mode.

◆ **View information on object dependencies (p. 63-64)** View information on dependencies between database objects. Viewing a list of objects that use a specific object helps maintain a database over time and avoid errors related to missing record sources. For example, the Quarterly Orders query in the Sales database is no longer needed, but before deleting it, you might want to find out which other objects in the database use the query. You can either change the record source of the dependent objects, or delete them, before deleting the Quarterly Orders query. Viewing a complete list of dependent objects helps you save time and minimize errors. In addition to viewing the list of objects that are bound to a selected object, you can also view the objects that are being used by the selected object.

◆ **Propagating field properties (P. 71)** In previous versions of Access, whenever you modified a field's inherited property, you had to manually modify the property of the corresponding control in each of the forms and reports. Now, when you modify an inherited field property in Table design view, Access displays an option to update the property of all or some controls that are bound to the field.

◆ **Autocorrect options (p. 92-93)** The AutoCorrect Options button appears near text that was automatically corrected. If you find on occasion that you don't want text to be corrected, you can undo a correction or turn AutoCorrect Options on or off by clicking the button and making a selection.

◆ **Smart tags (p. 94-95)** Use the Smart Tags property to add a smart tag to any field in a table, query, form, report, or data access page in a database.

◆ **Enhanced sorting in controls (p. 150-151)** Specify the ascending or descending sort order of up to four fields in the List Box and Combo Box Wizards in forms and reports, and the Lookup Wizard in an Access database. The sort page added to these wizards looks and behaves like the sort page in the Report Wizard.

◆ **Microsoft Windows XP theme support (p. 156)** The Windows XP operating system offers you several themes. If you have chosen a theme other than the default, Access will apply the chosen theme to views, dialog boxes, and controls. You can prevent form controls from inheriting themes from the operating system by setting an option in the database or project.

◆ **Error checking in forms and reports (p. 178-179)** Enable automatic error checking to locate common errors in forms and reports. Error checking points out errors, such as two controls using the same keyboard shortcut, and the width of a report being greater than the page it will be printed on. Enabling error checking helps you identify errors and correct them.

◆ **Make a local table from a linked table (p. 234-235)** Make a local copy of the structure or data and structure contained in a linked table.

◆ **XML support (p. 240-241)** XML (Extensible Markup Language) is a universal language that enables you to move information across the Internet and programs where the data is stored independently of the format so you can use the data more seamlessly in other forms. Access allows you to import and export XML data as well as transform the data to and from other formats using XML related files.

◆ **Back up a database or project (p. 262)** Back up the current database or project before making major changes to it. The backup will be saved in the default backup location, or in the current folder.

◆ **Support for ink devices (p. 298-299)** Quickly provide input by adding your own handwriting to Office documents on a Tablet PC as you would using a pen and a printout. Additionally, view task panes horizontally to help you do your work on the Tablet PC.

◆ **Importing, exporting, and linking to a Microsoft Windows SharePoint Services list from Access (p. 331)** Export the contents of a table or a query to a Windows SharePoint Services list, import the contents of a Windows SharePoint Services list into a table, and link a table to a Windows SharePoint Services list.

◆ **Exporting and linking to Access data from Windows SharePoint Services (p. 331)** Export a list in its Datasheet view from Windows SharePoint Services to a static table or to a linked table in Access. When you export to a static table, you create a table in Access. You can view and make changes to the table independent of the original list in Windows SharePoint Services. Similarly, you can change the list in Windows SharePoint Services, and that will not affect the table in Access. When you export to a linked table, you create a table in Access and establish a dynamic link between the table and the list such that changes to the table are reflected in the list, and changes to the list are reflected in the table as well.

◆ **Enhanced font capabilities in SQL views** Change the font and font size of text by using the Query design font option added to the Tables/Queries tab of the Options dialog box under the Tools menu in the SQL and query Design views of a query in both an Access database and Access project. These settings apply to all databases and work with the high-contrast and other accessibility settings of your computer.

◆ **Context-based Help in SQL view** Get help specific to Jet SQL keywords, VBA functions, and Access functions in the SQL view of a query in a Microsoft Access database. Simply press F1 to bring up the help that corresponds to the text near the cursor. You can also search the Jet SQL and VBA function reference topics.

Troubleshooting

Clip art and objects

I want to paste our company logo into
   a form   195

I'd like to add an employee photo to my
   employee database   198

I inserted a Chart from Excel, and now
   I'd like to change the type of chart   203

I brought in an object, but now I need
   to move it   206

How can I analyze my Pivot data that
   I got from the Web   230

Columns

When I'm entering data, I'd like to be
   able to have a column closer   102

As I fill up more records in my database
   I lose the view of my field titles   103

Can I change the size of my rows and
   columns once data has been entered   104

I just realized that I left out a column in
   my design, can I add it now   105

Database

I'm told I should set up a database for
   my project, what can it do for me   1

What's the difference between a query
   and modules   2,15

There are so many sections on my
   screen, how do they all work together   8, 14

Before I get started, can I look at a
   sample database to get ideas   28

What is a switchboard   29

How do I set up a database   40

I'm not sure about all the Access
   wizard screens   42

Can I set up a database using something
   that Access might have created   43

How much planning needs to happen
   in order for me to start my design
   from scratch   45

How can I best determine object
   dependencies   63

Entering and editing data

How can I enter data accurately   92

I want to make sure that I enter my
   e-mail addresses correctly   94

How do I change my text   96

Can I copy some material from another
   application and paste it into Access   98

I'd like to have a different background
   color for my datasheet to help make
   it easier to enter data   106

I've renamed a form, and now I have
   some errors   107

Now that I've created a form, how do
   I enter a new record   155

Fields

Are there certain elements I can build
   into my field designs   65

Can I modify my fields in design view   66

I need to change my original field data
   type   68

Input mask, captions, validation rules,
   it's all very confusing   69

When determining my fields, is there a
   way to estimate field size that is
   stored   72

Can I set up a format so that data is only
   displayed that way in the field   73

There are certain field that I want to be
required entries   78

How can I make sure that the correct
information is entered   82

What are look up properties   86

I need to add a field to a query   122

Can i pull other fields from different
tables to do a query   123

How do I specify a criteria for
multiple fields   125

What is Expression Builder and how
does it work with my fields   128

Is there a way to find out if my database
has duplicate fields   130

Formatting

Is there a fast way to format my form
that I just created   184

Sometimes the headers and footers are
in the way   185

I need to break up my form a bit, can
I add some lines to separate   186

I'd like to set my required fields to a
certain color   189

What is conditional formatting   191

I need to add an overall theme to my
Web page that I created for my
Access database   225

Forms

How are forms used in Access   139

Is there an easy tool to use to create
a form   140

Bound, Unbound and Calculated
controls, how do these relate
to forms   141

What is the difference between
AutoForm and the Form Wizard   142-145

I need to change my form   147

Can the Control Wizard help me with
my form   150

How can I create a form that uses a
one-to-many relationship   152

I need to line up my controls better   192

What's a switchboard   271

Is there a way that I can make my
opening database screen more
exciting   273

Help

Is there a way I can get help without
the Clippit appearing   16

The Office Assistant is in my way   19

I can't find the Help topic I want in the
Office Assistant   20

Importing and exporting

Is there a way I can import data into my
tables so I don't have to re-type it   55

I want to put an Excel chart into my
Access database   194, 200

I want to insert a Graph Chart into my
Access database   202

I need to export a database to a Web
page   217

How do I export my database as an
ASP file   218

What formats are supported for data
sources   232

Can I link one database to another   234

I'd like to be able to use my contact
information in Outlook in my Access
database   237

Can I import or export XML data   240

I'd like to develop a form letter with my
Access data on my clients in Word   244

Language, voice and handwriting options

I'm having a tough time using the
Language feature   295

Am I actually able to control Access with
my voice   296

I want to insert some handwritten text
into my database   298

Am I able to have a duplicate table
translated in another language   300

Macros

What is a macro and can it really save me time 283

Once I've created a macro, do I save it 284

My macro isn't doing what I want it to do 286

Is there a way that I should catalog or group my macros 288

What is a conditional expression 289

There's a macro I run all the time, can I create a button to push on my form 290

As my macro runs, is there something I can display to notify the database user on what's happening 294

Managing

Now that the database is up and running what are the areas I need to manage 247

What are user and work groups 248

Is there a way to encode a confidential a database 249

Should I create a workgroup information file 250

How do I go about setting up users for the databases 252

Is there a way to change account permissions 254

I'd like to set a password on my Access database 257

How do I make sure that two people don't pull up the same record 259

Should I replicate my database for our other offices to use 260

I need to perform a backup 262

Our database seems to be crashing more, is there a problem 263

The database file is getting very large, can we split out some older data 264

Menus, toolbars, and task panes

I can't find a task pane 5

How come a shortcut menu shows up 10

I'm not sure about all the options on a dialog box 11

How do I open a button on a toolbar 12

What do all the various Toolbox buttons do 166-167

How do I use the Favorites button on the Web toolbar 216

What does this toolbar do that has people's faces on it 221

There are some buttons I just don't use on some toolbars, can I delete them 277

I'd like to have my own toolbar for the buttons I use all the time in Access 278

Now that I have all these macros, can I put them on their own menu 280

Is there a special toolbar for Languages 295

Microsoft Office Specialist

What is the Microsoft Office Specialist certification program 333

What are some of the requirements to get certified 334

How do I get certified in Access 2003 335

Are there any tips for taking the exam 336

Printing

Can I print mailing labels from Access 170

I need to change my report to print out in landscape instead of portrait 180

Before printing my large report, can I see what it's going to look like 181

Everything looks great in preview, so can I print it 182

Queries and reports

How can I print out what I just queried 39

What is a query 115

How do I know what type of query to use for my reporting 116

Is there another way to do a query besides using the wizard 117

Can I save a query to use later in the week to monitor my sales 118

I'm having trouble finding the Query Wizard 120

What are comparison operators and how can I use them in my query   126

I need to set up a query using different parameters   129

Can I use SQL to perform a query   138

Records

How can I move to a specific record   89

I need to find some text and replace it with other text   90

Errors showed up once I renamed a form in my table   107

I'd like to sort my records in a different order than when I first entered them   108

I have a record that is almost duplicate of another, can I copy it   110

How can I view a record that is in two different tables   111

Can I filter records to only show a certain criteria   112, 114

Can I match two tables together and see which has missing records   131

I need to delete all my records from a sales rep   134

How do properties affect my records   171

I need to group records together for a special report   174

Reports

What are some of the items I can include on a report   157

Are there any wizards available to help create reports   158

I'd like to be able to rearrange the controls on my report   163

The page breaks at an awkward part of my report, can I adjust it   169

What are object properties   171

I need to perform a calculation in my report   172

My report would be complete if I could just get a header and footer to print   176

How can a shortcut key help me with my reporting   177

Searching

When I search, I'm not sure I'm doing it correctly   7

I need to check for errors   178

SharePoint

What is SharePoint   317

How do I know which Page views to use   318

How can I control who views what documents   320

What tools are available in the Site Settings page   320

Is there a way to maximize all of our company documents, workbooks, and databases   322

How can you control who has access to the files   323

Is there a way that I can be notified if a certain database has been updated   324

Can I manage my employees' projects online   325

I'd like to notify our company about stock holders meeting   326

Spelling

Is there a way I can add our company specific information into the spell checker program   93

I accidentally added a word as an AutoCorrect entry, and I want to delete it   93

Is there a way I can check the spelling of records in my database   100

Tables

What's the difference between a table and a database   34

How do I use a form   36

How do I begin to create a table   48

What's a primary key   48

Is there a way that Access can walk me through creating my first table   50

How do I determine what table relationships to use 58

How can I ensure referential integrity 62

I performed a large query and want to make a new table with the data 132

Can I send a table through e-mail 243

Visual Basic (VBA)

What is Visual Basic Application (VBA) and how is it used in Access 301

Do I need to know how to program to use VBA 303

How do I get started with my first module 304

Is there a summary of all the parts of the Visual Basic Editor 305

Where do I write VBA commands 307

What is a custom function 310

My VBA procedure is not performing correctly, how can I check it 314

How can I make a MDE file 316

Views

Can I do a query in Design view 117

I need to change a query that I did last month, can I do it in Design view 119

Can I create a form to enter data in Design view 146

I need to make some changes to my form controls, is there a view I can use 154

I'm only seeing certain sections of my report in Design view 162

How can Design view help me with my data access page 224

I need to view my data access page 228

How do I know what view to use when I'm using SharePoint 318

Web

How can my Access database and the Web work together 208

What is HTML and how can I use it with my Access database 209

How can I use a hyperlink to jump between my Access database and my company Web page 210

I need to set up a link from one database to another 213

What do all the buttons do on the Web toolbar 216

I need to hold an online meeting with some of my clients 220

I need to create a data access page for the Web 222

Now that I've created my data access page, I'd like to see how it's going to look on the Web 229

Can I export my Access data into an XML format 241

I need to hold a Web discussion 330

Index

A

access keys in reports, assigning, 177
account logons, 249
actions, 283
    queries, action, 116
ActiveX Server, 309
Add-In Manager, 270
add-ins, using, 270
Address Book switchboard, 29
Admin accounts, using, 252
administrator permission in SharePoint Team
        Services, 323
Admins group, 249
alignment for form input boxes, 154
All Programs menu, My Recent Documents, 6
All Records, locking, 259
Analyze It With MS Excel command, 246
analyzing databases, 266-267
AND filters, creating, 114
AND queries, 126-127
append query, 133
Apply button, 11
arguments, 283
arrows, up/down, 11
ascending order sorts, 108
ASP (Active Server Pages), 209
    exporting database objects to, 218-219
Assistance Home Web page, 21
asterisk (*) wildcard, searching with, 7
attachments
    database objects to e-mail, 242-243
    with SharePoint Team Services, 325
AutoCorrect
    adding entries to, 93
    database objects, renaming, 31
    editing entries in, 93

tables, entering data in, 92-93
AutoExec macro, 274, 284
AutoFormat
    forms, formatting, 184
    reports, formatting, 184
AutoForm command, 140
AutoForm:Datasheet Wizard, 142
AutoForm:Tabular Wizard, 142
AutoForm Wizards, 140
    creating forms with, 142-143
AutoNumber, 35
    data type, 68
    field, 88
    for fields, 35
AutoReport command, 160
AutoReport Wizards, 158
    creating reports with, 160
average function in queries, 128

B

back-end database, 264
    backgrounds
    colors, adding, 188
for datasheets, 103
backing up
    databases, 262, 264
    Design Master, 261
Back Up Database command, 262
blank database, creating, 46
borders
    colors, changing, 188
    thickness, adjusting, 187
bound columns, 84
bound form controls, 141
Bound Object Frame button, 167
bound report controls, 163, 164-165

builders. *See also* Expression Builder
    availability, checking on, 173
buttons, 11
    macro to button, assigning, 290-291
byte size of field, 72

C

calculated form controls, 141
calculated report controls, 163, 172-173
calculations
    form controls for, 141
    queries performing, 128
    report controls for, 163, 172-173
Calendar events in Outlook, linking to, 327
Cancel button, 11
capitalization errors, AutoCorrect for, 92
captions
    for fields, 69, 79
    for group sections, 227
Cascade Delete Related Records check box, 62
Cascade Update Related Fields check box, 62
cells
    deleting contents of, 97
    editing contents of, 96
    inserting contents in, 97
    moving contents of, 97
    selecting, 110
certification exam
    Microsoft Office Specialist program,
      333-336
characters
    in captions, 79
    formatting symbols, 73-74
    input mask symbols, 77
charts
    chart area, 204
    customizing, 205
    Excel, inserting, 200
    formatting chart objects, 204-205
    graph charts, creating, 202-203
    plot area of, 204
    selecting chart objects, 204
    3-D charts, changing view of, 205
Chart Wizard, 202-203
Chat for online meetings, 220-221
Check Box button, 166

chiseled effect, 190
class modules. *See* VBA (Microsoft Visual
    Basic for Applications)
Click event, 292
clip art object, inserting, 199
Clipboard, 98-99
    copying records in, 110
    deleting items from, 99
    options, changing, 99
    pasting with, 98, 110
Clippit, 18
    changing character, 19
closing databases, 26
code for VBA, 302
collaborating in online meetings, 221
colors
    for datasheets, 103
    fill color, changing, 188
    for form input boxes, 154
    line or border color, changing, 188
    text color, changing, 189
columns and rows
    arranging columns, 102-103
    bound columns, 84
    crosstab query, changing headings in, 137
    Datasheet view, managing columns in, 105
    deleting columns in relationship, 105
    displaying hidden columns, 103
    freeze column feature, 102-103
    height of rows, changing, 104
    hiding columns, 102
    joining types of, 61
    for lookup fields, 84
    moving columns, 102
    renaming columns, 105
    resizing, 34, 54, 104
    selecting, 34, 110
    width of columns, changing, 104
Combo Box button, 167
combo boxes
    with Control Wizards, 150-151
    help for customizing, 151
Command button, 167
Command Button Wizard, 290-291
commands
    adding commands to, 281
    AutoReport command, 160

choosing menu commands, 10

copying to toolbars and menus, 281

groups of commands on menus, organizing, 282

from shortcut menu, 10

toolbar buttons, choosing with, 12

VBA (Microsoft Visual Basic for Applications) commands, writing, 307

commas, dictating, 297

common fields. *See* fields

compacting databases, 263

comparison operators for queries, 117, 126-127

conditional expressions

formatting with, 191

macros, creating, 289

consecutive numbers option for primary key, 52

contact lists with SharePoint Team Services, 328-329

content manager permission in SharePoint Team Services, 323

contributor permission in SharePoint Team Services, 323

controls. *See* form controls; report controls

Control Wizards, 141, 150-151

Control Wizards button, 166

copying

cell contents, 97

commands to toolbars and menus, 281

objects, 195

part of object, 243

records, 110

text, 97

count function in queries, 128

cropping graphics, 199

crosstab queries, 116, 136-137

currency

data type, 68

values formats, 74

customizing

charts, 205

combo boxes, 151

introduction to, 275

list boxes, 151

menu bars, 280-281

spell checking, 101

startup, 9

toolbars, 278-279

Cyrillic keyboard layout, 300

D

dash characters, 76

data access pages, 209

Design view, working in, 224

Excel spreadsheets, inserting, 230

grouping of, 226-227

hyperlinks to, 224

PivotTable, inserting, 230

properties of groups, 227

Startup, displaying at, 273

themes, adding, 225

viewing, 228-229

Web browser, viewing in, 228-229

wizard, creating with, 222-223

database objects. *See also* dependencies; hyperlinks; specific objects

deleting, 31

e-mail message, attaching to, 242-243

files, inserting objects from, 197

grouping, 32

list of objects, viewing, 15, 63

managing, 30-31

moving, 206

new objects

creating, 31

inserting, 196

opening, 30

pasting, 195

renaming, 31

resizing, 206

viewing, 14-15, 30

list of objects, viewing, 15, 63

database passwords, 249

deleting, 257

databases, 88. *See also* Database Wizard; Switchboard Manager

Admins group, 249

analyzing database, 266-267

backing up, 262, 264

blank database, creating, 46

closing, 26

compacting databases, 263

custom databases, creating, 45-64

defined, 1

databases *(continued)*
  documenting database, 265
  encryption of, 249, 258
  existing database, creating new database
    from, 47
  hyperlinking to objects in, 212-213
  importing data from, 234
  linking data from, 234-235
  locking records, 259
  management of, 247
  MDE format, converting to, 316
  names for, 40
  new database, creating, 46-47
  normalization process, 266
  opening, 6
  optimizing database performance, 266-267
  previous version of Access, converting
    database to, 269
  repairing databases, 263
  replicating, 260-261
  sample databases, 6, 28
  security for, 248-249
  splitting databases, 264
  storage of data, understanding, 2-3
  system database, 248
  templates for, 43
  upgrading older databases, 268-269
Database title bar, 8
Database toolbar, 8
Database window, 8
  macros, running, 286
  switching to, 28
  toolbar, 15
  viewing, 14
Database Wizard
  choices in, 42
  creating database with, 40-41
data-definition queries, 138
Datasheet Formatting dialog box, 103
datasheets
  appearance, controlling, 103
  fonts in, 103, 106
  formatting, 106
  for graph charts, 202
  gridlines, showing/hiding, 106
  subdatasheets, viewing, 110

Datasheet view
  columns, managing, 105
  copying and pasting records in, 110
  filters in, 112
  opening tables in, 34
  switching to Design view, 14
  tables, creating, 49, 54
Datasheet View button, 134
data types
  indexing, 81
  specifying, 68
date and time
  data type, 68
  formatting values for, 75
  predefined formats, 75
Dbl Click event, 292
debugging VBA procedures, 314-315
decimal places in fields, setting, 70, 74
decrypting databases, 258
default values, specifying, 69, 78
deleting. *See also* queries;
    relationships; tables
  cell contents, 97
  Clipboard, items from, 99
  columns in relationships, 105
  data access page groups, 226
  database objects, 31
  database passwords, 257
  encryption from database, 258
  fields, 67
  filters from tables, 112
  form controls, 148
  forms, records from, 37, 155
  group shortcuts, 32
  hyperlinks, 215
  passwords, 253
    database passwords, 257
  text in tables, 97
  toolbar buttons, 277
dependencies
  information on, 63
  modifying, 64
  viewing, 63
descending order sorts, 108
Design Master, 260-261
Design view. *See also* forms; queries;
    reports; tables

data access pages, working with, 224
fields, working with, 66-67
form controls, 159
primary keys, setting, 57
queries, viewing, 38
switching to Datasheet view, 14
desktop
shortcuts to, 4
starting Access from, 4
Detect and Repair feature, 24-25
automatically running, 25
dialog boxes, 11
help in, 17
in Table Wizard, 50
Dictation function, 297
dictionaries. *See* spell checking
displaying. *See* showing/hiding
docked toolbars, 278
moving, 13
Documenter utility, 265
documenting database, 265
Document Library, SharePoint Team
Services, 322
Domain Accounts, 318
double size fields, 72
drag- and- drop
Excel objects, 200
toolbars, moving, 13
duplicate records, finding, 130
dynamic Web pages, 209
dynaset, opening, 118

E

Edited Records, locking, 259
editing. *See also* forms
AutoCorrect entries, 93
Excel worksheets, 200
foreign languages, 101
form controls, 149
in Form view, 154
graphics, 196
hyperlinks, 215
indexed fields, 80-81
macros, 285
menu entries, 282
switchboards, 272

text, 96-97
toolbar buttons, 282
Edit Relationships check box, 62
ellipsis (...), 11
e-mail. *See also* attachments; SharePoint
Team Services
alerts, setting up, 324
importing data from mail program, 237
linking data, 211, 237
embedding. *See also* OLE (object linking and
embedding)
with pasting, 195
programs, sharing information in, 194
encryption
of data, 249
of database, 258
error checking
in forms, 178-179
in reports, 178-179
etched effect, 190
events. *See also* SharePoint Team Services
macros, assigning, 292-293
VBA (Microsoft Visual Basic for
Applications) events, 302, 303
Excel. *See* Microsoft Excel
existing database, creating new database
from, 47
Export command. *See* importing
and exporting
exporting. *See* importing and exporting
Expression Builder
calculated fields, creating, 128
queries, creating, 126
reports, performing calculations in, 172-173
using, 83
validation rule, creating, 82
VBA functions, accessing, 311
expressions. *See also* conditional expressions
in VBA (Microsoft Visual Basic for
Applications), 302

F

Field List box, showing/hiding, 164
field properties, 68
changing, 70
numeric field sizes, 72
size of field, 69, 72

field properties *(continued)*
  text field properties, 69
  turning off, 71
  updating, 71
  viewing, 69
fields, 34, 88. *See also* field properties;
    indexed fields; input masks; Lookup
    fields; queries; reports; tables
  with append query, 133
  bound columns, 84
  captions, adding, 69, 79
  common fields
    defining relationships with, 60-61
    specifying, 58
  Database Wizard, choice in, 42
  data type, choosing, 48
  decimal places, setting, 70, 74
  default values, specifying, 78
  deleting fields, 67
  entering data in, 37
  hyperlink fields, creating, 210
  joining types of, 61
  multiple fields, sorting records based
    on, 109
  new fields, inserting, 66
  numeric field sizes, 72
  order of fields
    changing, 67
    selecting in, 50
  primary keys, 48
  with Query Wizard, 120-121
  referential integrity, maintaining, 58-59
  requirements
    data for fields, 69
    specifying required fields, 78
  size, setting, 69, 72
  Smart Tags for, 70
  summarizing field contents with queries,
    135-136
  uses of, 65
  validation rule for, 82
  zero-length strings, setting, 79
files
  attaching objects to e-mail messages as,
    242-243
  finding files, 7
  HTML files, exporting database objects
    to, 217

hyperlinks, inserting, 211
  MDE files, creating, 316
  objects from files, inserting, 197
  workgroup information file, 248, 250
Filter By Form feature, 112, 114
filters, 112-113
  for data access page groups, 227
  AND filters, creating, 114
  forms, complex filters with, 114
  OR filters, creating, 114
  query, saving filters as, 112-113
  for SharePoint Team Services alerts, 324
Find dialog box, 90
Find Duplicate Query Wizard, 130
finding. *See also* help; queries
  contents in files, 7
  files, 7
  with Object Browser, 309
  tables, text in, 90-91
flat effect, 190
floating toolbars, moving, 13
floppy disks for blank databases, 46
fonts
  for datasheets, 103, 106
  foreign language fonts, 101
footers. *See* headers and footers
foreign languages. *See* languages
formats and formatting. *See also*
    forms; reports
  columns and rows, 104
  conditional formatting, 191
  for controls, 187
  currency values formats, 74
  datasheets, formatting, 106
  date and time values, formatting, 75
  for fields, 69
  finding formatted text, 91
  number formats, 74
  pasting information in specified format, 195
  for query fields, 123
  for text data, 73
formatting symbols, 73
  numeric and currency symbols, 74
Formatting toolbar, 12
  for forms, 184
  for reports, 184
form class modules in VBA, 303

form controls, 141
  adding, 148
  aligning objects and, 192
  Control Wizards, 150-151
  deleting, 148
  in Design view, 159
  editing, 149
  grouping controls and objects, 193
  properties, modifying, 149
  size of controls and objects, changing, 193
  special effects to controls, applying, 190
form letters
  importing data for, 237
  merging databases with, 244-245
forms, 2. *See also* borders; charts;
  dependencies; fields; Form Wizard;
  headers and footers; lines; rectangles
  alignment for input boxes, 154
  AutoFormat, formatting with, 184
  AutoForm command, 140
  AutoForm Wizards, 140, 142-143
  colors for input boxes, 154
  complex filters with, 114
  creating forms, 140
  deleting records from, 37, 155
  description of, 15
  Design view
    creating, 146
    form controls in, 141
    modifying, 141
    opening forms in, 36
  editing
    data in form, 155
    existing forms, 147
    form controls, 149
    in Form view, 154
  entering data in, 37, 155
  error checking in, 178-179
  Excel charts and worksheets, inserting,
    200-201
  fill color, changing, 188
  filters, creating, 114
  formatting, 184-185
    conditional formatting, applying, 191
  Form Wizard, 144-145
  graph charts, creating, 202-203
  grouping controls and objects, 193

  horizontal spacing, changing, 192
  hyperlinks to objects in, 212-213
  introduction to, 139
  linked forms, creating, 152
  main forms, 152
  new records, entering, 36
  one-to-one relationship, forms with tables
    in, 152
  renaming errors, repairing, 107
  saving
    AutoForm Wizard, saving new form
      with, 143
    Form Wizard, forms created with, 145
  Startup, displaying form at, 273
  styles for input boxes, 154
  subforms, creating, 152-153
  switching between views, 147
  themes with Windows XP and, 156
  vertical spacing, changing, 192
Form view
  editing forms in, 154
  input boxes, formatting, 154
  opening forms in, 36
Form Wizard, 140
  creating forms with, 144-145
  linked forms, creating, 152
  one-to-one relationship, forms with tables
    in, 152
freeze column feature, 102-103
functions. *See also* VBA (Microsoft Visual Basic
  for Applications)
  queries, performing with, 128

G

Get External Data submenu, 223
Getting Started task pane, 6
graph charts, creating, 202-203
graphics
  cropping, 199
  Database Wizard, choice in, 42
  editing original graphics, 196
  inserting graphic files, 198-199
Greek keyboard layout, 300
gridlines
  in datasheets, 106
  report grid, showing/hiding, 165

group accounts
  creating, 252
  ownership, setting, 256
  permissions, setting, 254
groups
  Admins group, 249
  controls, grouping objects and, 193
  for data access pages, 226-227
  for database objects, 32
  form controls, grouping objects and, 193
  macros, creating groups of, 288
  menu groups of commands, starting, 282
  renaming, 32
  for report records, 174-175
  shortcuts, removing, 32
  user groups, 248-249
Groups bar, 15, 32

H

handwriting
  input devices, 298
  recognition, 298-299
hard disks for blank databases, 46
headers and footers, 162
  colors, adding, 188
  to group sections, 227
  inserting, 176
  for reports, 162, 176
  showing/hiding, 185
headings for columns in crosstab queries, 137
Hebrew keyboard layout, 300
height of rows, changing, 104
help, 16-17. *See also* Office Online Help system
  combo boxes, help for customizing, 151
  in dialog boxes, 17
  Office Assistant for, 18-19
  updates on Web, obtaining, 20-21
hiding. *See* showing/hiding
horizontal spacing, changing, 192
HTML (Hypertext Markup Language), 209. *See also* importing and exporting
  attaching object to e-mail as HTML file, 242-243
  for data access pages, 222
  exporting database objects to HTML files, 217
  templates, 209, 217

hyperlinks, 212-213
  creating, 208
  to data access pages, 224
  data type, 68
  deleting, 215
  editing, 215
  fields, creating, 210
  for help, 16
  inserting hyperlinks, 211
  navigating, 215
  to new objects, 214
hypertext field, 208

I

icons in macro message box, 294
Image button, 167
Import command, 233
Import From Exchange/Outlook Wizard, 237
importing and exporting. *See also* tables
  ASP (Active Server Pages) files, exporting database objects to, 218-219
  data access page, exporting to, 223
  database, importing data from, 234
  e-mail program, importing data from, 237
  Excel spreadsheet, importing data from, 236
  HTML file, exporting to, 217
  information on, 232-233
  introduction to, 231
  other programs
    exporting data to, 242-243
    importing data from, 238
  SharePoint Team Services, importing and exporting data to, 331
  tables, 49
  XML (Extensible Markup Language), 240-241
Import or Link dialog box, 233
indexed fields, 69
  creating, 80-81
  editing, 80-81
  multiple-field indexes, 81
input masks, 69
  creating, 76-77
  for passwords, 77
  symbols, 77

Input Mask Wizard, 76-77
insertion point for text, 96
Insert Object command, 197
Insert Object dialog box, 196
installing
    SharePoint Server 2003, 332
    Windows 2003, 332
integer size of field, 72
Internet. *See also* hyperlinks; Office Online
        Help system; Web pages
    integrating Access and, 208-209
    meetings online, holding, 220-221
    SharePoint Team Services, Web discussions
        with, 330
    Smart Tags, finding, 94-95
    updates on Web, obtaining, 20-21

J

joining tables, 61
Join Meeting dialog box, 221

K

keyboard. *See also* shortcuts
    foreign language layouts, 300
    VBA Sub procedures, running, 308

L

Label button, 166
labels. *See also* mailing labels
    forms for creating, 155
Label Wizard, 170
landscape orientation for reports, 180
Language bar, 295
    dictating text, 296
    executing Voice commands, 296
    handwriting options, 298-299
    working with, 295
languages
    keyboards, foreign keys on, 58
    multiple languages, using, 300
    proofreading in foreign languages, 101
Layout Preview for reports, 159
libraries of objects, 309
Line button, 167
lines

adding to forms and reports, 186
    colors, changing, 188
    thickness of line, adjusting, 187
Linked Table Manager, 270
linking. *See also* hyperlinks; SharePoint Team
        Services; tables
    converting linked tables, 235
    database, linking data from, 234-235
    deleting linked tables, 234
    e-mail program, linking data from, 211, 237
    Excel spreadsheet, linking data from, 236
    forms, creating linked, 152
    identifying linked tables, 239
    information on, 232-233
    other programs
        data, linking, 238-239
        sharing information in, 194
    tables, 49
Link Table command, 233
Link To Exchange/Outlook Wizard, 237
List Box button, 166
list boxes, 11
    with Control Wizards, 150-151
    with custom values, 151
    specific records, displaying, 151
lists, 84-85
    of database objects, 15, 63
literals, 73
    with input masks, 76
locking database records, 259
logical operators for queries, 126-127
logons. *See also* passwords
    activating, 249
long integer size of field, 72
Lookup fields, 84-85
    manually creating, 85
Lookup list, 84
Lookup Wizard, 84-85
    data type, 68
Lotus 1-2-3. *See* importing and exporting

M

Macro Design toolbar, 285
Macro Design view, 286
Macro Name column, displaying, 288

macros, 2
  AutoExec macro, 274,284
  button, assigning macro to, 290-291
  conditional macros, creating, 289
  creating macros, 284
  description of, 15
  editing macros, 285
  event, assigning macro to, 292-293
  forms for running, 155
  groups of macros, creating, 288
  introduction to, 283
  message box for, 294
  running macros, 286
  saving macros, 284
  security levels, 44
  stopping, 287
  testing macros, 286-287
  toolbars, placing on, 286
  views for displaying, 287
mailing labels
  Address Book switchboard, access with, 29
  creating, 170
main forms, 152
Main Switchboard, 41
maintenance on programs, performing, 25
make-table query, 132
many-to-many table relationships, 58
margins in reports, changing, 180
Maximize button, 9
MDE files, creating, 316
meetings
  Meeting Workspace, 326
  Microsoft NetMeeting, 220-221
  online meetings, 220-221
Meeting Workspace, 326
member permission in SharePoint Team
  Services, 323
menu bar, 8
  adding commands, 280
  customizing, 280-281
  deleting commands from, 280
menus
  accelerator keys, assigning, 280
  choosing commands, 10
  copying commands to, 281
  editing entries, 282
  groups of commands, starting, 282

  naming new menus, 281
  new menus, creating, 281
  options, setting, 277
  shortcut menu commands, choosing, 10
merging
  Address Book switchboard, merging
    with, 29
  Microsoft Word document, merging data
    with, 244-245
  with Microsoft Word Mail Merge
    Wizard, 237
message box for macro, creating, 294
methods for VBA, 302
microphones, 295
Microsoft Access Desktop Driver, 309
Microsoft Active Directory, 323
Microsoft Active Server 3.0, 309
Microsoft Excel. *See also* importing and
    exporting; SharePoint Team Services
  analyzing data in, 246
  attaching object to e-mail as Excel file,
    242-243
  data access page, inserting spreadsheets
    in, 230
  forms, inserting charts and worksheets into,
    200-201
  hyperlinks to spreadsheets, 214
  importing data from spreadsheet, 236
  linking data from spreadsheet, 236
  reports, inserting charts and worksheets
    into, 200-201
Microsoft Exchange. *See* importing
    and exporting
Microsoft NetMeeting, 220-221
Microsoft Office Application Recovery
    program, 23
Microsoft Office Specialist program, 333-336
Microsoft Outlook
  events, linking to, 327
  importing or linking data from, 237
  Meeting Workspace, 326
Microsoft Paint, creating objects with, 196
Microsoft PowerPoint. *See also* SharePoint
    Team Services
    hyperlinks to presentations, 214
Microsoft Proofing Tools Kit, 101
Microsoft SharePoint technology. *See*
    SharePoint Team Services
Microsoft SQL Server database, 3

Microsoft Windows XP themes, 156, 185
Microsoft Word. *See also* SharePoint
Team Services
creating document from Access
database, 245
merging data with, 244-245
part of object into document,
converting, 245
Microsoft Word Mail Merge Wizard, 237
Minimize button, 9
minimizing, 9
Language bar, 295
modules, 2. *See also* VBA (Microsoft Visual
Basic for Applications)
description of, 15
Modules Objects list, 312
Modules window, 303
More Controls button, 167
mouse pointer, 9
moving. *See also* tables
cell contents, 97
columns, 102
objects, 206
report controls, 168
text in tables, 97
toolbars, 13
windows, 9
MsgBox action, 294
multiple-field indexes, 81
multiple languages, using, 300
My Recent Documents, 6

N

Name AutoCorrect, 63, 107
names. *See also* renaming
for data access pages, 223
for databases, 40
Database Wizard, choice in, 42
new menu, naming, 281
navigating
group sections, navigation boxes for, 227
hyperlinks, 215
NetMeeting, 220-221
New button, 47
New Database task pane templates, 43
No Locks strategy, 259
normalization process, 266

Northwind Traders sample database, 28
NOT queries, 126-127
numbers
data type, 68
formats, 74

O

OBDC (Open Database Connectivity). *See*
importing and exporting
Object Browser, 303
copying commands from, 309
object dependencies. *See* dependencies
Object Dependencies task pane. *See*
dependencies
object-oriented programming languages, 302
objects. *See also* database objects; VBA
(Microsoft Visual Basic for Applications)
libraries of, 309
Objects bar, 15
organization of objects on, 30
Office Assistant, using, 18-19
Office Clipboard. *See* Clipboard
Office Online Help system, 16
updates, obtaining, 20-21
Office Online Web site, templates on, 43
OLE DB component architecture, 3
OLE (object linking and embedding)
data type of OLE object, 68
working with, 194
On Enter event, 292
one-to-many table relationships, 58
one-to-one relationships, 58
forms with tables in, 152
Online Meeting toolbar, 221
Open button, 6
Open dialog box, 7
opening
database objects, 30
databases, 6
Language bar, 295
previous version, databases in, 269
queries, 118
sample database, 28
switchboards, 29, 272
tables, 34
Visual Basic Editor, 304
Open Table macro action, 283

optimizing database performance, 266-267
Option buttons, 11, 166
Option Group button, 166
Order Date field, 38
OR filters, creating, 114
Outlook. *See also* Microsoft Outlook
ownership, 249
    setting object ownership, 256

P

Page Break button, 167
pages, 2. *See also* Web pages
    description of, 15
page setup in reports, 180
Page Wizard
    groups, creating, 227
    themes, choosing, 225
paper settings for reports, 180
parameter queries, 116, 129
parenthesis characters, 76
pass-through queries, 138
passwords. *See also* database passwords
    activating user logons, 253
    for Admin accounts, 249
    deleting, 253
        database passwords, 257
    disabling passwords, 253
    input masks for, 77
    for VBA projects, 313
Paste button, 195
paste linking objects, 197
Paste Special command, 195
    for paste linking objects, 197
pasting
    Clipboard, items from, 98
    Object Browser, pasting commands
        from, 309
    objects, 195
    part of object, 243
    programs, sharing information in, 194
    records, 110
    in specified format, 195
Performance Analyzer, 266-267
    results of, 267
periods, dictating, 297
permissions

setting, 254
    for SharePoint Team Services members, 323
personal IDs for user accounts, 255
pictures. *See* graphics
PivotCharts, 224
PivotTable and PivotChart Wizard, 230
PivotTables, 137, 224
    data access page, inserting in, 230
plot area of charts, 204
portrait orientation for reports, 180
preview boxes, 11
previewing report data, 159, 181
previous version of Access, converting
    database to, 269
primary keys, 48
    Design view, specifying in, 57
    multiple primary keys, selecting, 57
    options for, 52
    referential integrity, maintaining, 58-59
    with Table Wizard, 51-52
primary tables, 58
Print button, 39
Print command, Standard toolbar, 12
printing. *See also* reports
    Documenter information, 265
    forms for, 155
    permissions lists, 255
    queries, 39
    Relationships window, 61
    tables, 39
Print Preview for reports, 159, 181
problems, deleting and repairing, 24-25
procedures in VBA, 303
programs
    Detect and Repair feature for, 24-25
    maintenance, performing, 24
    recovering, 23
Project Explorer, 303, 312
projects. *See also* VBA (Microsoft Visual Basic
    for Applications)
    defined, 3
properties. *See also* reports
    of data access page groups, 227
    Language bar properties, changing, 295
    list, 68-69
    report properties, setting, 171
    toolbar properties, changing, 279

Property Update Options button, 71
Publish It With MS Word command, 245
punctuation marks, dictating, 297

Q

queries, 2. *See also* dependencies; fields; indexed fields; Query Wizard
    action queries, 116
    adding
        fields to queries, 122
        records with queries, 133
    append query, 133
    calculations, performing, 128
    changing query fields, 122-123
    comparison operators for, 117, 126-127
    creating, 116
    crosstab queries, 116, 136-137
    custom queries with Design view, creating, 117
    data-definition queries, 138
    deleting
        fields from queries, 122
        records with query, 134
        tables, 119, 123
    description of, 15
    duplicate records, finding, 130
    dynaset, opening, 118
    filters as query, saving, 112-113
    formatting fields in, 123
    introduction to, 115
    logical operators for, 126-127
    make-table query, 132
    modifying in Design view, 119
    multiple fields, specifying criteria for, 125
    new tables with query, creating, 132
    NOT queries, 126-127
    opening, 38, 118
    order of fields, changing, 123
    other tables, adding fields from, 123
    parameter queries, 116, 117
    pass-through queries, 138
    printing, 39
    AND queries, 126-127
    renaming
        errors, repairing, 107
        fields, 129
    running, 38, 118
    single field, specifying criteria for, 124
    sorting retrieved records, 119
    SQL-specific queries, 138
    summarizing field contents with, 135-136
    types of, 116
    union queries, 138
    unmatched records, finding, 131
    update query, 135
    updating records with, 135
    viewing, 38, 138
Query Design window, 124-125
Query Wizard, 116
    simple queries with, 120-121
question mark (?) wildcard, searching with, 7
quitting Access, 26

R

raised effect, 190
reader permission in SharePoint Team Services, 323
records, 34. *See also* forms; queries; tables
    adding records with queries, 133
    append query, 133
    copying, 110
    deleting
        forms, records from, 37, 155
        query, deleting records with, 134
        tables, records from, 35
    duplicate records, finding, 130
    filtering, 112-113
    joining types of, 61
    list boxes displaying specific records, 151
    locking database records, 259
    multiple fields, sorting records based on, 109
    new records in table, entering, 35
    pasting, 110
    sorting, 108-109
        to second field, 175
    subdatasheets, 110
    updating records with queries, 135
recovering
    programs, 23
Rectangle button, 167

rectangles
  adding to forms and reports, 186
  colors, adding, 188
referential integrity, 58-59
  ensuring, 62
relationships. *See also* dependencies;
    referential integrity
  building, 58
  columns, deleting, 105
  defining, 60-61
  deleting, 61
    columns in relationships, 105
    data, related, 35
  options for, 53
  planning, 58-59
  subdatasheets, 110
  tables, related, 58
  with Table Wizard, 53
  unmatched records, finding, 131
Relationships window, printing, 61
renaming. *See also* queries; VBA (Microsoft
    Visual Basic for Applications)
  AutoCorrect for renaming database
      objects, 31
  columns, 105
  database objects, 31
  errors, repairing, 107
  groups, 32
repairing
  databases, 263
  renaming errors, 107
replacing text in tables, 91-92
replicating databases, 260-261
replication ID fields, 72
report class modules in VBA, 303
report controls
  adding, 164-165
  aligning objects and, 192
  formatting, 187
  moving, 168
  selecting, 169
  shortcut keys, assigning, 177
  size of controls, changing, 168, 193
  using, 166-167
  working with, 163, 169

reports, 2, 157-182. *See also* AutoReport
    Wizards; borders; charts; dependencies;
    headers and footers; lines; objects;
    rectangles; Report Wizard
  access keys, assigning, 177
  aligning objects and controls, 192
  AutoFormat, formatting with, 184
  bound controls, 163, 164-165
  calculated controls, 163
  clip art object, inserting, 199
  creating, 39
  Database Wizard, choice in, 42
  description of, 15
  Design view
    creating report in, 164-165
    form controls, working with, 159
    sections in, 162
  error checking in, 178-179
  Excel charts and worksheets, inserting,
      200-201
  Expression Builder for calculations, 172-173
  fill color, changing, 188
  formatting, 184-185
    conditional formatting, applying, 191
    values in reports, 173
  graph charts, creating, 202-203
  graphics, inserting, 198
  grid, showing/hiding, 165
  groups
    controls, grouping, 193
    records, grouping, 174-175
  horizontal spacing, changing, 192
  hyperlinks to objects in, 212-213
  introduction to, 157
  landscape orientation in, 180
  Layout Preview for, 159
  long information, setting properties for, 171
  mailing labels, creating, 170
  margins, changing, 180
  methods for creating, 158
  moving controls, 168
  page setup, changing, 180
  page spacing, adjusting, 169
  paper settings, changing, 180
  portrait orientation in, 180
  previewing reports, 159, 181
  printing, 39
    data from reports, 182

Print Preview for, 159, 181
properties
    general properties, setting, 171
    group properties, setting, 175
ruler, showing/hiding, 165
saving
    with AutoReport Wizard, 160
    with Report Wizard, 161
sections
    in Design view, 162
    spacing, adjusting, 169
selectors in sections, 162
shortcut keys to controls, assigning, 177
showing/hiding boxes in, 164
size of controls and objects, changing, 168, 193
snapshots, creating, 182
special effects to controls, applying, 190
Toolbox
    buttons, using, 166-167
    showing/hiding, 164
unbound controls, 163, 164-165
vertical spacing, changing, 192
Report Wizard, 158
    creating and saving reports with, 161
    grouping records with, 174-175
reshaping toolbars, 13
resizing
    columns and rows, 34, 54, 104
    objects, 206
    report controls, 168, 193
    windows, 9
Restore Down button, 9
restoring Language bar, 295
RTF (Rich Text Format)
    attaching object to e-mail as RTF file, 242-243
    saving files in, 245
ruler in reports, showing/hiding, 165

S

sample databases, 6, 28
Save button, Form View toolbar, 145
Save command, Standard toolbar, 12
saving. *See also* forms; reports; VBA
    (Microsoft Visual Basic for Applications)

AutoForm Wizard, saving new form with, 143
with AutoReport Wizard, 160
blank databases, 46
data, 22
on closing database, 22, 26
Documenter output, 265
graph charts, 202-203
macros, 284
on quitting Access, 26
RTF (Rich Text Format), files in, 245
screen style choice in Database Wizard, 42
ScreenTips
    for help, 17
    for hyperlinks, 211
scrolling in tables, 89
searching. *See* finding
Search task pane, 7
secondary sorts, 108
sections. *See* reports
security. *See also* encryption; passwords
    database passwords, 257
    for databases, 248-249
    macro security levels, 44
    ownership, assigning, 249
    for templates, 44
Security Wizard, 251
selection criteria, 115
    fine-tuning, 127
selection handles for objects, 206
Select Objects button, 166
shadowed effect, 190
shared documents library, 322
SharePoint Team Services
    administering, 320-321
    alerts, setting up, 324
    Calendar events, linking to, 327
    Change Settings Page, 320-321
    contact lists, creating, 328-329
    Document Library, 322
    Documents and Lists Page, 318-319
    events
        creating, 326-327
        Outlook events, linking to, 327
    filters for alerts, 324
    Home Page, 318
    importing and exporting data to, 331

SharePoint Team Services *(continued)*
  installing, 332
  introduction to, 317
  linking
    to contacts in Outlook, 329
    to events in Outlook, 327
  Manage Users Page, 318-319
  Meeting Workspace with, 326
  new team members, adding, 323
  Portal Site Navigation Page, 320
  Site Settings Page, 320-321
  tasks, assigning, 325
  uploading documents, 322
  Web discussions, holding, 330
shortcut menu commands, choosing, 10
shortcuts
  accelerator keys to menus, adding, 280
  group shortcuts, deleting, 32
  speed of, 12
  from Start menu, 4
Show Direct Relationships button, Relationship
    toolbar, 61
showing/hiding
  columns, 102-103
  graphics, 199
  gridlines in datasheets, 106
  headers and footers, 185
  hidden objects, showing, 64
  Language bar option buttons, 295
  Macro Name column, displaying, 288
  Office Assistant, 19
  reports boxes in, 164
  Smart Tags, 94
  subdatasheets, 110
  toolbars, 13
  windows, 33
single size fields, 72
size. *See also* resizing
  of data access page groups, 227
  field size, setting, 69, 72
  of report controls, 168, 193
sizing handles for report control, 168
Smart Tags
  adding, 95
  for fields, 70
  showing/hiding, 94
  using, 94-95

snapshots in reports, 182
Snap To Grid, turning off, 193
social security number fields, 48
sorting. *See also* reports
  data access page groups, 227
  designating sort order, 109
  multiple fields, sorting records based
    on, 109
  queries, records retrieved by, 119
  secondary sorts, 108
Sorting And Grouping box in report,
    showing/hiding, 164
Speak Text button, 296
special effects to controls, applying, 190
Speech command, 295
Speech Recognition Wizard, 295
spell checking, 100-101. *See also* AutoCorrect
  customizing, 101
  in foreign language, 101
  in tables, 100
Spelling button, Table Datasheet toolbar, 100
splash screens, creating, 273
splitting databases, 264
SQL. *See also* importing and exporting
  queries, SQL-specific, 138
standard class modules in VBA, 303
Standard toolbar, 12
  New button, 47
Start menu, starting from, 4
Startup options, 9
  Access, starting, 4
  changing, 274
  data access page at Startup, displaying, 273
  forms at Startup, displaying, 273
  ignoring, 273
static Web pages, 209
status bar, 8
  field descriptions in, 66
string of text for primary keys, 52
styles for form input boxes, 154
subdatasheets, viewing, 110
subforms, creating, 152-153
Subform/Subreport button, 167
Sub procedures. *See* VBA (Microsoft Visual
    Basic for Applications)
sunken effect, 190

Switchboard Manager, 247
  creating switchboards with, 271
  editing switchboard with, 272
switchboards, 8
  as add-in, 270
  automatically opening, 272
  creating, 271
  default page, defining, 272
  options, selecting, 29
  pages, adding, 272
  using, 29
switching
  to Database window, 28
  between Datasheet and Design view, 14
  between form views, 147
  between task panes, 5
symbols. *See also* formatting symbols
  input mask symbols, 77
syntax for VBA, 302
system crashes, repairing database after, 263
system database, 248

T

Tab Control button, 167
Tab order, 148
Table Analyzer, 266-267
Table Design view. *See* field properties
tables, 2. *See also* cells; columns and rows;
    dependencies; fields; indexed fields;
    linking; primary keys; queries; records;
    referential integrity; relationships
  analyzing design of, 267
  AutoCorrect, entering data with, 92-93
  common fields, specifying, 58
  converting a linked table, 235
  copying text and cell contents, 97
  creating, methods for, 49
  current field, searching for text in, 90
  deleting
    linked tables, 234
    queries, deleting from, 119, 123
    records, 35, 88
    relationships, 61
    text, 97
  description of, 15
  Design view
    creating tables in, 49, 54

  working with table in, 56
  editing text in, 96-97
  entering data to create, 54
  filtering records in, 112-113
  finding text in, 90-91
  formatted text, searching for, 91
  hyperlink field, creating, 210
  hyperlinks to objects in, 212-213
  identifying linked tables, 239
  importing and exporting
    data into tables, 55
    new tables, 49
  introduction, 87
  joining types of, 61
  linking, 49
    identifying linked tables, 55
  make-table query, 132
  modifying table in Design view, 56
  moving, 88
    to specific records, 89
    text, 97
  new records, entering, 88
  new tables with query, creating, 132
  normalization process, 266
  opening, 34
  planning, 48-49
  primary tables, 58
  printing, 39
  related tables, 58
  renaming errors, repairing, 107
  replacing text in, 91-92
  scrolling in, 89
  sort order, designating, 109
  specific records, moving to, 89
  spell checking in, 100
  subdatasheets, inserting, 110
Tablet PC, 298
Table Wizard, 49
  primary keys with, 51-52
  relationships, defining, 53, 60-61
  using, 50-51
tabs in dialog boxes, 11
target of link, 208
task panes, 5
  Getting Started task pane, 6
tasks with SharePoint Team Services, 325

templates
  for databases, 43
  foreign language templates, 101
  HTML templates, 209, 217
  warnings about, 44
text. *See also* tables
  color, changing, 189
  copying text, 97
  data type, 68
  deleting text in tables, 97
  dictating text, 297
  editing text, 96-97
  field properties, 69
  handwriting text, 298-299
  moving text in tables, 97
  reading back text, 296
  validation text, specifying, 82
Text Box button, 166
text boxes, 11
  renaming errors, repairing, 107
themes from Windows XP, 156, 185
3-D
  charts, changing view of, 205
  effects, creating, 190
time. *See* date and time
Toggle button, 166
Toolbar Options list arrow, 12
toolbars. *See also* docked toolbars; Formatting
    toolbar; Standard toolbar
  adding buttons, 276
  copying commands to, 281
  customizing, 278-279
  Database toolbar, 8
  Database window toolbar, 15
  deleting buttons, 276
  editing buttons, 282
  macros on, 286
  moving, 13
  new toolbars, creating, 278
  Online Meeting toolbar, 221
  options, setting, 277
  properties, changing, 279
  quickly displaying, 13
  reshaping, 13
  showing/hiding, 13
  Undo button with, 279

  working with, 12-13
Toolbox. *See* reports
Track Name AutoCorrect Info, 63. *See also*
    dependencies
turning on/off
  field properties, 71
  Office Assistant, 19
  Snap To Grid, turning off, 193
Type A Question For Help box, 16-17

U

unbound form controls, 141
Unbound Object Frame button, 167, 196
unbound report controls, 163, 164-165
underscore character, 76
Undo button, 279
undoing mistakes, 96-97, 279
unicode compression of fields, 69
union queries, 138
unique numbers for primary keys, 52
unmatched records, finding, 131
update query, 135
updating
  field properties, 71
  queries, updating records with, 135
  replicas, 261
  Web updates, obtaining, 20-21
up/down arrows, 11
upgrading older databases, 268-269
uploading documents with SharePoint Team
    Services, 322
URLs (uniform resource locators), 208
user accounts
  creating, 252
  ownership, setting, 256
  permissions, setting, 254
  personal IDs for, 255
user logons, activating, 253

V

validation rule, 69, 82
validation text for fields, 69
Value list, 84
  creating fields based on, 85
variables with VBA functions, placing, 310

VBA (Microsoft Visual Basic for Applications), 2
    class modules, 303
        creating class modules, 312
    copying commands from Object
        Browser, 309
    debugging procedures, 314-315
    event procedures, 303
    functions, 303
        creating custom functions, 310
        running custom functions, 311
    introduction to, 301-302
    MDE files, creating, 316
    modules, 303
        MDE files, creating, 316
        new standard module, creating, 304
        renaming, 308
        saving, 311
    passwords for projects, 313
    procedures, 303
    projects, 303
        properties for project, setting, 313
    renaming
        errors, repairing, 107
        modules, 308
    saving
        modules, 311
        project passwords, 313
    Sub procedures, 303
        creating, 306
        running, 308
    variables with functions, placing, 310
    writing
        code, 302
        commands, 307
vertical spacing, changing, 192
views and viewing, 34. See also
        database objects
    Access window, 8
    data access pages, 228-229
    Database window, 8, 14
    dependencies, 63
    field properties, 69
    indexed fields, 80-81
    macros, views for displaying, 287
    queries, 38, 138
    relationships, 61
    SQL queries, 138

    subdatasheets, 110
    tables, 34
viruses, protection from, 44
Visual Basic Editor, 303. See also VBA
        (Microsoft Visual Basic for Applications)
    opening, 304
Voice commands, 295-297
    dictating text, 297
    executing, 296

W

Web browsers, 208
    data access pages, viewing, 228-229
Web pages. See also data access
        pages; hyperlinks
    ASP pages, 209
    creating, 209
    static Web pages, 209
    themes, adding, 225
    Web toolbar, navigating with, 216
Web toolbar, 208-209
    working with, 216
Whiteboard for online meetings, 220-221
width of columns, changing, 104
wildcards, searching with, 7
windows. See also switchboards
    arranging windows, 9
    showing/hiding, 33
Windows 2003, installing, 332
Windows Explorer, starting Access from, 4
Windows SharePoint Services Wizard, 321
wizards, 40-41. See also Database Wizard;
        Table Wizard
    AutoForm Wizards, 140, 142-143
    AutoReport Wizards, 158, 160-161
    Chart Wizard, 202-203
    Command Button Wizard, 290-291
    Control Wizards, 141, 150-151
    data access pages, creating, 222-223
    Find Duplicate Query Wizard, 130
    Form Wizard, 144-145
    Import From Exchange/Outlook Wizard, 237
    Input Mask Wizard, 76-77
    Label Wizard, 170
    Link To Exchange/Outlook Wizard, 237
    Lookup Wizard, 84-85
    Microsoft Word Mail Merge Wizard, 237

wizards *(continued)*
    PivotTable and PivotChart Wizard, 230
    PivotTable Wizard, 137
    Report Wizard, 158, 160-161
    Security Wizard, 251
    Speech Recognition Wizard, 295
    Windows SharePoint Services Wizard, 321
Word. *See* Microsoft Word
Workgroup Administrator, 248
    locating, 251
workgroup IDs (WIDs), 250
workgroup information file, 248, 250
workgroups, 248
    joining, 251
worksheets from Excel, inserting, 200-201
World Wide Web, 208
Write Anywhere option, 299
Writing Pad, handwritten text with, 299

X

XML (Extensible Markup Language), 232
    importing and exporting, 240-241
XML Schema (XSD), 240
XSL (Extensible Stylesheet Language), 240

Y

year 2000 compliant date values, 75
yes/no data type, 68

Z

zero-length
    fields, 69
    strings, setting, 79